AF473931

ANGELICA KAUFFMAN

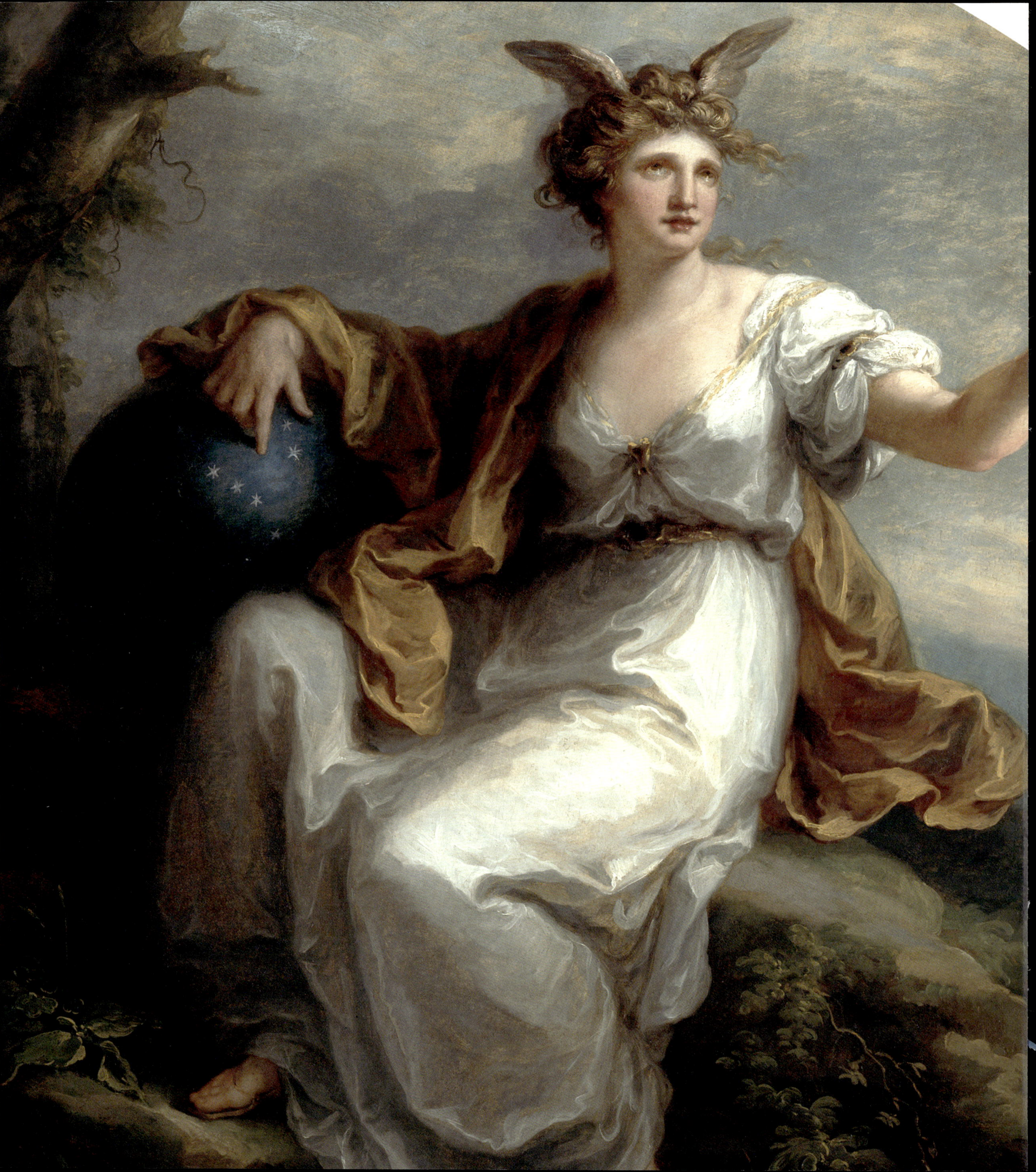

ANGELICA KAUFFMAN

ROYAL ACADEMY OF ARTS

First published on the occasion of the exhibition
'Angelica Kauffman'

Royal Academy of Arts, London
1 March – 30 June 2024

Supported by Christian Levett and Musée FAMM, with additional support from Kathryn Uhde, Antigone Theodorou and Stefan Bollinger, the Glenbevan Trust, the International Music and Art Foundation, Miss Rosemary Lomax-Simpson, and the Dr Lee MacCormick Edwards Charitable Foundation

This exhibition has been made possible as a result of the Government Indemnity Scheme. The Royal Academy of Arts would like to thank HM Government for providing indemnity and the Department for Digital, Culture, Media & Sport and Arts Council England for arranging the indemnity.

Department for
Digital, Culture,
Media & Sport

DIRECTOR OF EXHIBITIONS
Andrea Tarsia

EXHIBITION CURATORS
Bettina Baumgärtel
Per Rumberg
Annette Wickham
Rebecca Bray
assisted by Natasha Fyffe

EXHIBITION MANAGEMENT
Joanna Weston
with Helena Cooper

PHOTOGRAPHIC AND COPYRIGHT CO-ORDINATION
Caroline Arno
Giulia Ariete

EXHIBITION CATALOGUE
Royal Academy Publications
Florence Dassonville, Production and Distribution Co-ordinator
Carola Krueger, Production and Distribution Manager
Peter Sawbridge, Head of Publishing and Editorial Director

Translation from the German (Baumgärtel): Fiona Elliott
Copy-editing and proofreading: Caroline Ellerby
Design: Maggi Smith
Colour origination and print: Gomer Press, Wales
Printed in Wales by Gomer

British Library Cataloguing-in-Publication Data
A catalogue record for this book is available from the British Library

ISBN 978-1-915815-03-3

Distributed outside the United States and Canada by ACC Art Books Ltd, Riverside House, Dock Lane, Melton, Woodbridge, IP12 1PE

Distributed in the United States and Canada by ARTBOOK | D.A.P., 75 Broad Street, Suite 630, New York, NY 10004

EDITORIAL NOTE
All works illustrated are by Angelica Kauffman (1741–1807) unless otherwise stated.

Dimensions of all works of art are given in centimetres, height before width.

ILLUSTRATIONS
Pages 2–3: detail of p. 80
Page 7: detail of cat. 4
Page 9: detail of cat. 6
Pages 34–5: detail of cat. 31

CONTENTS

PRESIDENT'S FOREWORD

Described by a contemporary as 'perhaps the most cultivated woman in Europe', Angelica Kauffman was an artist of originality, elegance and erudition. Overcoming the considerable barriers faced by women artists at the time, she painted professionally from an early age and forged an international reputation for her portraiture and Neoclassical history paintings, which broke new ground with their focus on female protagonists from literature and mythology. Painting for and befriending influential figures of her day, from Goethe to Catherine the Great, Kauffman became one of the most celebrated artists of the late eighteenth century.

This exhibition is the first in this country since the 1950s to survey the whole of Angelica Kauffman's distinguished career, from her formative years in Italy to her success in London – where she lived for fifteen years – and finally to Rome. Originally scheduled to open at the Royal Academy in June 2020, the exhibition was regrettably cancelled due to the Covid-19 pandemic. We are very pleased indeed to have been able to bring it back into the programme in 2024, especially as Kauffman holds particular significance at the Royal Academy as one of the institution's founding Royal Academicians (she and the painter Mary Moser being the only women among the group). We thank Tim Marlow, former Artistic Director, and Axel Rüger, Secretary and Chief Executive, for programming the exhibition, and Andrea Tarsia, Director of Exhibitions, and Dr Adrian Locke, Chief Curator, for their unwavering support and guidance during its development.

The exhibition has been curated by Dr Bettina Baumgärtel, Director of the Angelika Kauffman Research Project and former head of the paintings collection at the Museum Kunstpalast, Düsseldorf, with Dr Per Rumberg, Jacob Rothschild Head of the Curatorial Department at the National Gallery (and formerly Curator at the Royal Academy), and the Royal Academy curators Annette Wickham and Rebecca Bray, assisted by Natasha Fyffe. We thank the curators for their thoughtful selection, Joanna Weston and Helena Cooper for their expert organisation of the exhibition, and Caroline Arno, who oversaw the photographic rights. For the elegant exhibition design, graphics and lighting, we thank EBBA Architects, Patrick Morrissey and Sanford Lighting respectively. Thanks are due to the many staff at the Royal Academy who have contributed to the exhibition's development and delivery. We are grateful to the RA Collections team, in particular Edwina Mulvany, Martha Graves and Mark Pomeroy, and to Peter Sawbridge and the publishing team for producing this beautiful catalogue.

The exhibition at the Royal Academy would not have been possible without generous support, and we are much indebted to Christian Levett and Musée FAMM, with additional support from Kathryn Uhde, Antigone Theodorou and Stefan Bollinger, the Glenbevan Trust, the International Music and Art Foundation, Rosemary Lomax-Simpson, and the Dr Lee MacCormick Edwards Charitable Foundation. Not least we are immensely grateful to the many lenders, both public and private, who have entrusted their works to our care during the exhibition.

Rebecca Salter PRA
President, Royal Academy of Arts

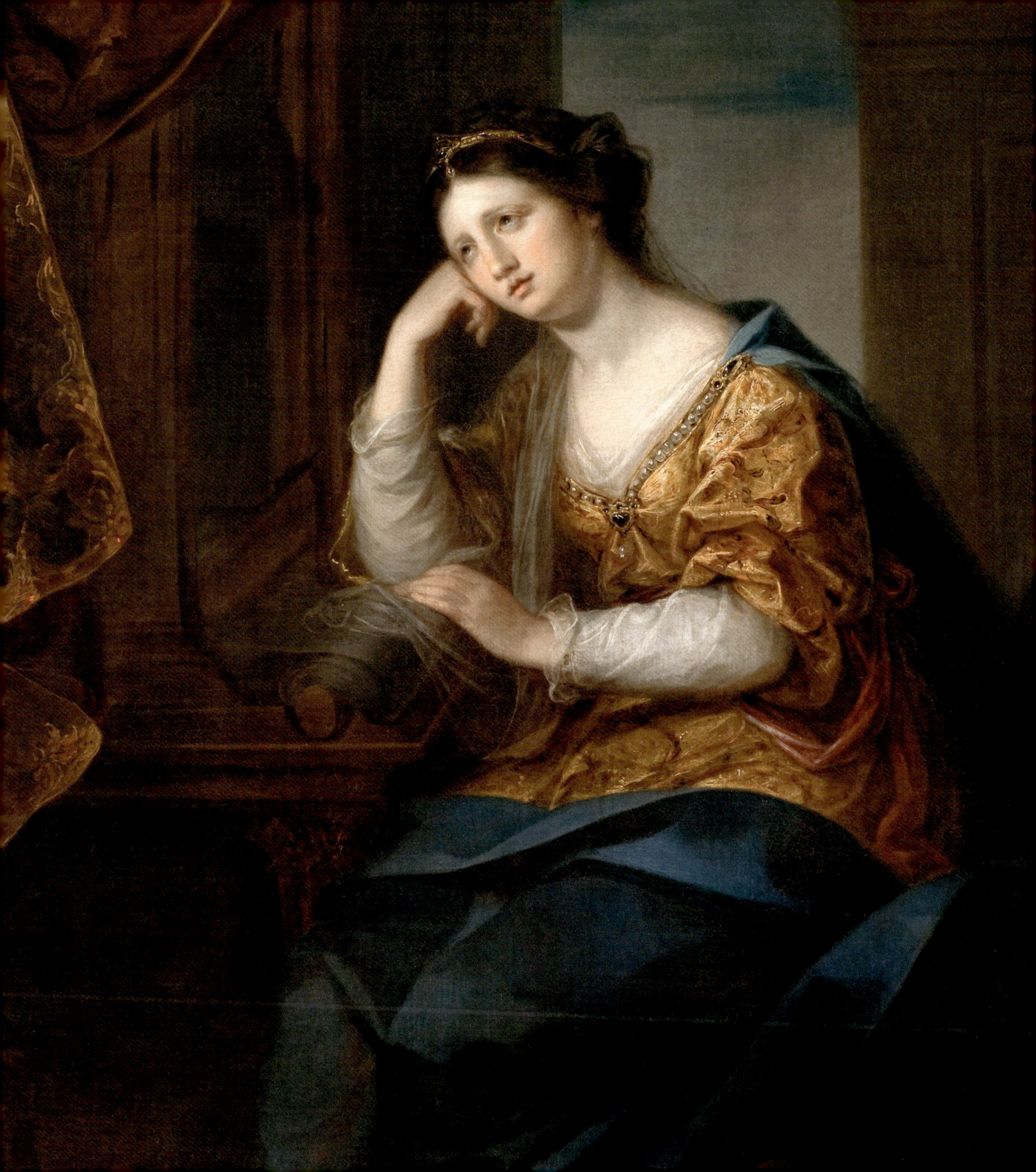

ACKNOWLEDGEMENTS

The Royal Academy is extremely grateful to the following individuals for their assistance during the making of this exhibition and its catalogue:

Kathie Armstrong
Peter Assmann
Emma Barker
Christoph Becker
Antonia Boström
Alexander Brockhoff
Hugo Chapman
Delphine Charpentier
Polly Chiapetta
Catherine Coates
Louise Cooling
Nicholas Cullinan
Jon Culverhouse
Ann Demeester
Rebecca England
Gabriele Ewenz
Lucy Faithful
Jenny Gaschke
Łukasz Gaweł
Kurt Grabher
Richard Hart
Jana Hess
Thomas Hirtenfelder
Inken M. Holubec
Tristram Hunt
Damian Jurt
David Ker
Tim Knox
Felix Krämer
Stephan Kunz
Alastair Laing
John Leighton
Lowell Libson
Alexandra Loske
Anne Lyden
Bernhard Maaz
Hilary McGrady
Karin Marti
Inge Maruyama
Kate Mavor
Fabrizio Mecozzi
Nick Merriman
Jerzy Miziołek
Francesca Montanaro
Martin Myrone
Florence Mytum
Tina Neuner
Andrea Parow
Giada Pasqualini
Alice Peters
Justin Piperger
David Preece
Michał Przygoda
Verena Rayer
Anna Reynolds
Christine Riding
Miranda Rock
Orlando Rock
Steffi Roettgen
Herbert Rott
Andreas Rudigier
Eike Schmidt
Svenja Schütte
Tico Seiffert
Hedley Swain
Sarah Talbot Capes
Charlotte Topsfield
Cecilia Treves
Sarah Victoria Turner
Lan Tyszka-Drozdowska
Helen Valentine
Simon Verde
Monika Wagner
Wendy Wassyng Roworth
Madeleine Whicheloe
Jonny Yarker

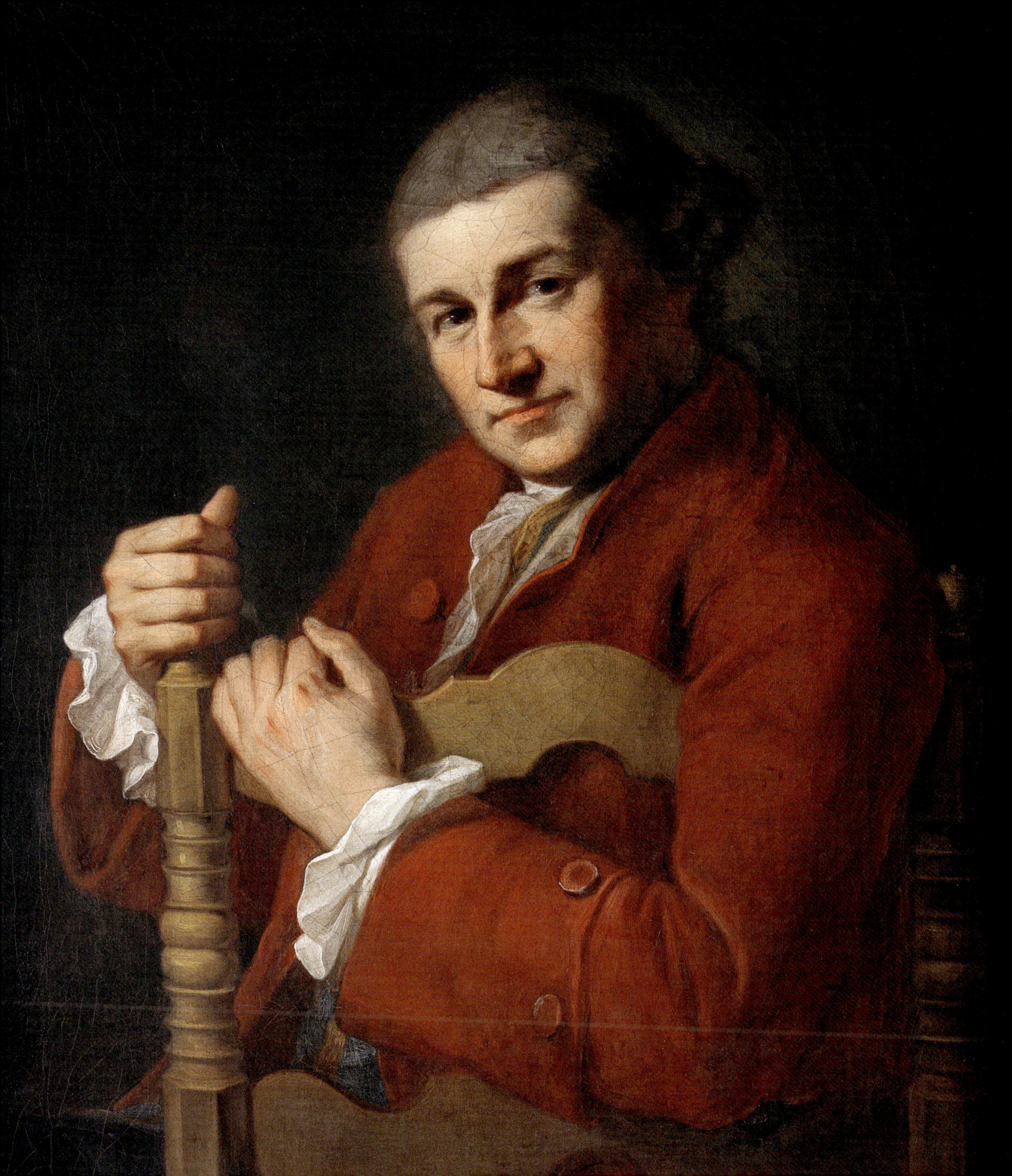

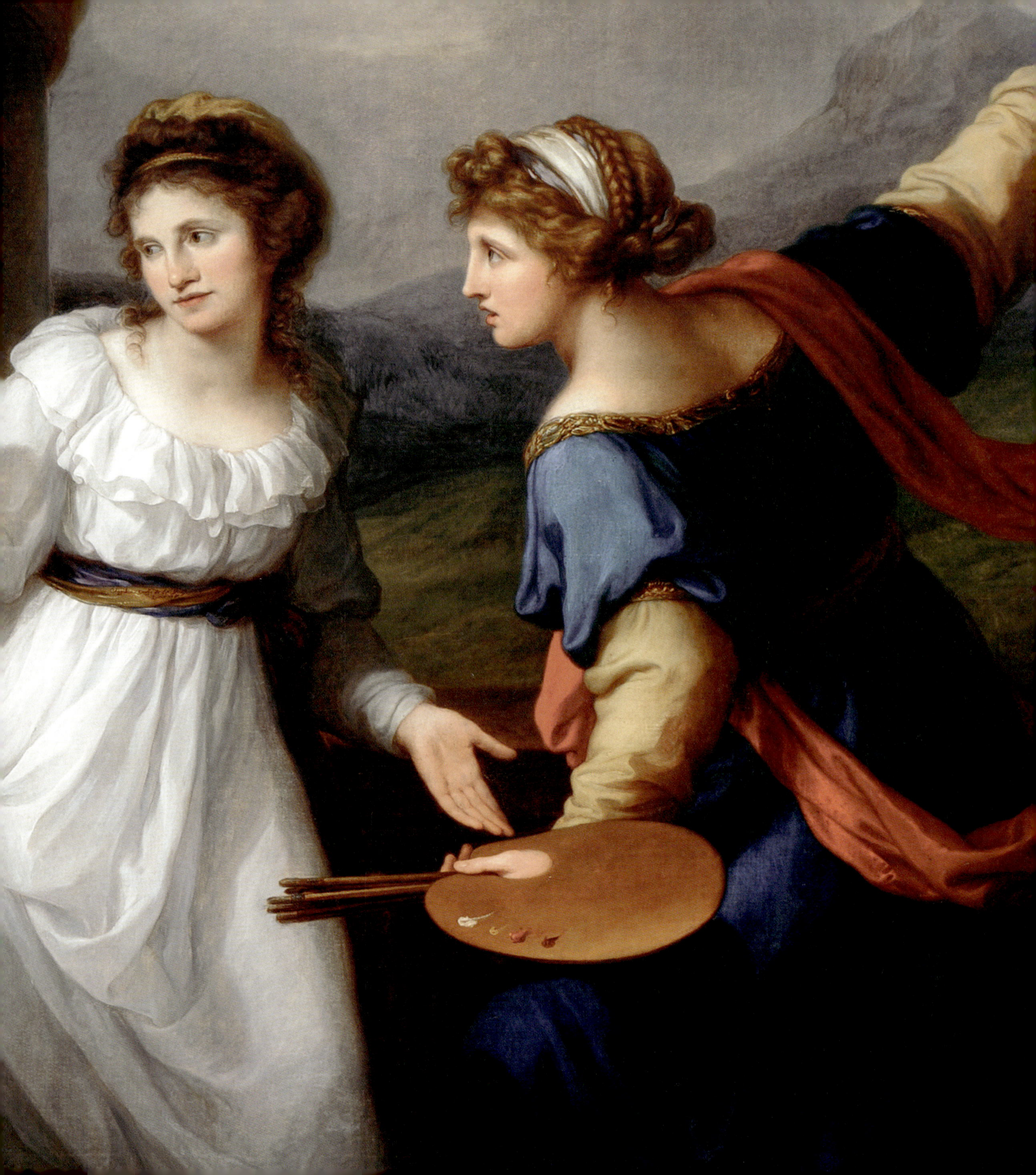

'SHE WAS OF HER TIME AND THE TIME WAS MADE FOR HER'

BETTINA BAUMGÄRTEL

LEGEND HAS IT that we owe the invention of art – or, more precisely, of drawing, as the wellspring of all the visual arts – to the daughter of Butades of Sicyon, a Corinthian potter. As the youth she loved was preparing to leave, she traced his shadow onto a wall. This origin myth is the only one in which the leading role is played by a woman. In the Pygmalion myth, for instance, a work of art comes about through an almost divine act of creation. Pygmalion, using his own imagination, sculpts his ideal of womanly beauty and thereby attains the highest level of original creativity. By contrast Butades' daughter only engages in imitation, the lowest level of creativity: she merely copies nature. It is not by chance that the highest and lowest levels of creativity are associated with concepts of masculinity and feminity in that order.[1]

Nevertheless, in the eighteenth century certain women artists became fascinated with the Butades myth; it helped to strengthen their self-image.[2] In the Age of Enlightenment more women than ever before made their names as artists. Many now abandoned their roles as anonymous craftswomen in family businesses and ventured into the realms of professional art. Women were employed at princely courts as drawing teachers for the children of the nobility and participated in academy exhibitions as 'amateurs'. The story of Butades' daughter provided a context for women to make female art practice image-worthy; it gave their work art-historical legitimacy and placed it within an ancient tradition.

And yet, there is no denying that the image of a young woman tracing an outline in Classical Greece was at times reframed in a way that can only have hampered women's efforts to be accepted as artists. Joseph Wright of Derby's painting *The Corinthian Maid* (1782–84; fig. 1), for instance, reflects the then prevailing assumption that women – in keeping with their 'feminine nature' – only ever created reproductive art, in the same way that they bore children.[3] Even Angelica Kauffman's artistic career was overshadowed by that particular prejudice and other stereotypical concepts of femininity. Her compositions were often seen as the emotion-led 'diversions' of what was understood to be the female mind. In Wright's painting, Butades' daughter trustingly rests her leg against that of the sleeping youth in a pose that recalls the iconography of lovers. She engages in the creative process as if she were making love. At the same time the traditional concept of inspiration from a muse also infiltrates this composition. It is as if the two figures exchange roles: the female artist becomes the muse and the sleeping male model becomes the artist, with his Corinthian 'muse' appearing before him as a dream image.

But of course Angelica Kauffman – as living proof that a woman could in fact have a career as an artist – was more important to aspiring women artists than any references to the Butades myth. She became someone to identify with and had a major, enduring influence on the 'professional

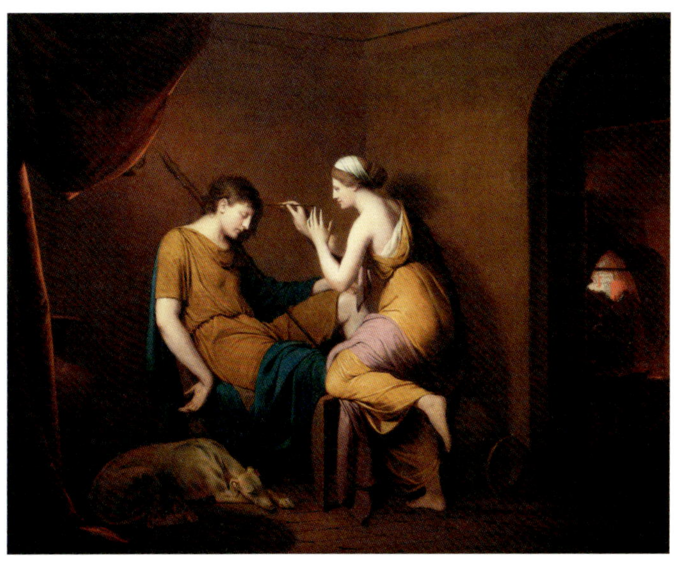

Fig. 1 JOSEPH WRIGHT OF DERBY *The Corinthian Maid*, 1782–84. Oil on canvas, 106.3 × 130.8 cm. National Gallery of Art, Washington DC, Paul Mellon Collection, inv. 1983.1.46

Detail of cat. 33

development' of subsequent generations of women artists. Elisabeth Vigée Le Brun, writing in her *Souvenirs*, tells how the sight of a self-portrait (1787; cat. 3) by her illustrious role model, Kauffman, at the Uffizi in Florence gave her courage.[4]

While the usual narrative of the wholly exceptional woman artist does not properly apply to Kauffman, she was nevertheless one of the first women to establish herself as a 'European' artist, representing a new kind of artistry with connections throughout Europe and a cosmopolitan approach to artistic work. Her wide-ranging oeuvre embraces all the main aspects of international Neoclassicism in the era of *Empfindsamkeit* – sensibility. Kauffman adeptly turned notions of femininity to her advantage and – intelligently and elegantly – took control of her own image. She actively promoted herself as the 'pittrice delle grazie' ('painter of the Graces'), as a 'female Raphael', as a 'beautiful soul'.[5] An example of her meaningful play of self-promotion in the dual role of artist and muse is seen in her *Self-portrait in the Character of Design Listening to the Inspiration of Poetry* (1782; cat. 26 and fig. 2).[6] Kauffman portrays her own creative potential – confidently brushing aside the clichés associated with women artists. And in so doing she adroitly takes advantage of the potentially awkward fact that as a rule allegories appear in the form of a 'borrowed' female figure and would normally be difficult to distinguish from a self-portrait by a woman.[7] The customary practice of alluding to an art-historical issue or an artistic concept by dint of a female representative works very well – thanks to ancient cultural codes – as long as the artist is a man and his model is a woman. If a woman replaces the male artist, there is no longer a clear-cut distinction, and misunderstandings arise. Even now Kauffman's female figures in history paintings, allegories and portraits are still regularly misinterpreted as 'covert self-inscriptions' or even as concrete self-portraits.[8]

However, in *Self-portrait in the Character of Design Listening to the Inspiration of Poetry*, Kauffman deliberately opens up multiple readings of the two female figures; by presenting her own self-portrait as an allegory of drawing (*disegno*) she creates a dynamic interplay between the real and an ideal world. This is unusual: *disegno* is generally represented as a male figure. But in this case the artist herself personifies drawing. Kauffman thus fends off the critics who maintain that she, as a woman, is by definition unable to draw correctly.[9] She invites the viewer to make the connection between herself and the concept of *disegno*, despite its male connotations – it was considered as the 'Father of all the Arts', on the highest level of original creativity, according to Giorgio Vasari.[10] By thus asserting her own capacity, as a woman artist, for *disegno* and *inventio*, she lays claim to the same creative potential as her male colleagues. As she sits listening to Poetry's inspiring words, her right hand is poised in a telling gesture – with her stylus in mid-air, she pauses as inspiration comes to her (fig. 2 and cat. 26). It is a moment of self-invention.[11] Kauffman thus depicts the emergence of her own creative artistic self. She also redefines the well-worn trope of the artist and his muse. She does not merely reverse their roles and provide herself with male inspiration, she creates a muse of her own. And yet the close link between the two figures does not indicate a love relationship of the kind that tends to pervade depictions of a male painter and his muse; this is a pact between friends.

In fact Kauffman was a typical representative of the cult of friendship that flourished in the eighteenth century. She gave paintings away as tokens of friendship; she cultivated intense epistolary friendships and was always ready to help others. She was widely regarded as the epitome of a 'beautiful soul'. The poet Johann Gottfried Herder was effusive in his praise of Kauffman: she 'is an angel of a woman, who, in her great beneficence, sevenfold recompenses me and removes the ills that others of her gender have done me'.[12] Many people made reference to the meaning of her first name, Angelica, which came to be regarded as a synonym for her angelic appearance, her 'gentle nature' and her beautiful soprano voice ('She sang like an angel').[13] Francesco Bartolozzi's print after Joshua Reynolds's portrait of Angelica Kauffman, whom he affectionately named 'Miss Angel', even includes a drawing of an angel (fig. 3).

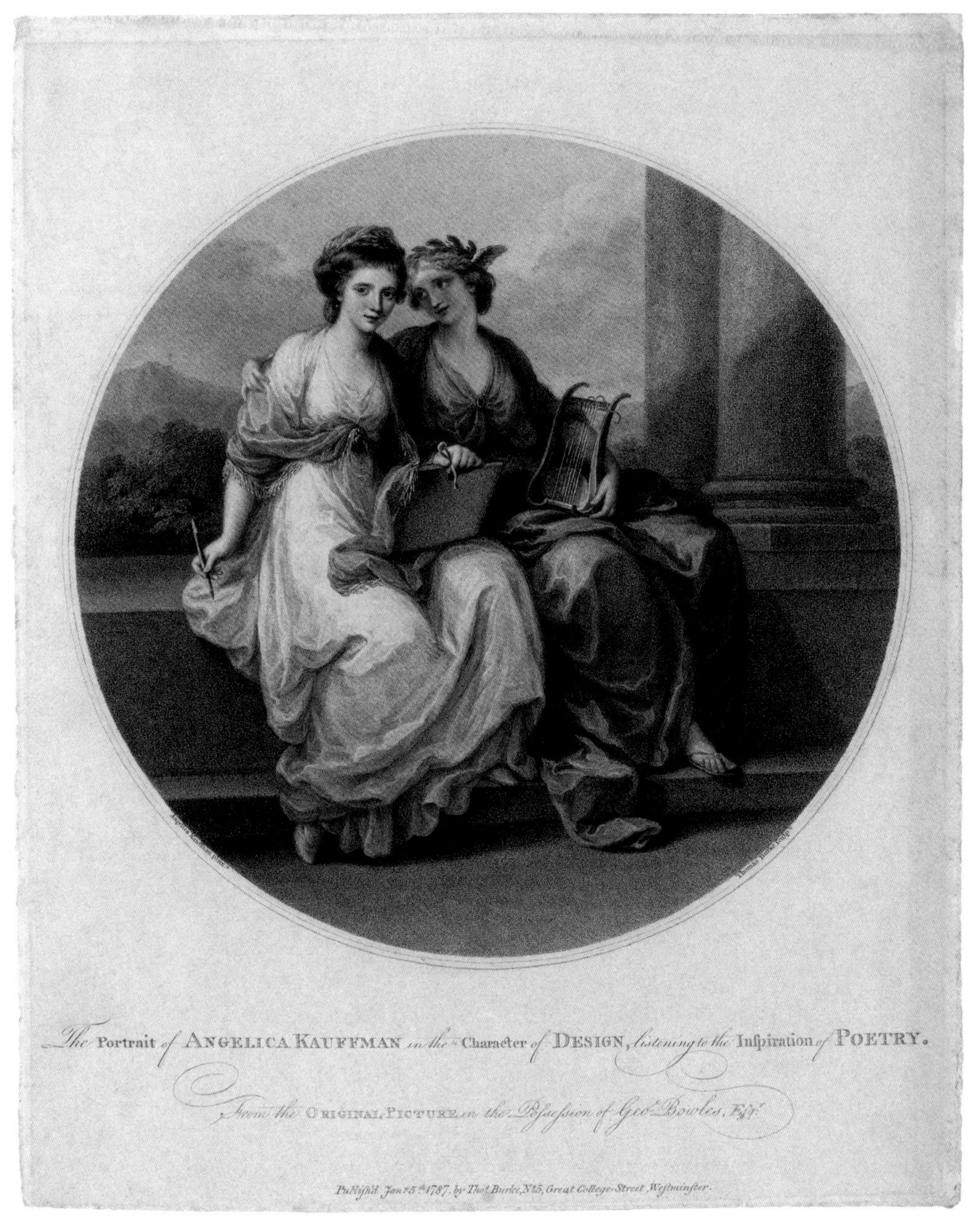

Fig. 2 THOMAS BURKE, after ANGELICA KAUFFMAN *Self-portrait in the Character of Design Listening to the Inspiration of Poetry*, 1787. Stipple engraving, 45.5 × 35.8 cm. vorarlberg museum, Bregenz, inv. no. A.K. St 95

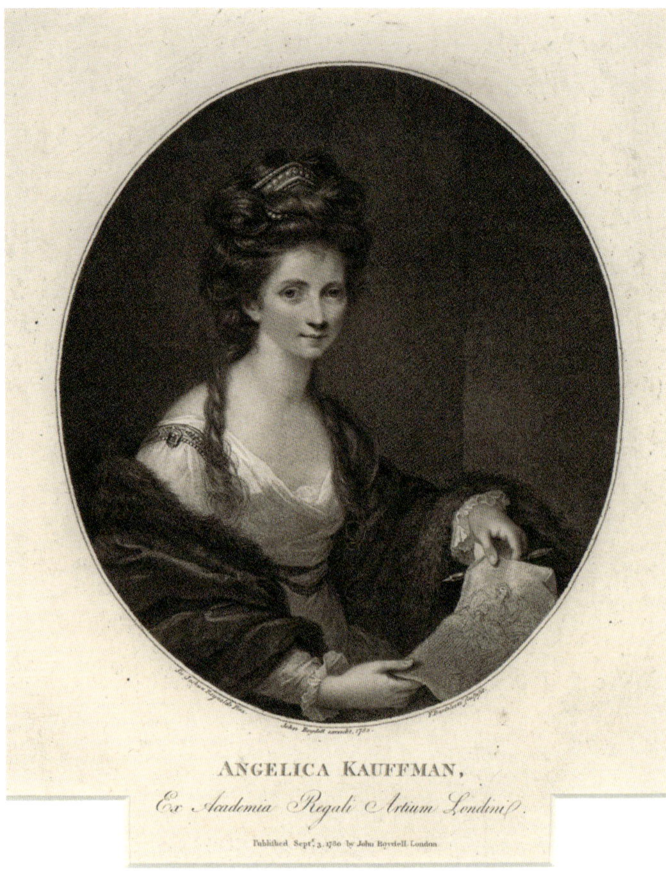

Fig. 3 FRANCESCO BARTOLOZZI, after JOSHUA REYNOLDS *Portrait of Angelica Kauffman*, 1780. Stipple engraving, 32.5 × 26.2 cm. vorarlberg museum, Bregenz, inv. A.K. St 44

The creation of these clichés of femininity arises from a combination of self-assertion and external input. In her self-portrait in the Uffizi (cat. 3), Kauffman takes the idealised notion of a chaste *virgo*, a Vestal virgin clad in white, and elevates herself to a priestess in the temple of fame. And in her most important self-portrait, *Self-portrait at the Crossroads Between the Arts of Music and Painting* (1794; cat. 33), she again alludes to notions of beauty and virtue.[14] In the guise of a Grace she chooses the virtuous path of painting. More importantly, however, the allusion to the masculine myth of Hercules at the crossroads highlights her capacity to take her own decisions as a woman artist.

'Possibly the most cultured woman in Europe'[15]

Angelica Kauffman owed her international success not only to her cosmopolitanism, her business acumen and her surefooted career planning, but also to the fact that – very unusually for a girl at that time – her talent was already recognised and encouraged early on. As an only child she received instruction in a wide range of subjects from both her father, Johann Joseph Kauffman (1707–1782) – a painter from Vorarlberg, Austria – and her Swiss mother, Cleophea Lutz (1717–1757). As a skilled linguist with a wide knowledge of art, music and literature and a charming demeanour, Kauffman was much admired in all social circles. Although she was clearly an exceptional figure in various ways, above all she had an outstanding dual talent as a singer and a painter.

As 'possibly the most cultured woman in Europe', to quote Herder, Kauffman carved out a remarkable career for herself. She was one of the wealthiest bourgeois women of her day and amassed a considerable fortune entirely through her own efforts. And whereas it was customary at that time for a man to treat his wife's assets as his own, Kauffman ensured that, even after her marriage to the painter Antonio Zucchi (1726–1795), she still kept control of her own income.[16] A short-lived previous marriage to a confidence trickster, and idle gossip about alleged liaisons – supposedly with Johann Wolfgang von Goethe, among others – provided ample material for novels, but also distracted attention from Kauffman's artistic achievements as one of the most important exponents of Neoclassicism in the art centres of Europe.[17]

A European avant la lettre

Born in Chur in Switzerland in 1741 and with family roots in Vorarlberg in Austria, Kauffman was already exposed to different environments at a young age as her family moved from Switzerland to Valtellina (Lombardy), Como in northern Italy to Schwarzenberg in Austria and to Lake Constance. And as a celebrated prodigy she soon had a network of clients in up to twenty nations in Europe and across the Atlantic, and counted many of the intellectual giants of the day as her friends. Later on she lived and worked in England for fifteen years, during which time she also spent some months in Ireland. Clearly those years were crucial to her career, but it was in her beloved Rome – 'Roma mi è sempre in pensiero' – that she spent the longest time: around thirty-eight of her sixty-six years.

It has never been easy to assign Kauffman to any one nation, and art historians have sometimes appropriated her as the whim took them. At one moment hailed as a Swiss artist (*Allgemeines Künstler-Lexicon*, 1767), at the next a 'British artist' (*London Encyclopaedia*, 1829), she was described as an Austrian artist in Constantin von Wurzbach's *Biographisches Lexikon des Kaiserthums Österreich* (1864). However, more often than not she was seen as a German who subscribed to Weimar Classicism in the shadow of Goethe. Ultimately it was Kauffman herself who reinforced the perceived multinationalism of her persona. Clearly regarding herself as a European *avant la lettre*, she once noted: 'My fatherland is every inhabited world.'[18]

For all that the internationalism of her career brought her recognition, in certain areas of dispute it has also served as convenient grounds for exclusion. And with old prejudices against female talent added to the mix, it is striking to note that Kauffman has had to wait over 250 years for a solo exhibition celebrating her work at the Royal Academy, despite her being one of the founding members of the institution.

'Fashion of the hour'

Yet it was in London during her own lifetime that Kauffman first had an exhibition dedicated solely to her work. A glance at her exhibition history shows that it is more extensive than that of any other woman artist in the historical period. Between 1779–80 and the present day her work has been presented in around thirty solo exhibitions.[19] Kauffman's first solo show in London was organised by her engraver and publisher William W. Ryland when she was 38. On 30 April 1779 Thomas Robinson, 2nd Baron Grantham, wrote, not without a critical undertone, to his brother Frederick Robinson about this very well-attended sales exhibition of Kauffman's work: 'Angelica's sale is stopped I do not know the reason, it is said that she is marry'd to Zucchi. She has great defects but I think posterity will value her works. The exhibition is always crouded'.[20] In May 1780 Ryland presented an important exhibition of the artist's work at 'Mr. Pollard's Room, in Piccadilly' with no less than 146 exhibits, including eighteen paintings.[21]

And it was in England in 1892 that the first reliable biography of Kauffman, with an extensive list of works (not a critical catalogue raisonné), was published by the Irish writer Geraldine Penrose Fitzgerald under the pseudonym Francis A. Gerard.[22] Her biographer pointed out that it was in England, where Kauffman had been the 'fashion of the hour', that she had also been soonest forgotten after her death. In Germany and Austria her memory was still alive in the twentieth century, albeit cast in an increasingly critical light. The first fictional biography of Kauffman was published by Armand François Léon de Wailly as early as 1832. The Swiss were the first to devote an encyclopaedia entry to the 25-year-old artist (written by Henry Fuseli in 1767), but what is still the most credible account of her life and work was published in Italy. That first biography was written during her lifetime, by her brother-in-law Giuseppe Carlo Zucchi (1721–1805),[23] who had arrived in London in 1766 – like Kauffman – and had observed her career with great interest. Zucchi's manuscript, finished in 1788, served as the basis for Giovanni Gherardo de Rossi's *Vita di Angelica Kauffmann, Pittrice* (1810).[24] Like Zucchi, de Rossi, a poet and an art historian, drew on what he knew from his close friendship with Kauffman; both of their accounts could be regarded as autobiographies at one remove. De Rossi's *Vita*, translated into German in 1814 by Alois Weinhart, an Austrian author, made an early impact in the German-speaking world. Subsequent biographies – regardless of the nationality of their authors – were largely novelesque; they sensationalised Kauffman's love life and paid scant attention to her artistic work. As Neoclassicism lost its hold in the nineteenth century, Kauffman's popularity declined, prompting Fitzgerald to conclude that 'Angelica has not quite kept her place as an artist.'[25]

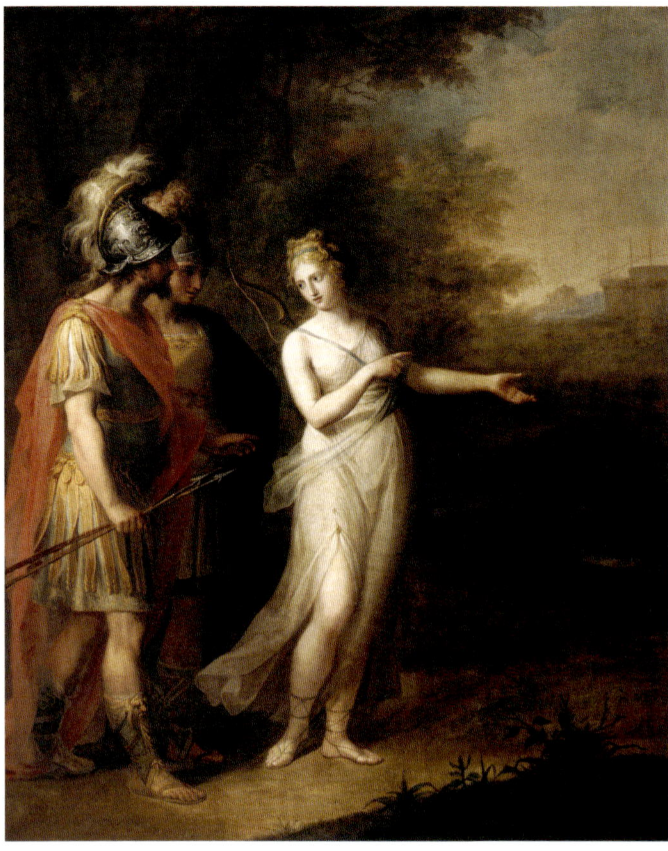

Fig. 4 *Venus Showing Aeneas and Achates the Way to Carthage*, 1768. Oil on canvas, 127 × 101.6 cm. National Trust Collections (Saltram House, The Morley Collection [accepted in lieu of tax by H.M. Treasury and transferred to the National Trust in 1957]), inv. NT 872180

However, closer examination reveals a more nuanced picture. Admiration for her work and the life she chose never completely ebbed away. And the motifs she created, which have been used to such a very considerable extent in arts and crafts over the last 250 years, are still appreciated as keenly as ever, even if Kauffman's authorship has sometimes been overlooked.

The history painter

Any survey of Kauffman's work as a whole shows that history painting was the main focus of her activities. Two-thirds of her paintings portray historical, mythological, literary and allegorical scenes. Portraiture, on the other hand, was in her view merely a useful and necessary source of income and artistic prestige.

In the early 1770s various commentators reflected on the lack of interest in history painting in Great Britain. However, in 1775 the *Public Advertiser* identified some progress in this matter:

> *It has long been a matter of complaint in this Country, that there is very little Encouragement for Historical Paintings; and that most Men extend their Ideas of Painting no farther than to get their own Portrait executed, and perhaps that of their Wife, or favourite Child... However well founded the above-mentioned complaint might be some Years ago, yet it is certainly not so at present... The public Exhibitions have kindled an Emulation among the Encouragement to the Rich and Great; so that at present when artists arise in the historical Line (of such acknowledged Merit as Mr West and Signora Angelica) there can be no doubt of their being fully employed and amply rewarded.*[26]

Yet Kauffman's sales of classicist subjects to the wider public in Britain were in fact relatively modest. Her early Homeric scenes did not sell at all until Theresa Parker, Lady Boringdon, a sister to the aforementioned Robinson brothers, enthusiastically purchased them; soon *Venus Showing Aeneas and Achates the Way to Carthage* (1768; fig. 4) and another four multi-figure scenes graced the interior of Saltram House in Devon.[27] Kauffman had to accept that in the English-speaking world she was mainly appreciated for her skills as a portraitist.

On her extended study trip through Italy, which lasted from around 1759 to 1765, Kauffman had already been determined to gain recognition as an exponent of history painting, the most noble genre. During that first phase of creative work in Italy she combined the virtuosity and saturated colours of Baroque art from Rome and Bologna with the strictly classicist forms favoured by artists such as Gavin Hamilton. Her earliest large-format history paintings, such as *Penelope at Her Loom* (1764, cat. 4), embrace the sublime and are peopled with suitably monumental heroes and heroines. At the same time Kauffman also studied the works of Dutch and Flemish Old Masters, such as Rembrandt and Van Dyck, whose expressive handling of paint still fascinated her in later life, as in her depiction of *Agrippina Mourning Over the Ashes of Germanicus* (1793; Kunstpalast, Düsseldorf). Similarly, her admiration for Raphael and Correggio never waned. Right up until her last composition, *St Maria Magdalena* (1807; private collection)[28] – which was only rediscovered in 2013 – Kauffman painted in a highly sophisticated, Raphaelesque style. Finely worked paints and subtle glazes render the flesh of Kauffman's figures especially delicate and smooth. Her lively brushwork – manifesting a certain ease known as *sprezzatura* – and the soft modulations of her colours never lost their vigour.[29]

Kauffman is thus one of the few eighteenth-century women who were already established exponents of history painting by the early 1760s. In London she became one of the first artists to depict scenes from early British history and thus provided an important catalyst for British art. Her theatrical scenarios, with new heroines such as Eleanor of Castile (cat. 11), Lady Jane Grey and Margaret of Anjou, Queen of England, alerted her host country to its own history. By thus significantly contributing to the new interest in British history that flourished in the nineteenth century, Kauffman laid the first foundations for the 'Gothick Picturesque'.[30] The many artists who followed her lead included John Deare, John Downman, John Opie, John Francis Rigaud and Richard Westall.

It is also worthy of note that Angelica Kauffman was the only woman to be explicitly recognised by the Royal Academy for her history paintings. Other women who became members of various academies, such as Marguérite Gérard, Adélaïde Labille-Guiard, Therese Concordia Mengs, Anna Dorothea Therbusch, Anne Vallayer-Coster, Elisabeth Vigée Le Brun and Kauffman's protégée Maria Cosway, were all exponents of the lowlier genres of still-life and portraiture. It was only towards the end of that era that certain women, students of Jacques-Louis David, such as Marie-Guilhelmine Benoist, started to compete for attention in the sublime realms of history painting by openly taking Kauffman as their role model (fig. 5).

It therefore made complete sense that Kauffman only showed history paintings at Royal Academy exhibitions between 1769 and 1772, all the more so given that it was the declared intention of the Royal Academy to establish a school of history painting focusing on British subjects. As early as 1767 her Homeric scenes were already contributing to the rejuvenation of Antiquity in painting. And that phase of her work was by no means completed during her second Roman period; on the contrary, from 1782 onwards she mainly worked on strictly Classical scenes – with stylistic influences from the School of David – taken from Homer, Ovid, Plutarch, Tasso and Virgil. At the same time she skilfully replaced the cool detachment of *gravitas romana* with a more elegant style of her own.

In London, the 'portrait capital of the world', Kauffman – thanks to her wide-ranging, very fashionable repertoire – was soon able to hold her own with Reynolds and George Romney as a much sought-after portrait artist. Although she set new trends with her portraits of women dressed *à la turque* and men in Van Dyck costumes (cats 7 and 29), she still regarded portraiture merely as a means to earn a living. Even in her portraits she was keen to historicise her subjects. Her portraits go beyond pure mimesis and exploit the idealisation and role-plays of history painting that Reynolds had recommended in his *Seven Discourses on Art* (1769).[31]

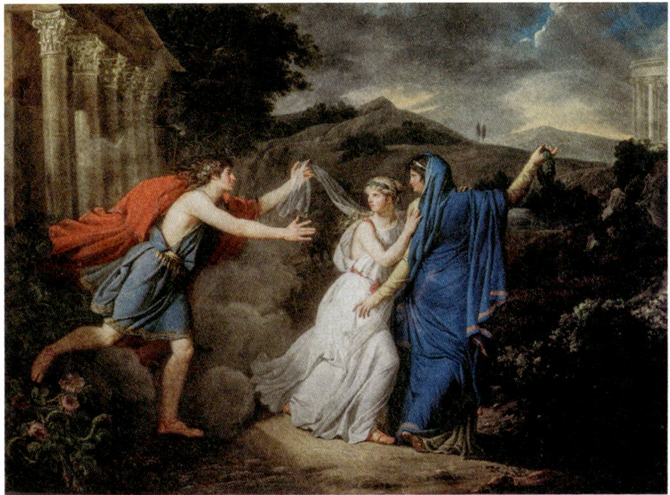

Fig. 5 MARIE-GUILHELMINE BENOIST *Innocence Between Vice and Virtue*, 1791. Oil on canvas, 87 × 115 cm. Private collection

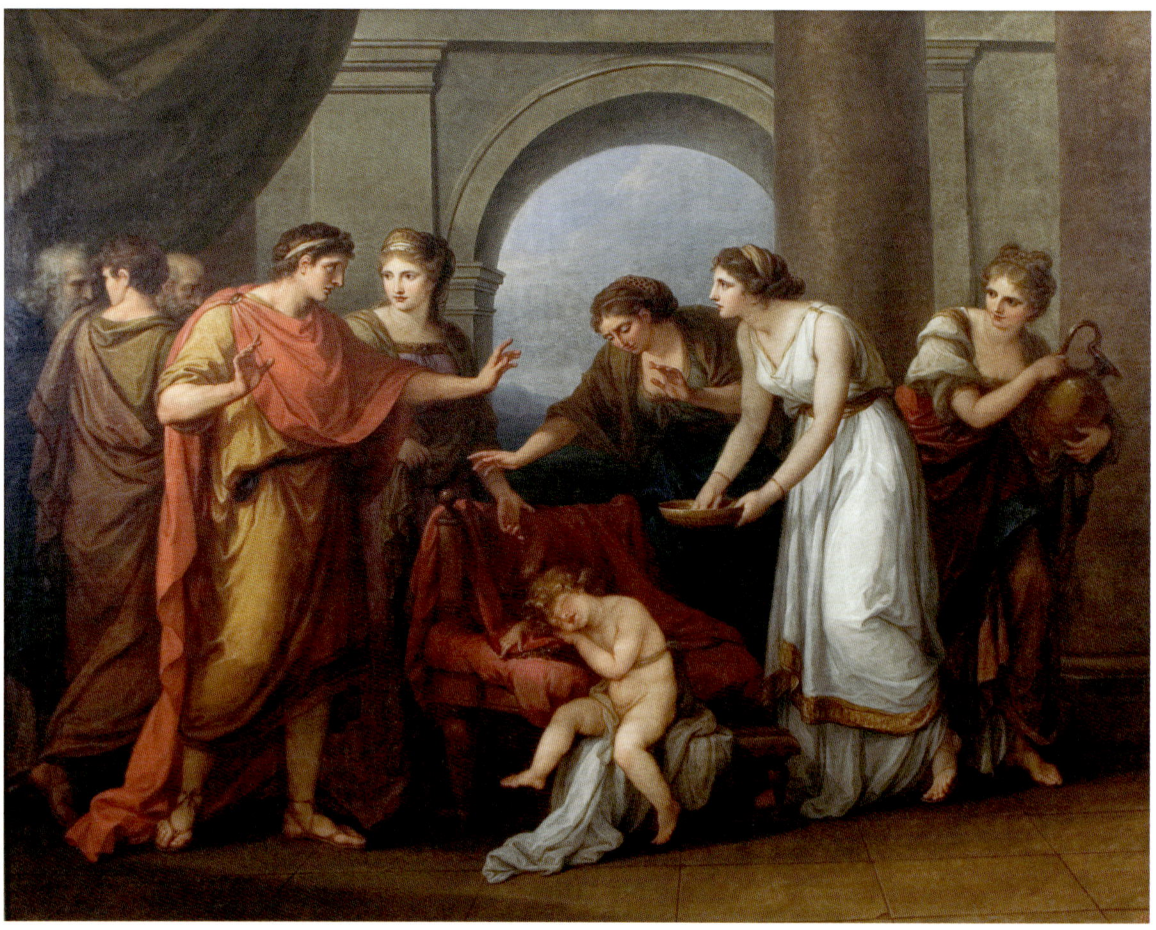

Fig. 6 *Servius Tullius as a Child, Asleep Beneath the Miraculous Flame*, 1785. Oil on canvas, 257 × 317 cm. Scientific-Research Museum of the Academy of Arts of Russia, St Petersburg, inv. N-J-171

Young, emancipated women from privileged backgrounds, such as the sculptor Anne Seymour Damer (*née* Conway), were her first portrait clients, and numerous artistically active women followed in their wake. These sitters delighted in being ennobled and cast in the allegorical or mythological role of a Muse or of goddesses such as Hebe and Ceres. In Rome in the 1790s Kauffman developed this type of portrait into what might be described as 'Attitudes' portraits, capturing moments in dramatic scenes that were performed by female friends in her very well-attended salons. These friends included Emma Hart, Lady Hamilton (cat. 31), famously enacting an attitude as Thalia, and Fortunata Sulgher Fantastici, a renowned impromptu virtuoso, as an inspiring and inspired Muse.[32]

The wide range of Kauffman's subject matter was unusual for a woman in that era, as were her differentiated

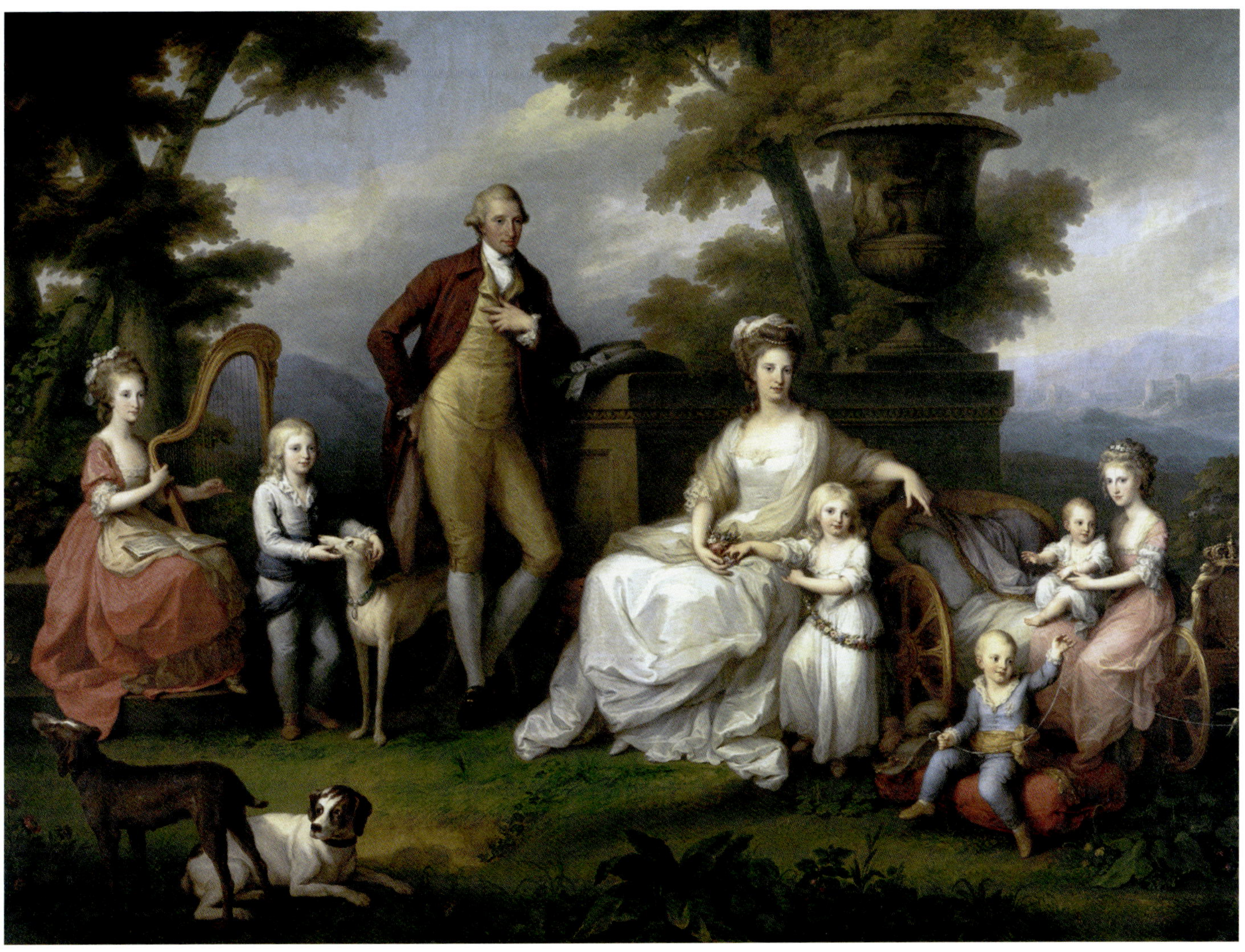

Fig. 7 *Portrait of the Royal Family of Naples*, 1783. Oil on canvas, 310 × 426 cm. Museo Nazionale di Capodimonte, Naples, inv. O.A.6557

handling of paint and drawing techniques and her choice of picture formats and canvas sizes. Besides standard vertical and horizontal formats, she also had a fondness for tondi painted on rectangular canvases (reminiscent of Raphael); occasionally she would create elongated friezes, which served as overdoors. Her formats cover the full range, from miniatures to full-wall history paintings. She painted two monumental, strictly classicist scenes from Greek history for Catherine the Great of Russia, which measured around 2.5 × 3 metres (fig. 6).[33] These compositions and her *Portrait of the Royal Family of Naples* (fig. 7),[34] at around 3 × 4 metres, and her *Portrait of Augusta, Duchess of Brunswick-Lüneburg (1737–1813), with Her Son Prince Charles George Augustus (1766–1806)* (fig. 10, p. 25),[35] at around 3 × 2 metres, suggest that Kauffman had a high-ceilinged studio space and was confident working on a ladder – something of a challenge for an artist treading

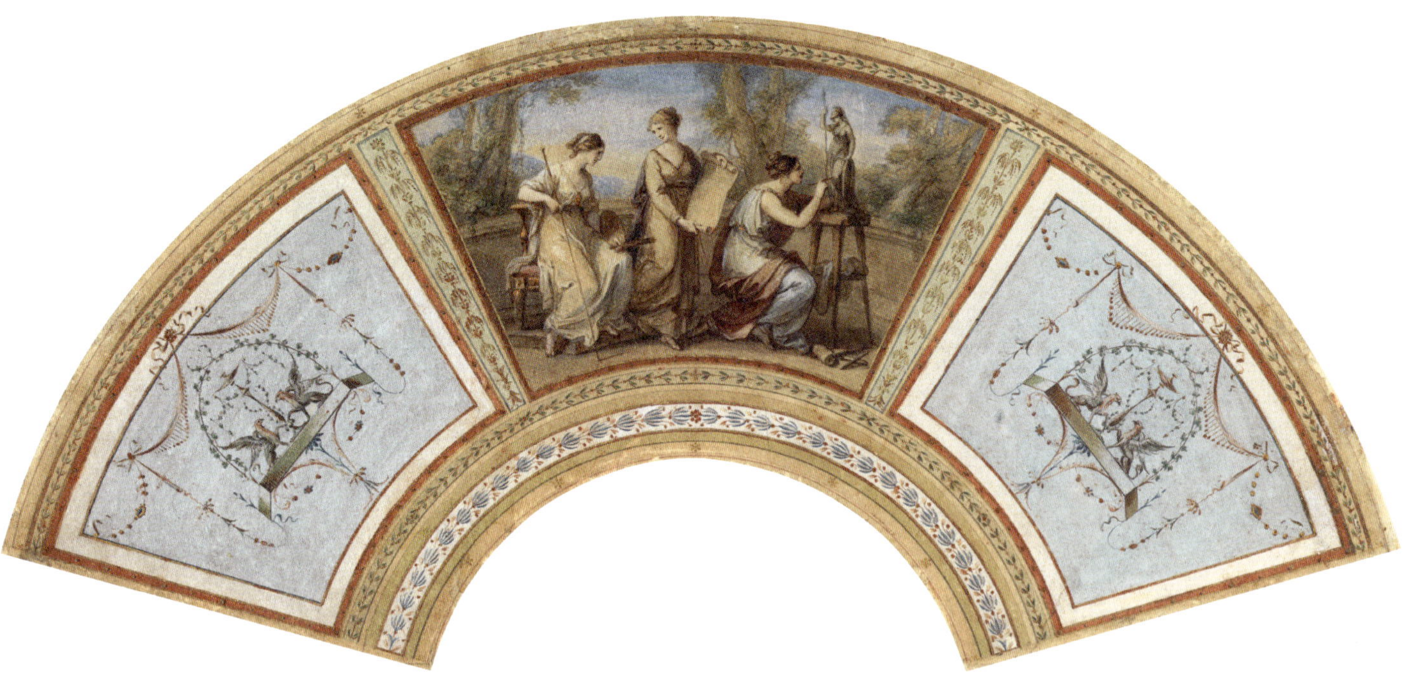

Fig. 8 *The Three Fine Arts: Painting, Architecture and Sculpture*, c. 1779–80. Design for a fan: watercolour, body colour, graphite, gold on paper, 17.1 × 53.3 cm. Yale Center for British Art, New Haven, Paul Mellon Collection, inv. B1975.3.1237

the fine line between decorous, feminine behaviour and her aims as a professional artist.

'She was of her time and the time was made for her'[36]

Kauffman's extended sojourn in London, from 1766 to 1781, marked a high point in her artistic career. Her works soon started to influence the fashions of the day and even led to a 'Kauffman cult'. She deliberately created a canon of motifs in the 'sentimental style' and produced some of her most popular compositions in the form of touching depictions of abandoned female figures in pleasing round formats, such as *Poor Maria* (cat. 13) from Laurence Sterne's 1768 novel *A Sentimental Journey Through France and Italy*.[37] These small scenes, mostly painted on copper, were primarily intended to adorn the interiors of great houses and sold more easily than larger formats.

It was thanks to stipple engraving – a new print technique – that from the 1770s Kauffman's work could be distributed throughout Europe and became enormously popular.[38] Besides the established engravers who produced prints after Kauffman's works – from William W. Ryland, Francesco Bartolozzi and his apprentices to John and Josiah Boydell – there were now ever more women working in this field: notably Ann Bryer, Elisabeth Chaillou, Rose Le Noir, Susanna Vivares and publishers' widows such as Jane Matthews[39] and Mary Ryland. Kauffman also benefitted from the fact that interior design was now attracting unprecedented interest, not least because swathes of new, female producers and buyers were emerging in both the upper and middle classes. And it was above all women who were buying prints after paintings by Angelica Kauffman for their homes. The leading interior architects of the time were Robert and James Adam, but Kauffman did not work for them, as far as we know, although some of her imagery served as models for wall, ceiling and fireplace decorations. Today, many decorations erroneously attributed to her can be given to Antonio Zucchi, who created extensive decorative programmes for the Adam brothers.[40]

Nevertheless, some of Kauffman's most popular works were reproduced as 'mechanical paintings' on an almost industrial scale by Matthew Boulton and Francis Eginton;[41] they also featured in designs painted on porcelain in such leading factories as Chelsea or Meissen, and on fans made by Antonio Poggi (fig. 8), on furniture made by George Brookshaw and in tapestries worked by aristocratic women and their

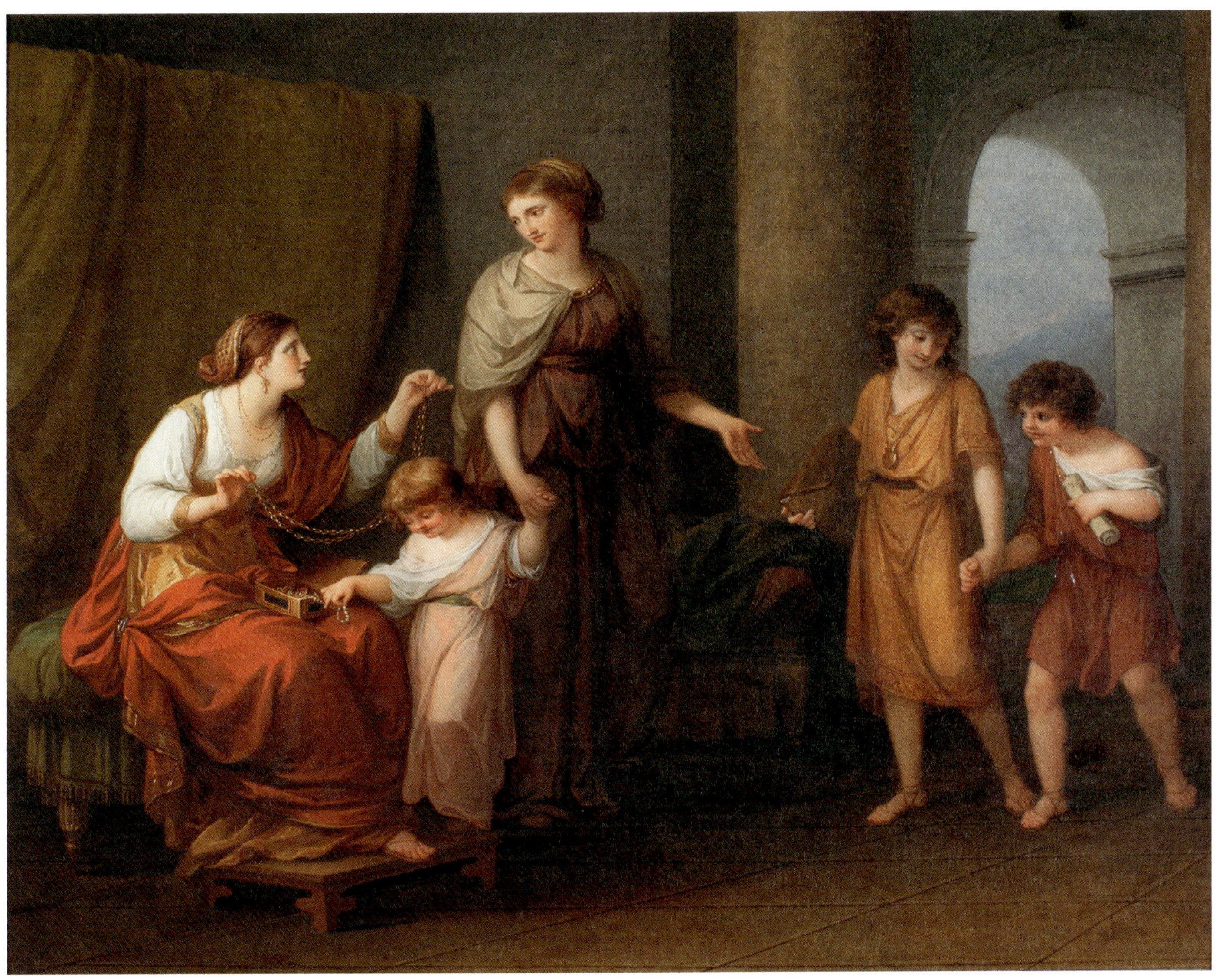

Fig. 9 *Cornelia, Mother of the Gracchi*, 1785. Oil on canvas, 100.6 × 127.8 cm. Klassik Stiftung Weimar, Museen, inv. G 2405

bourgeois counterparts alike.[42] People today are not always aware that Kauffman was also much in demand as an illustrator. She contributed no less than nine images to John Bell's *Edition: The Poets of Great Britain*,[43] two images to the Macklin Bible[44] and designed frontispieces for *Goethe's Schriften*.[45]

'Noble simplicity and serene grandeur'

Kauffman evidently had an instinct for being in the right place at the right time. Her aim when she returned to Italy in 1781 was to gain wider recognition for her history paintings by making her mark in Rome, the epicentre of progressive history painting. In Rome she also found new clients among members of the aristocracy from Poland, Russia, Scandinavia and France making their Grand Tour of Europe. In 1785, when Jacques-Louis David turned the spotlight on brave warriors in his much acclaimed *Oath of the Horatii* (Musée du Louvre, Paris), Kauffman responded within the year with an equivalent feminine world in *Cornelia, Mother of the Gracchi* (fig. 9) and *Julia, Wife of Pompey, Fainting* (Klassik Stiftung Weimar). Thus, well before the French Revolution, she was already exploring a female perspective on bourgeois virtue in the Roman republic. She also created Greek counterparts to these courageous Roman women: exemplary figures such as Penelope and heroic lovers such as Dido, Circe (cat. 35), Calypso and Sappho took centre stage in her compositions and thus significantly contributed to the formation of a new Enlightenment ideal of femininity. In these compositions, bearing in mind Johann Joachim Winckelmann's concept of 'noble simplicity and serene grandeur',[46] Kauffman avoided extreme imagery and portrayed the fates of her heroines in carefully calibrated emotional situations. And her figures also have the flowing outlines of William Hogarth's 'line of beauty'.[47] Although Kauffman adhered to the classicist rules of beauty, her art was frequently disparaged as work done by a woman. She had to withstand accusations that, as a woman, she lacked 'masculine powers of expression' and that her figures were debilitated due to feminisation. This dismissal of 'art by women' as gender-dependent 'women's art' has been commonplace ever since Giorgio Vasari published his *Lives of the Most Excellent Painters, Sculptors, and Architects* in 1550.[48]

Refined colourism

Close examination of Kauffman's paintings reveals the full extent of her painterly virtuosity. She had a particular talent for depicting colours and textiles, which she executed with a *penello volante* – a flying brush – and very fluid paints in contrasting areas of extremely sparse application or striking impasto. Her saturated yet finely attuned colours recall the finest Baroque masters in northern Italy and southern Germany. Her agile brushwork bespeaks her musicality; indeed she had a positively Mozartean dexterity. In works such as *Rinaldo and Armida in the Magic Garden* (c. 1772; cat. 9) echoes of French Rococo resonate in subtly tasteful, 'ancient' Classicism. As yet few are aware that Kauffman's approach to painting was also an expression of a new aesthetic: it utilises ground-breaking findings concerning not only the perception of the relationship between light and shade (chiaroscuro) but also the impact of shimmering colours, as in the Royal Academy ceiling painting *Colouring* (1780; see p. 81). According to Joseph Baretti:

> Colouring *appears in the form of a blooming young Virgin, brilliantly, but not gaudily dressed. The varied Colours of her garments unite and harmonize together. In one hand she holds a prism, and in the other a brush, which she dips in the Tints of the Rainbow. Under her feet is seen the Cameleon sporting on a bed of various flowers.*[49]

In fact her artistic practice partly informed the theories and aesthetics that were debated in the circle around Goethe, influencing his colour theory and also contributing to the idea of 'changeant' painting developed by Goethe's friend, the Swiss artist and art historian Johann Heinrich Meyer.[50]

In her final years Kauffman returned to her early 'Baroque classicist' period. Close-quarters monumentality in her figuration and strong local colours mark the onset of her late religious works, such as *Christ and the Samaritan Woman* (1796; cat. 36). In conclusion it could be said that Kauffman's strength lay in her virtuosic ability to combine aspects of Roman-Bolognese, Venetian, French and English styles in a highly sophisticated, sentimental and virtuously pathos-laden Classicism. In Kauffman's rhapsodic natural scenarios, content and form – so often inspired by Antiquity – coalesce in an ideal image of exalted humanity.

Detail of *Colouring*, 1780 (see p. 81)

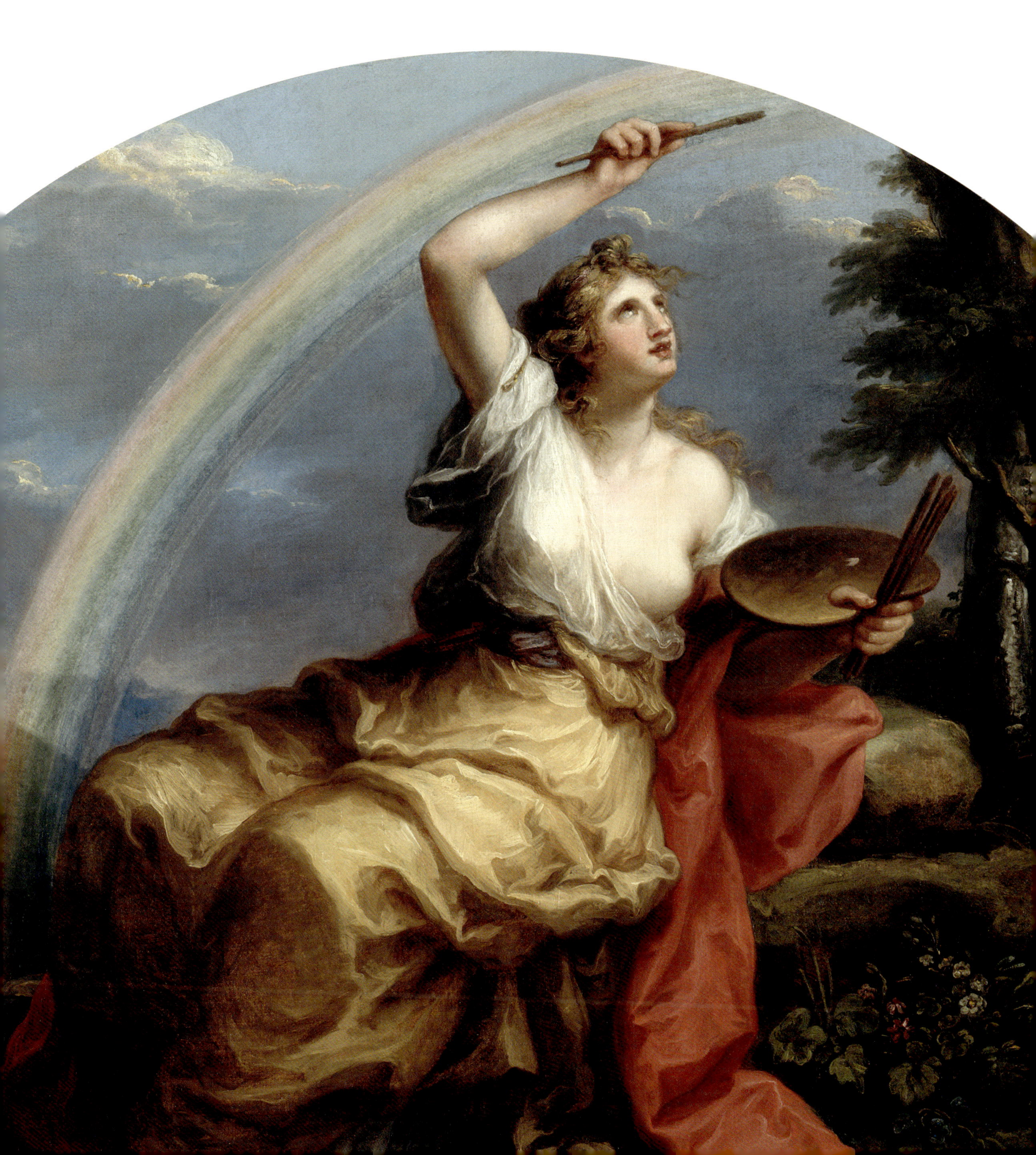

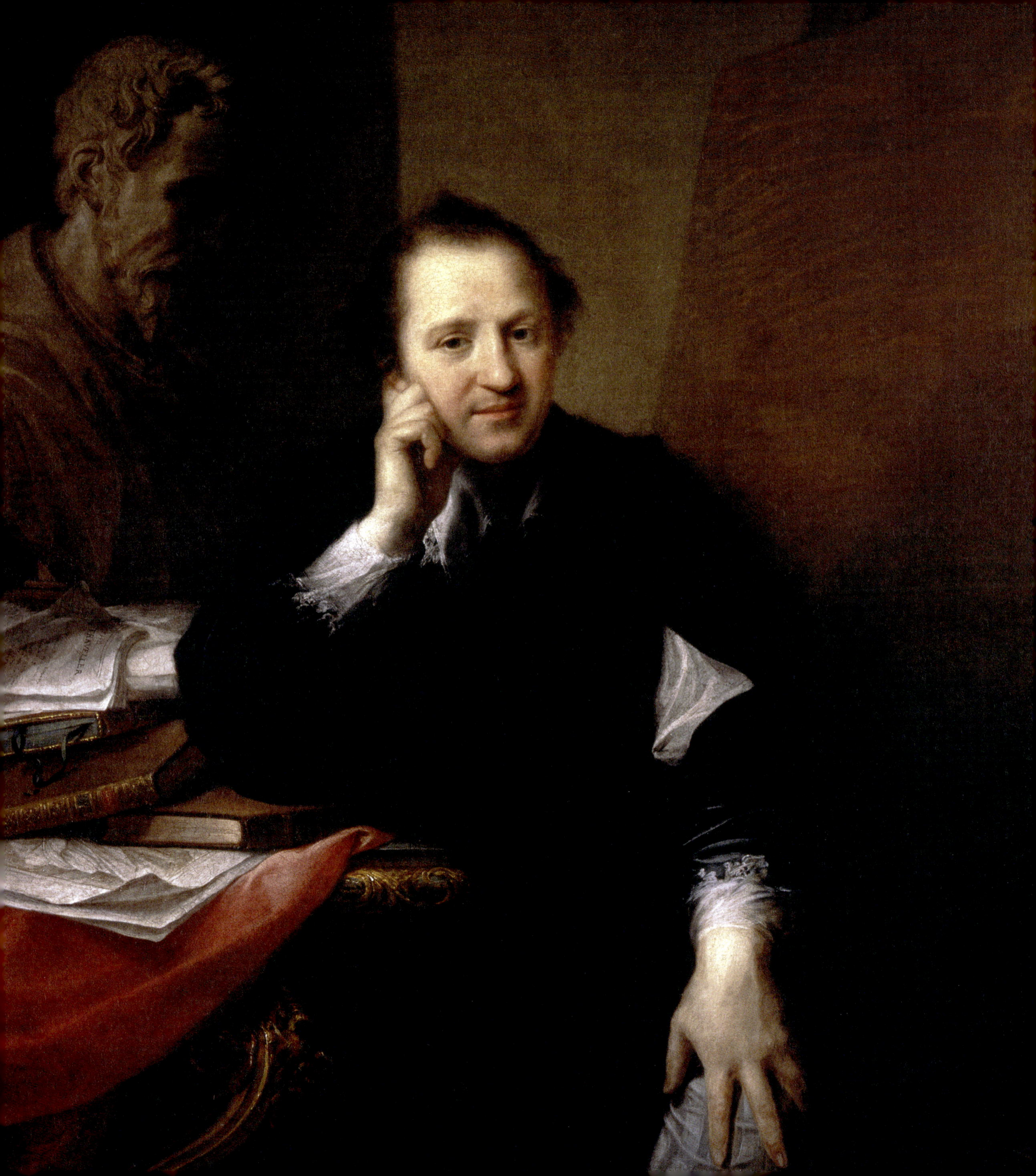

ANGELICA KAUFFMAN AND THE ROYAL ACADEMY

ANNETTE WICKHAM

WRITING FROM ROME in 1763, the English connoisseur Daniel Crespin praised the talents of the 'German paintress' Angelica Kauffman, adding 'I wish this Sigra [Signora] ... was in so good a part of the world as Great Britain.'[1] His wish was to be fulfilled when, encouraged by her popularity among Grand Tourists and expatriates in Italy, the artist moved to London in 1766. Just two years later, Kauffman's status as one of the leading lights of the British art world was officially confirmed by her inclusion among the 36 founding members of the Royal Academy of Arts on 10 December 1768. She remained a prominent member of the institution throughout her years in London, continuing to exhibit there even after moving to Rome in 1782. While remarkable in itself, this trajectory invites broader reflection given that, after Kauffman and Mary Moser as founding members, there was not to be another woman Royal Academician until the twentieth century.

In many ways Kauffman was an ideal candidate for membership of the new institution that sought to promote the 'Grand Manner' in emulation of Renaissance and Classical art.[2] Having trained with her father in Italy, she had studied both Classical sculpture and the works of the Old Masters at first hand, she had an international reputation both for history painting and portraiture, and she could already boast membership of several Italian academies.[3] Yet, as a young, Swiss-born woman only recently settled in England, there were several grounds on which she might easily have been omitted from the initial group of Royal Academicians – not least her recently annulled marriage to an imposter posing as the Swedish Count de Horn.

Two key connections made during her first months in London were crucial in ensuring her inclusion. Within weeks of her arrival, Kauffman was introduced to Joshua Reynolds, whom she described as 'the first English painter'.[4] They got on so well that within a few months she could report that he 'is one of my kindest friends ... As a proof of his admiration for me he has asked me to sit for my picture to him [fig. 3, p. 14], and, in return, I am to paint his'.[5] Concurrently, Kauffman secured, in quick succession, two prestigious commissions from Royal women: firstly, from the Queen Mother to paint her daughter, Augusta, Duchess of Brunswick-Lüneburg, sister of King George III, with the latter's son Charles George Augustus (commissioned 1766, painted 1767; fig. 10), and,

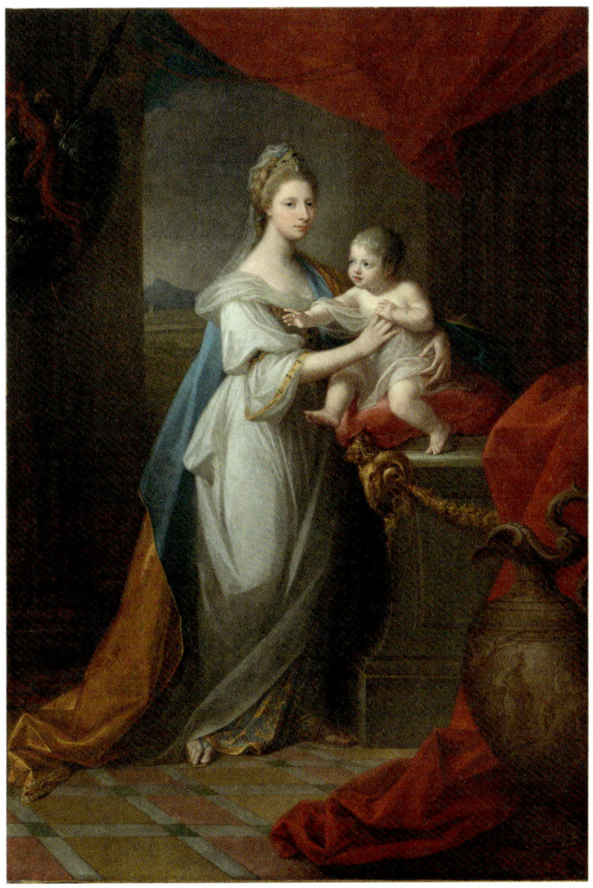

Fig. 10 *Portrait of Augusta, Duchess of Brunswick-Lüneburg (1737–1813) with Her Son Prince Charles George Augustus (1766–1806)*, 1767. Oil on canvas, 272 × 180.6 cm. Royal Collection, RCIN 405359

Detail of cat. 16

secondly, from Queen Charlotte herself (1767; the painting is untraced but it is known from Thomas Burke's later mezzotint of 1772 [cat. 17]). Kauffman and the Queen, both native German speakers, reportedly spent 'many hours of easy & familiar conference' together.[6] Although the Royals and Reynolds were not on good terms, both were prime movers in assembling the new Academy's founders between November and 10 December 1768 with Reynolds as the institution's first President and King George III as its patron.[7] Kauffman, as a close friend of the former who was in favour with the Queen, was a fitting and politic choice for membership.

By the 1760s, the question of a national academy of art in Britain had been debated for nearly a century but it was a dispute within the Incorporated Society of Artists that eventually triggered the foundation of the Royal Academy. The seceding Directors of the Society secured the King's support and brought together the founding membership without an election process. Based around several interconnecting circles of patronage and friendship, the initial group has been described as a 'hotch potch collection' including the most celebrated artists active in London at the time alongside a number of less prestigious but well-connected figures like the drapery painter Peter Toms.[8] The new Academy was – necessarily – fairly inclusive in terms of nationality, although most of the foreign-born artists had been established in London for some years, such as the Swiss George Michael Moser who moved to the city in the 1720s.[9]

Kauffman and the American Benjamin West, conversely, were recent arrivals via Italy at this time but both found rapid success in England, benefitting from their connections with Grand Tourists and Rome's Neoclassical luminaries. Kauffman's novelty was undoubtedly part of her initial appeal, but it is striking how she progressed from being hailed as a 'pleasing guest' in England to someone who could be described as being 'looked upon as an English artist'.[10] Numerous artists from around Europe and beyond lived and worked in Britain during the eighteenth century but some found themselves the focus of jealousy and discrimination. 'Signora Angelica' seems to have largely avoided this kind of attention and, while she continued to be variously referred to in England as Austrian, German, Italian and Swiss, her close identification with her adopted country surely helped to ease her path at the Academy.[11]

Kauffman's gender was, potentially, a much more substantial challenge to her academic ambitions in London than her nationality. As Amanda Vickery has pointed out, women were excluded entirely from most professional societies in Britain at this time and, against this backdrop, the inclusion of Kauffman and the painter Mary Moser (daughter of the Academy's first Keeper) among the founding Royal Academicians can be read as somewhat enlightened.[12] Frustratingly, there is no record of discussion on this subject among the first Royal Academicians and, in any case, the rapid formation of the original group left little time for debate. Kauffman's and Moser's close connections with key founder members seem to account for both their involvement at this pivotal moment and the omission of other eligible women, such as the painter Catherine Read.

The first Royal Academicians were presumably also looking to their continental counterparts and predecessors, in particular the Académie royale de peinture et sculpture in Paris, which had admitted Marie-Thérèse Reboul in 1757.[13] Only three further women were accepted into the Académie by 1789, however, and Hannah Williams has described the institution as approaching the admission of women with 'even more trepidation than that of foreigners and heretics'.[14] The Royal Academy demonstrated a comparable lack of confidence in its original decision, closing the doors firmly – albeit tacitly – behind Moser and Kauffman.[15] Despite numerous successes by women artists at Royal Academy exhibitions (and their occasional nomination for election) throughout the eighteenth and nineteenth centuries, there was not to be another woman Royal Academician until 1936.[16] The first record of this matter being officially debated appears only in the late nineteenth century but the exclusion of women beyond the founding members may be partially explained by the rapidly expanding

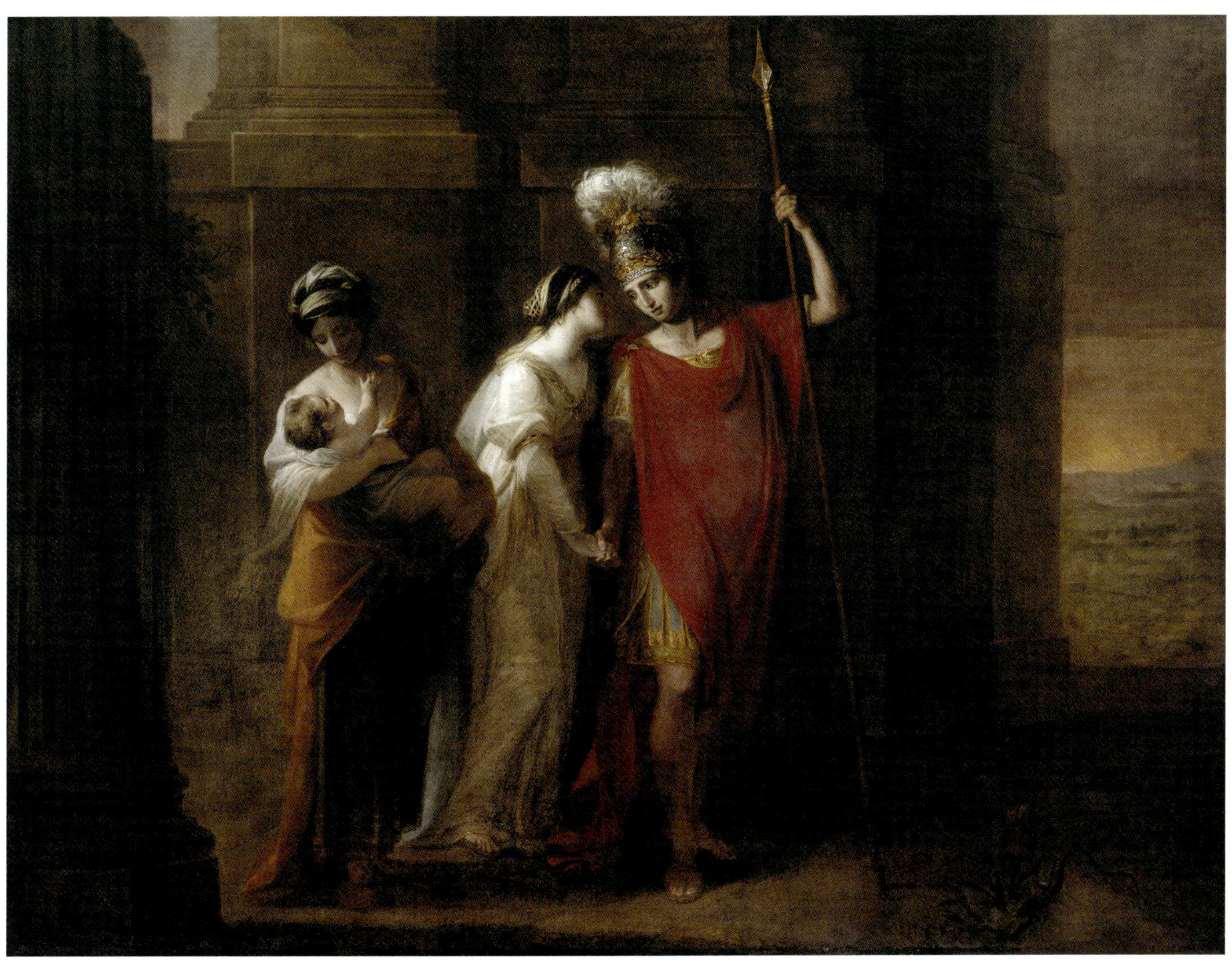

Fig. 11 *Hector Taking Leave of Andromache*, 1768. Oil on canvas, 134.6 × 177.8 cm. National Trust Collections (Saltram House, The Morley Collection [accepted in lieu of tax by H.M. Treasury and transferred to the National Trust in 1957]), inv. 872177

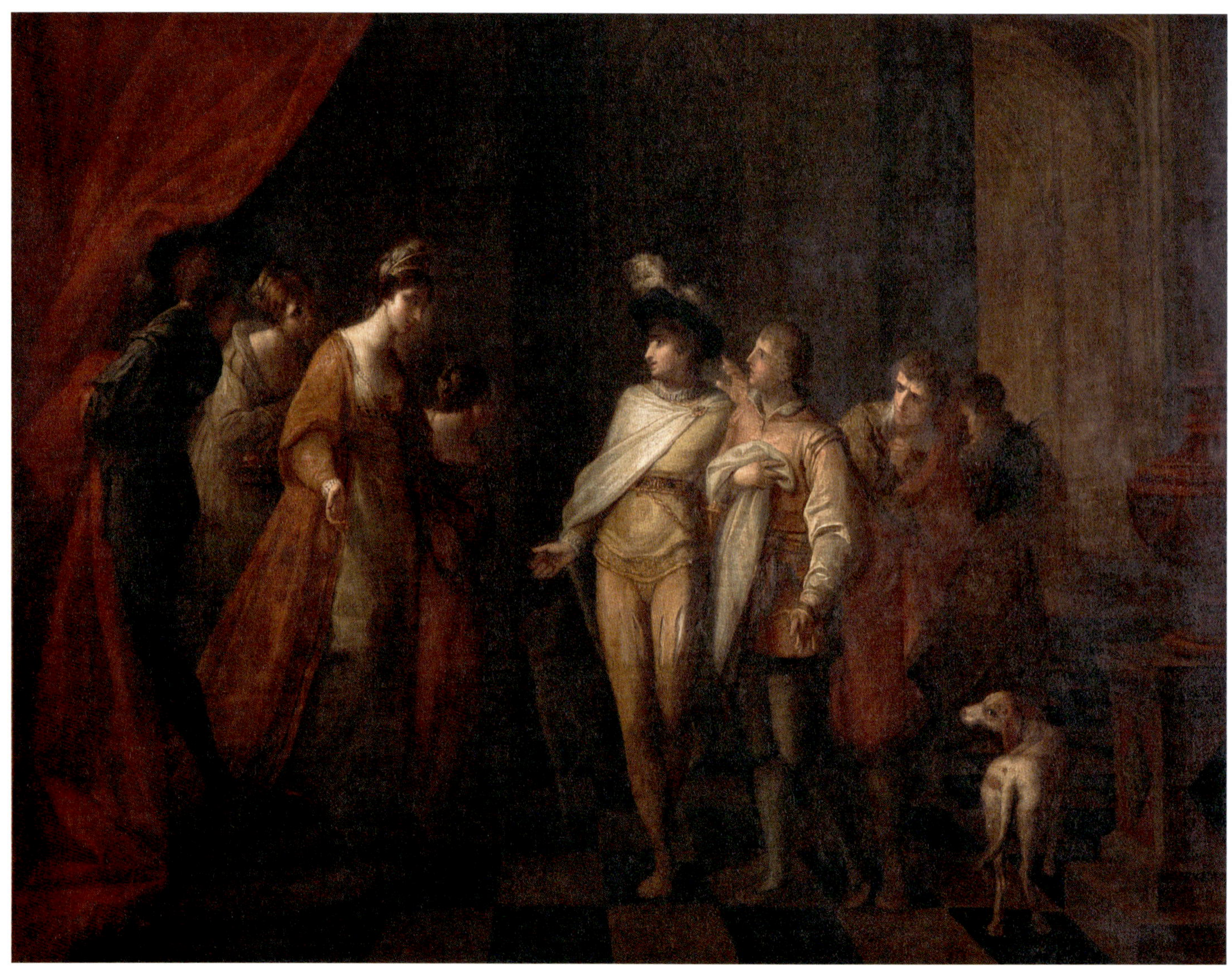

Fig. 12 *Interview of Edgar and Elfrida after Her Marriage to Athelwold*, 1769–70. Oil on canvas, 153.7 × 214.6 cm. National Trust Collections (Saltram House, The Morley Collection [accepted in lieu of tax by H.M. Treasury and transferred to the National Trust in 1957]), inv. 872179

field of artists eligible for election during this period – in one respect, an indication of the institution's success – and by the growing formality and reliance on precedent within the organisation.

Johan Zoffany's group portrait of the new Royal Academicians (1771–2; cat. 14) famously objectifies Kauffman and Moser, including their likenesses as portraits on the wall, almost comically observing the male-only life-drawing class at one remove. This tongue-in-cheek solution enabled Zoffany to feature the women in his scenario without censure. It is, perhaps, an indication of their importance that he did not simply leave them out. Nevertheless, this portrayal inevitably emphasises their difference and has been much analysed in these terms.[17] Memorably described by Angela Rosenthal as an 'icon of exclusion',[18] it certainly encapsulates the inherent contradictions in the women's status at the Academy. More recently, Paris Spies-Gans has acknowledged this duality while contending that there was more to their experiences than 'exclusion and discrimination'.[19] As far as their public image was concerned, Kauffman and Moser were indeed closely identified with the institution in much the same way as their male colleagues. They enjoyed the Royal Academicians' privilege of exhibiting their work at the prestigious Annual Exhibition, which served as a crucial 'barometer of reputations' for artists at this date.[20]

However, this contrasts sharply with their distinct lack of official involvement in the administration and inner life of the institution.[21] No written rule excluded them yet there was clearly an expectation that the women would have no say in the day-to-day running of the Academy. Mary Moser appears to have tested the boundaries by attending General Assembly on occasion from 1779 onwards but neither woman served on the Academy's governing Council or the Annual Exhibition's Hanging Committee, nor did they teach in its Schools or become Professors.[22] Official dinners and less formal dining clubs were also male preserves but both women were, nevertheless, involved in the institution's social circles, and Kauffman's friendships with Reynolds and others suggest that she would, at least, have been well appraised of Academy matters.[23]

Kauffman's public prestige as a founding Royal Academician was a crucial marker of her success in London and surely played a part in her decision to remain in the city for over a decade. She made full use of her status, setting her fees in line with those of successful fellow members like Reynolds and approaching the Annual Exhibitions as a strategic opportunity to demonstrate her abilities as a history painter.[24] This was fully in keeping with the institution's rhetoric but in contrast to the productions of many of its leading artists. At the Academy's inaugural Annual Exhibition in 1769, Kauffman showed four ambitious multi-figure scenes from Homer and Virgil.[25] These were well received, with the artist hailed as 'a young lady of uncommon genius and merit' and the paintings bought by Theresa and John Parker, Lord and Lady Boringdon, for Saltram House in Devon (for example, fig. 11).[26] Continuing in this vein throughout the 1770s, Kauffman displayed her erudition with innovative scenes from a broad range of literary sources both ancient and modern as well as exhibiting portraits.[27] Tapping into the cultural currents of her adoptive home, Kauffman was quick to engage with the growing interest in depicting Shakespearean subjects. Moreover, she was one of the first artists at the Royal Academy to portray episodes derived from accounts of British history rather than from literature.[28] Paul de Rapin's *History of England* (1724–27) was the source for several scenes from medieval history including *Eleanora Sucking the Venom Out of the Wound of Her Husband, King Edward I* (1776; cat 11), a striking example of Kauffman's originality in unearthing intriguing and infrequently depicted scenes featuring heroic female protagonists. The artist's English history paintings proved particularly rewarding in terms of reproductive prints which enhanced her fame.[29] In 1771, one of her Academy exhibits, *Interview of Edgar and Elfrida after Her Marriage to Athelwold* (fig. 12), was said to have 'raised her reputation in England to the highest point'.[30]

At the Royal Academy, Kauffman's dedication to history painting often received critical approval. In 1778 the *London*

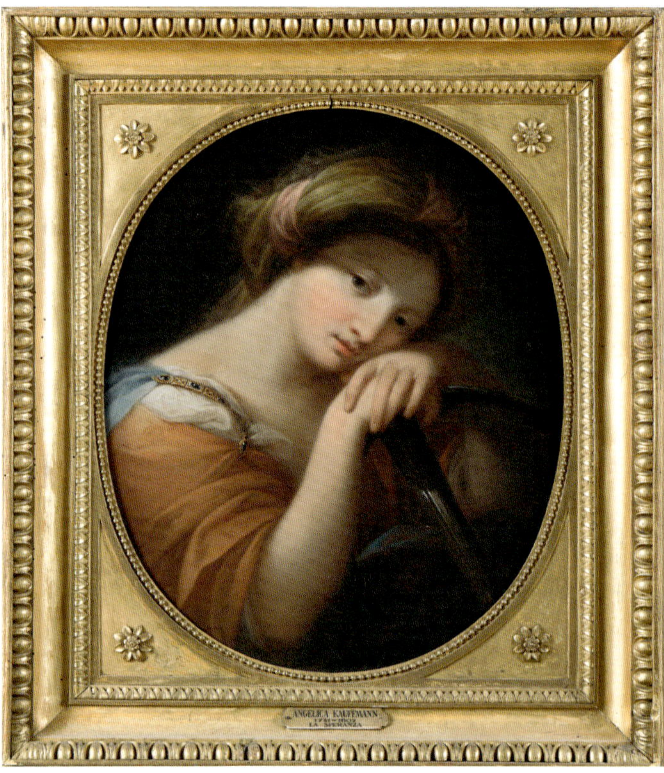

Fig. 13 *Hope*, 1765. Oil on canvas, 58 × 47.2 cm. Accademia Nazionale di San Luca, Rome, inv. 286

Chronicle observed, for example: 'It is surely somewhat singular that while so many of our male artists are employed upon portraits, landscapes and the other inferior species of painting, this lady should be almost uniformly carried, by the boldness and sublimity of her genius, to venture upon historical pieces.'[31] Her focus on female characters and domestic settings in her history paintings was also noted and generally interpreted by her contemporaries in terms of her 'natural' predisposition as a woman.[32] This reading possibly aided her acceptance as a history painter, situating her work as a variant of the genre that did not encroach on the 'male' territory of more epic scenes. More recently, scholars have argued for a nuanced analysis of features such as the domesticity of Kauffman's *Odyssey* scenes, suggesting that her compositions 'mediate between the artist's own subject position and the traditional forms of history painting'.[33] Whereas her historical works broadly reinforce traditional 'female' virtues, Bettina Baumgärtel has demonstrated how Kauffman consistently portrayed active rather than passive heroines, and her insistence on incorporating women into public life and historical and literary discourse through her choice of subjects in itself challenged the status quo.[34]

Kauffman's exceptional celebrity as a woman artist and a member of the Royal Academy did not come without a cost, however. In addition to gendered criticism, the flipside of her fame was a seam of gossip and innuendo.[35] This took on tangible form at the Academy in 1775 when the Irish artist Nathaniel Hone (1718–1784) sent *The Pictorial Conjuror, Displaying the Whole Art of Optical Deception* (National Gallery of Ireland, Dublin) to the Annual Exhibition. The painting depicts an old man, with a girl at his knee, conjuring a picture from an array of old prints. The most obvious target was Reynolds – known for his liberal recycling of motifs from the Old Masters – but the girl's pose also mimics Kauffman's painting *Hope* (1765; fig. 13), which was issued as a print in England in February 1775.

More scurrilously, Hone included a group of naked artists in the background cavorting in front of St Paul's Cathedral, one a woman holding a palette and wearing only black stockings which was thought to depict Kauffman herself. This mocked those artists – among them Kauffman and Reynolds – who were involved in a short-lived commission to paint the interiors of St Paul's in 1773.[36] Kauffman immediately took issue with this, and her subsequent letter to the Academy's Council (cat. 38) suggests that, initially, they attempted to placate her without removing the painting.[37] She was forced to exhort the Council to demonstrate 'a Respect to the Sex which it is their glory to support' and threatened to quit the Academy if they did not – 'withdrawing one object who never deserved his or their ridicule'.[38] Her warning shot prompted a ballot. The Royal Academicians voted in favour of Kauffman, and Hone was instructed to remove his painting.[39] The saga rumbled on.

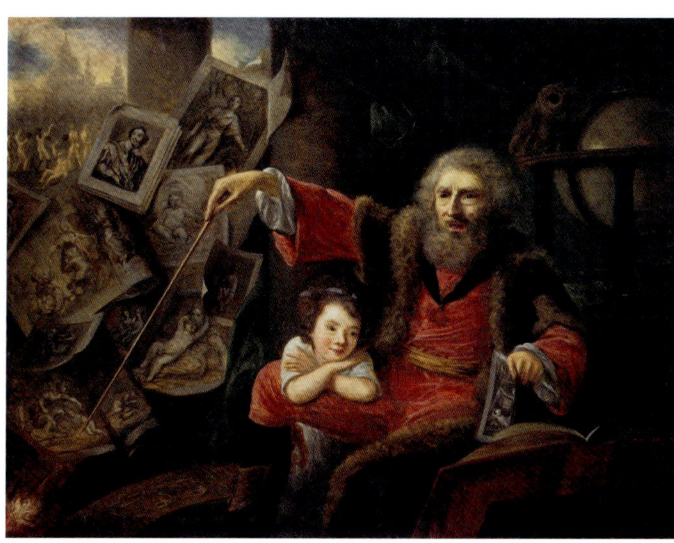

Fig. 14 NATHANIEL HONE *Sketch for 'The Conjuror'*, 1775. Oil on wood, 57.5 × 81.9 cm. Tate, inv. T00938

Hone insisted on exhibiting the work (with the naked figures transformed into a group of clothed gentlemen drinking wine at a table) in a one-man show, denying any intended slight on Kauffman.[40] The offending scene can, however, still be seen in his preparatory oil sketch for the work (fig. 14).

Having successfully asserted herself at the Academy both through her art and against moral slights, Kauffman was at the height of her powers and popularity in England during the late 1770s. A much more respectful representation of her appeared on the Academy's walls in the Annual Exhibition in 1779 in Richard Samuel's *Portraits in the Characters of the Muses in the Temple of Apollo* (1778; cat. 19), in which she features as the only artist among a group of 'bluestockings', distinguished female musicians, writers and scholars. Although this was a speculative work, produced without the involvement of any of the women depicted, it was evidently intended as a positive portrayal and is, as Elizabeth Eger has noted, a unique example of a 'group portrait of women united by their professional status' in Britain at this date.[41] Rather than presenting the women as otherworldly conduits of inspiration to great men, she adds that Samuel painted them with 'their feet firmly on the ground, demanding respect and provoking curiosity'.[42] The same exhibition featured seven of Kauffman's own paintings.

Kauffman's crowning accolade at the Academy, though, was the invitation to adorn the ceiling of one of its prestigious purpose-built apartments at New Somerset House, designed by Sir William Chambers, which were unveiled in 1780. The architectural and visual programme of the building has been described as fostering the sense of 'an ascent to Parnassus', leading the exhibition visitor up to the splendours of the Great Room.[43] However, as Helen Valentine has argued, Kauffman's works in the Royal Academicians' Council Room – alongside those of Benjamin West and others – were primarily for an audience of her peers. As part of a decorative scheme casting the Academy as 'collective arbiters of national taste… within their own palace of art' this was therefore a particularly significant honour within the institution.[44]

The four oval panels depict *Invention* (see p. 80), *Design* (cat. 24), *Composition* (cat. 25) and *Colouring* (p. 81) and are together known as *The Elements of Art* (1780). How much Kauffman personally determined their subject matter is not known but the presence of four preparatory grisaille drawings (cats 20–23) with only minor differences from the finished compositions suggests a possible consultative process between the artist, Reynolds, Chambers and other Royal Academicians. Kauffman's four cornerstones of art synthesise established academic art theory, referencing Reynolds, Johann Joachim Winckelmann, Jonathan Richardson and earlier writers. Bettina Baumgärtel has demonstrated that, in personifying all four as women, Kauffman deviates significantly from tradition, forging her own interpretation of the artistic process and visually identifying this with her own practice as an artist.[45] Kauffman also directly references the Royal Academy context: *Design* draws the revered Belvedere Torso, two plaster casts of which were among the prized possessions of the early Royal

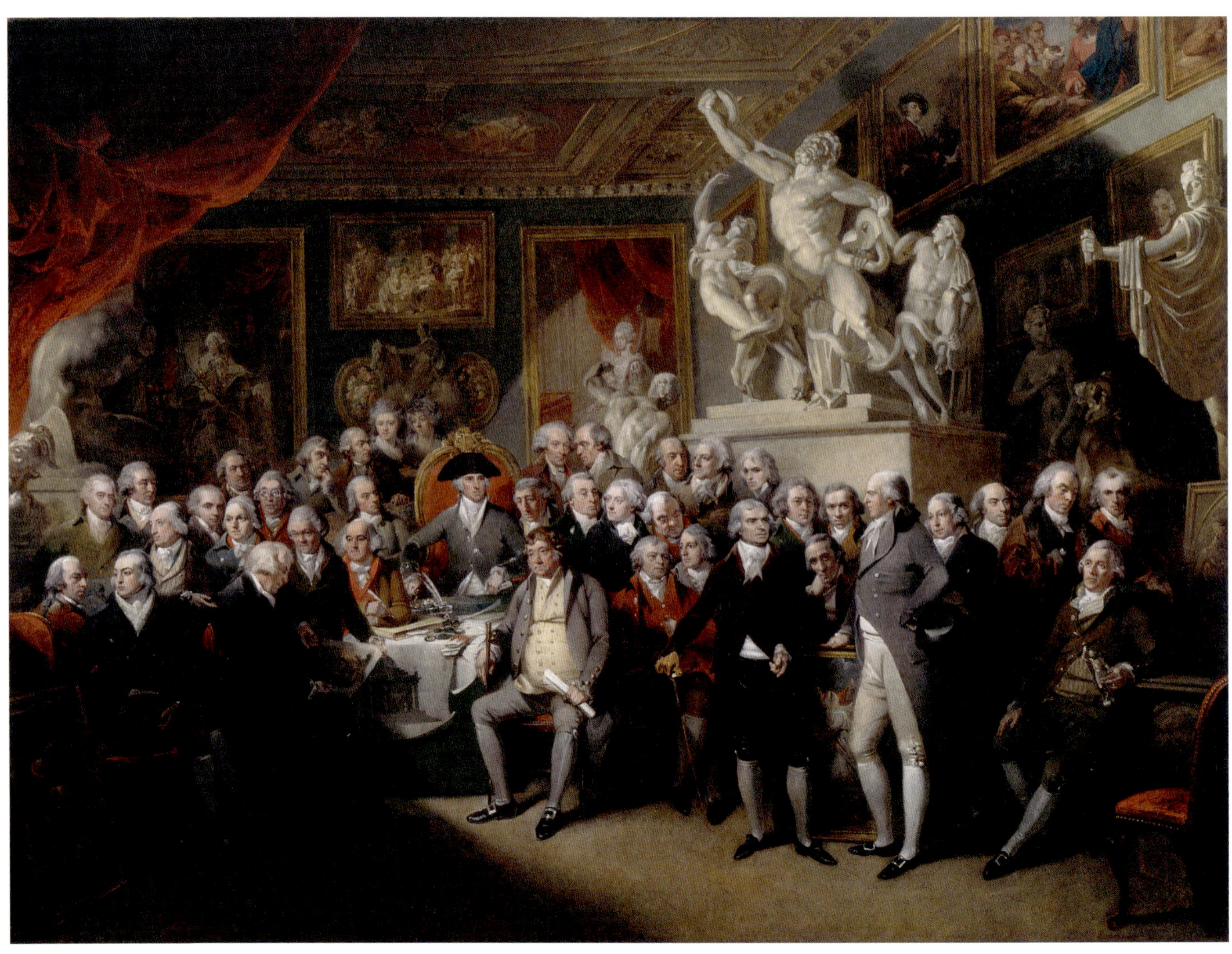

Fig. 15 HENRY SINGLETON *The Royal Academicians in General Assembly,* 1795. Oil on canvas, 198.1 × 259 cm. Royal Academy of Arts, London, inv. 03/1310

Academy. At this date, the Torso already featured on the RA Schools' silver medal under the title 'Study'. After Kauffman's evocative depiction, several Academy artists followed suit to the extent that it became emblematic of the institution; it features, for instance, in Henry Singleton's group portrait *The Royal Academicians in General Assembly* (1795; fig. 15) as well as in Benjamin West's *Self-portrait* of 1793 (Royal Academy of Arts). In his *Guide Through the Royal Academy* (1781), Joseph Baretti singles out Kauffman's works for praise. So famous is she that she is referred to only by her first name; the work of 'the celebrated Angelica' is hailed as being 'executed with all that grace, elegance and accuracy which distinguish the best productions of this Extraordinary lady'.[46]

Kauffman's *Elements of Art* can be seen in the original decorative scheme of the Council Room at New Somerset House in Henry Singleton's group portrait, situated directly above a portrayal of Kauffman herself. Ironically, she did not attend such gatherings and there is a poetic justice in the presence of her visualisation of academic art theory on the ceiling of this room, as Brigid von Preussen has observed.[47] By the time Kauffman and her work featured in Singleton's portrait, she had been living in Rome for nearly fifteen years. Her early biographer, Giovanni Gherardo de Rossi, attributed her decision to return to Italy mainly to her father's health, noting that it 'demanded her complete separation from a country with which she was connected, and which appreciated and honoured her and to which she confessed attachment and love'.[48] However, Wendy Wassyng Roworth has suggested that Kauffman's departure can also be explained by the lack of full-blooded support for history painting in England, despite the stated aims of the Royal Academy.[49] Kauffman's absence was keenly felt in London, and the *St James's Chronicle* suggested instead that the Academy was directly to blame for her decision to leave because it had not elected her husband, Antonio Zucchi, as a full Royal Academician.[50] If either counted among her motives for moving to Italy, Kauffman appeared to hold no significant grudge towards the institution and continued sending paintings to the Royal Academy's Annual Exhibitions until 1797.[51]

As Kauffman's inclusion in Singleton's group portrait suggests, her move to Italy did not diminish her standing as a founding member. Her enduring presence in the story of the Royal Academy, and of British art more generally, was bolstered by her continuing popularity among British patrons and visitors to her famous studio in Rome. If Kauffman's absence put her relationship with the Academy on a different footing, this seems to have been largely positive: she avoided involvement in the politics and rivalries that plagued the institution while continuing to enjoy the prestige and privileges of membership. In return, the Academy benefitted from its association with an artist of international standing. The sense of continuing interest in, and respect for, Kauffman among her fellow Royal Academicians is underlined by the fact that a detailed account of her grand funeral in Rome (cat. 39), arranged by the famous sculptor Antonio Canova, was not only read out to the General Assembly meeting in 1807 but also transcribed in full in the minutes for posterity. While it is clear that the institutional context of the Academy presented considerable barriers for Kauffman – and other women artists at this date – within this challenging framework, she successfully negotiated a place for herself as a Royal Academician. It seems particularly fitting that her visual legacy – the *Elements of Art* – continues to greet visitors in the Front Hall of Burlington House.

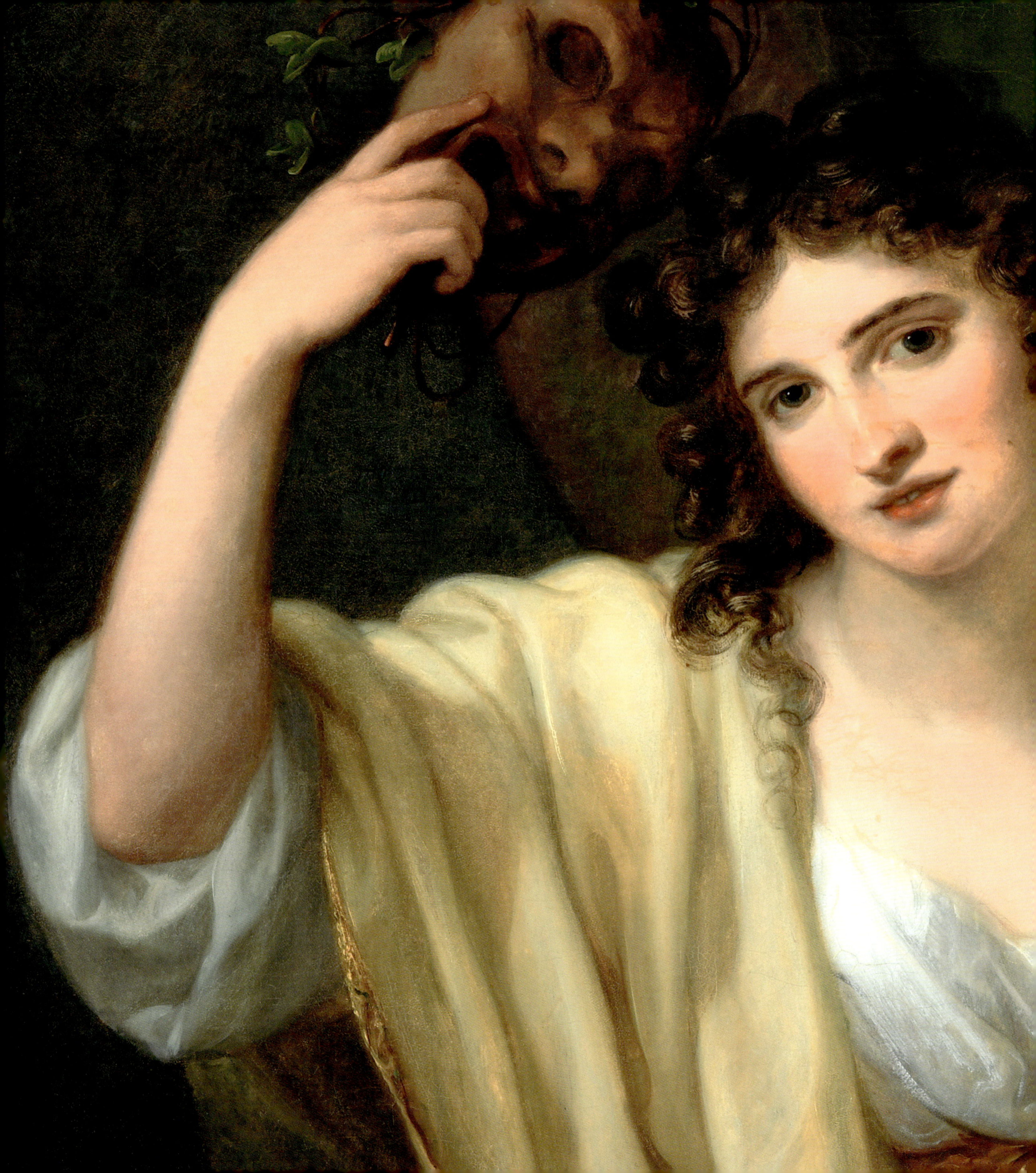

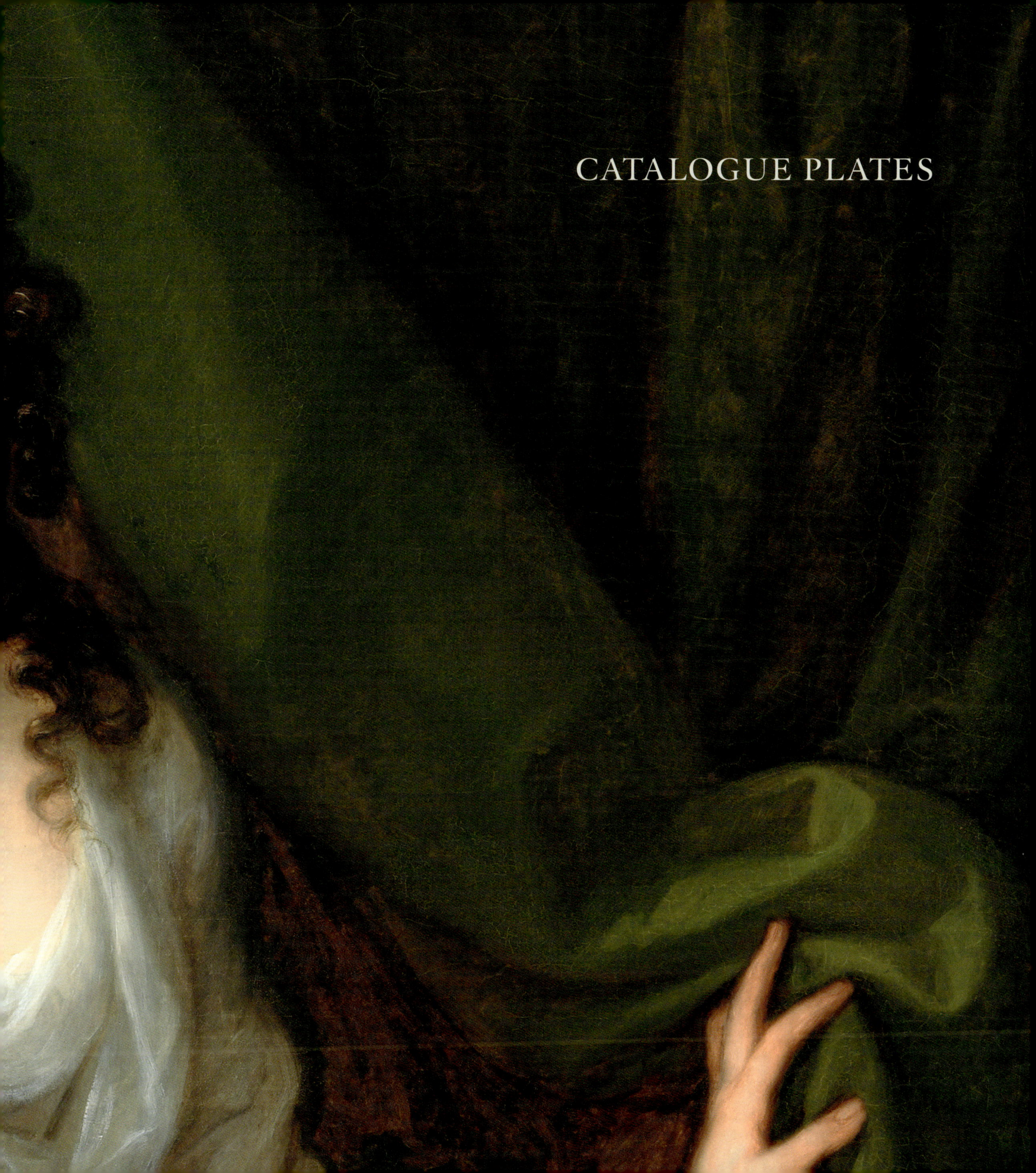

CATALOGUE PLATES

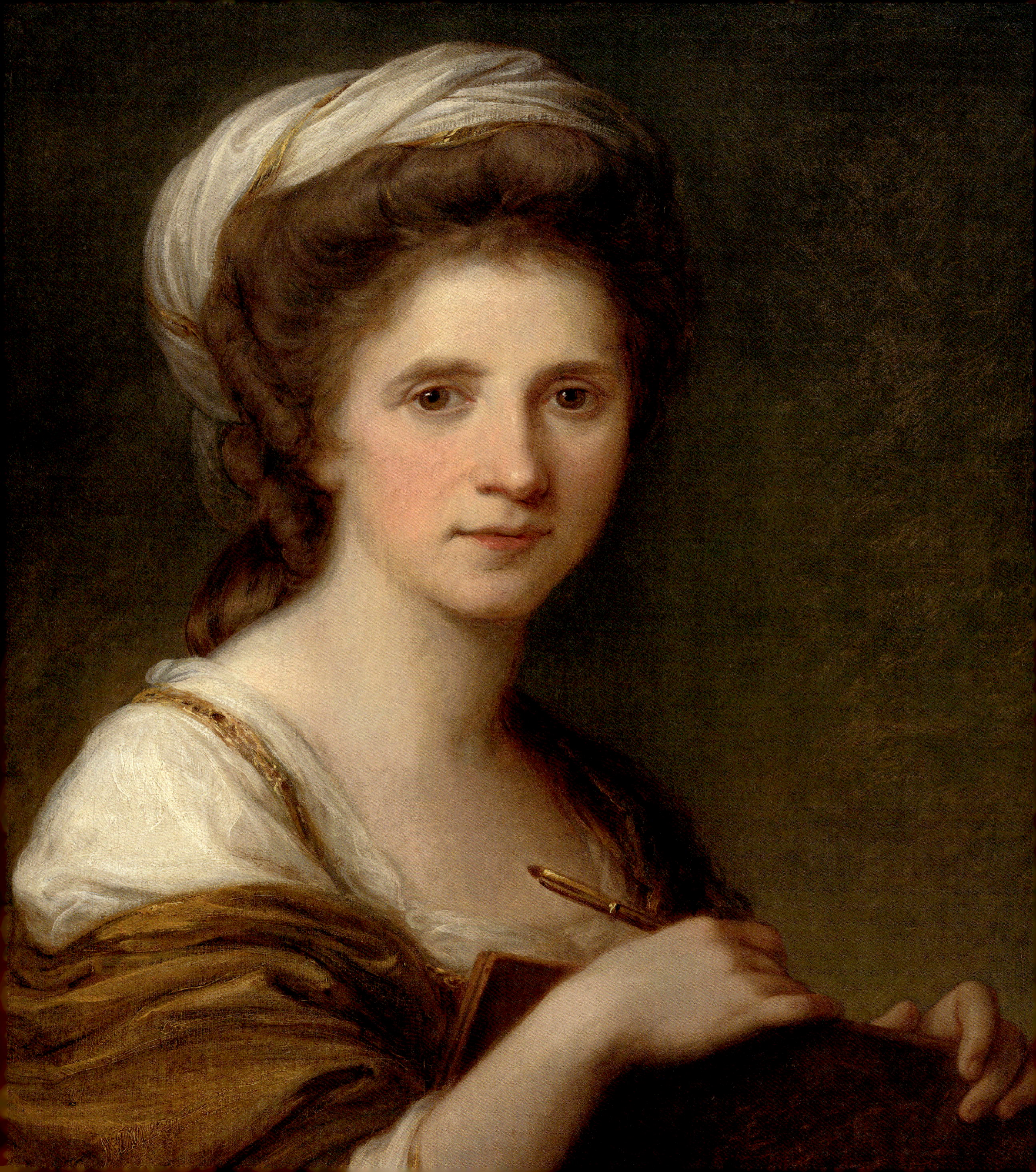

STAGING THE SELF

Angelica Kauffman's self-portraits are among her most confident, sophisticated and intriguing works. She returned to her own likeness throughout her career, producing at least 24 self-portraits in addition to various self-referential images, consciously blurring the distinction between self-portraiture and allegorical representations (cats 26 and 33).[1] Painting herself offered the perfect vehicle with which to control her own image and explore her identity as an artist. Kauffman's self-portraits shaped her reputation and enhanced her fame, especially through the circulation of reproductive engravings.

Several important self-portraits highlight pivotal moments in Kauffman's life.[2] Her 1781 portrayal in the traditional costume of the Bregenz Forest (cat. 1) initially appears to be a relatively straightforward representation of the artist's likeness. Her face and distinctive outfit are rendered with great delicacy and skill but the painting is otherwise plain, lacking any setting or accoutrements. Yet this work was of great personal significance to the artist. Kauffman regards the viewer with an intense, thoughtful gaze, appearing closer to her real age than the youthful features of her other self-portraits. Painted at a time of transition, between England and Italy, this image can be read as a meditation on both her familial and artistic heritage.

After fifteen years in London, Kauffman set out for Italy in July 1781 accompanied by her husband Antonio Zucchi and her elderly father. The group stopped en route at the latter's native Schwarzenberg in the Bregenz Forest, Vorarlberg, Austria, where Kauffman consciously identified herself with her paternal homeland by painting her own portrait dressed in the area's traditional costume.[3] This device visually reconnected the artist with her younger self and her aspirations, echoing two early self-portraits in similar attire, one showing her standing at her easel, sleeves rolled up and ready to paint (c. 1757–59; see p. 40).[4] The 1781 iteration also possibly alludes to her art-historical knowledge and alignments as a mature artist. Her distinctive black hat was an important part of the area's summer dress

Detail of cat. 2

which all women would have been expected to wear in public but its angle also seems reminiscent of some of Rubens's portraits including that of Helena Fourment (1630–32, Calouste Gulbenkian Museum, Lisbon; this work was at Houghton Hall in England during the eighteenth century), and his sombre self-portrait of 1623 (Royal Collection).[5]

Kauffman kept this painting in her studio for the rest of her life but it became widely known posthumously through the engraved frontispieces of Giovanni Gherardo de Rossi's 1811 biography of the artist and its German translation.[6] Despite the personal significance of this work, it was not the portrayal that Kauffman chose to represent her in the pantheon of artists' self-portraits at the Gallerie degli Uffizi in Florence, and her concern over this matter highlights the importance she placed on fashioning her public image for posterity. The gallery had already acquired a self-portrait of Kauffman in 1772 – one of the two early paintings depicting herself in traditional Bregenz Forest dress (1757–59; see p. 40) – but Kauffman wished to replace this small, early work with a portrayal 'less unworthy of myself'.[7] Her reflections were possibly spurred on by reports of the rapturous reception of Reynolds's self-portrait at the Uffizi in 1775.[8] Kauffman's proposal to paint a new work was accepted in 1782 and the painting delivered in 1788 (1787; cat. 3). The artist explained that other commissions delayed its completion but the time she spent on it also indicates the effort and thought she expended on this image.[9]

Kauffman's second Uffizi portrait of 1787 is a self-icon in her mature style, presenting herself as a 'vestal virgin'.[10] Dressed in a simple white robe – like those in which she portrayed most of her female sitters at this period – she tapped into fashionable Neoclassical taste while avoiding the vagaries of specific trends to create a timeless image. The only decoration is on her belt which, in a learned nod to the painting's destination, sports a cameo owned by the Medici family showing a contest between Minerva and Neptune.[11] This large and striking painting inhabits a liminal space between a literal – if somewhat rejuvenated – depiction of the artist's likeness and a powerful symbolic image of Kauffman as creator and muse combined. The portrait lives up to the artist's reputation as the 'pittrice delle grazie' ('painter of the Graces'), emphasising her virtue and elegance, but it subtly lays claim to more. While the portrait has been described as Kauffman in the guise of a 'muse of painting', Bettina Baumgärtel has pointed out that she holds a chalk and board so can be more specifically interpreted as a muse or personification of *disegno*, traditionally the 'father' of all the visual arts.[12] Kauffman's efforts paid off: her portrait was chosen to hang next to that of Michelangelo himself at the Uffizi.[13]

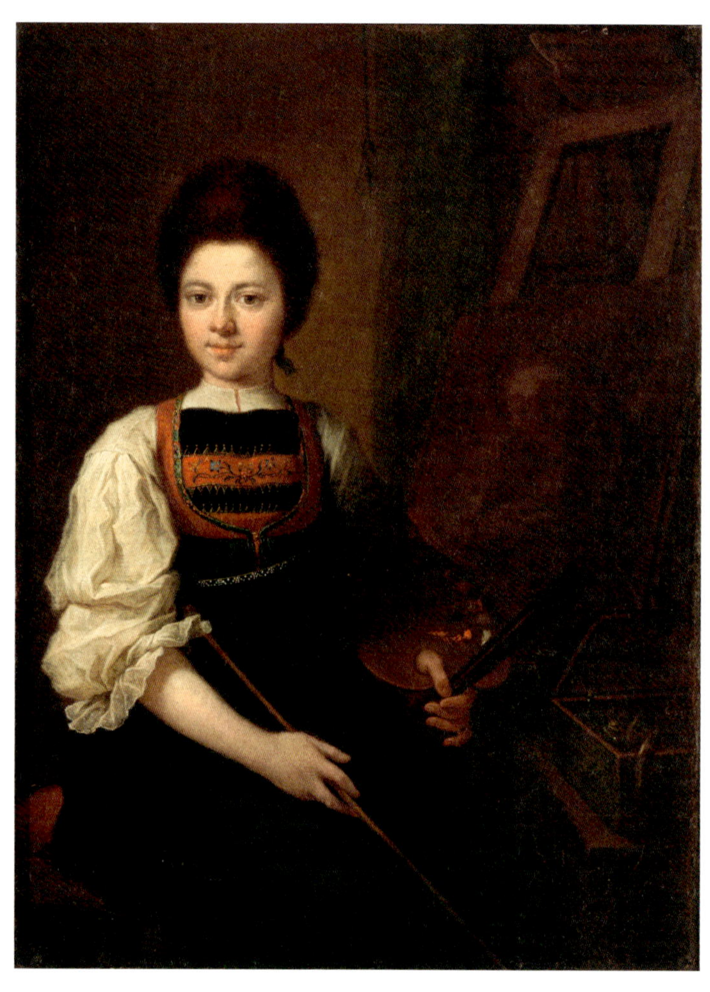

Self-portrait in the Traditional Costume of the Bregenz Forest, Seated at Her Easel, c. 1757–59 (NOT EXHIBITED)
Oil on canvas, 46 × 33 cm
Gallerie degli Uffizi, Florence, inv. 1890, no. 4444

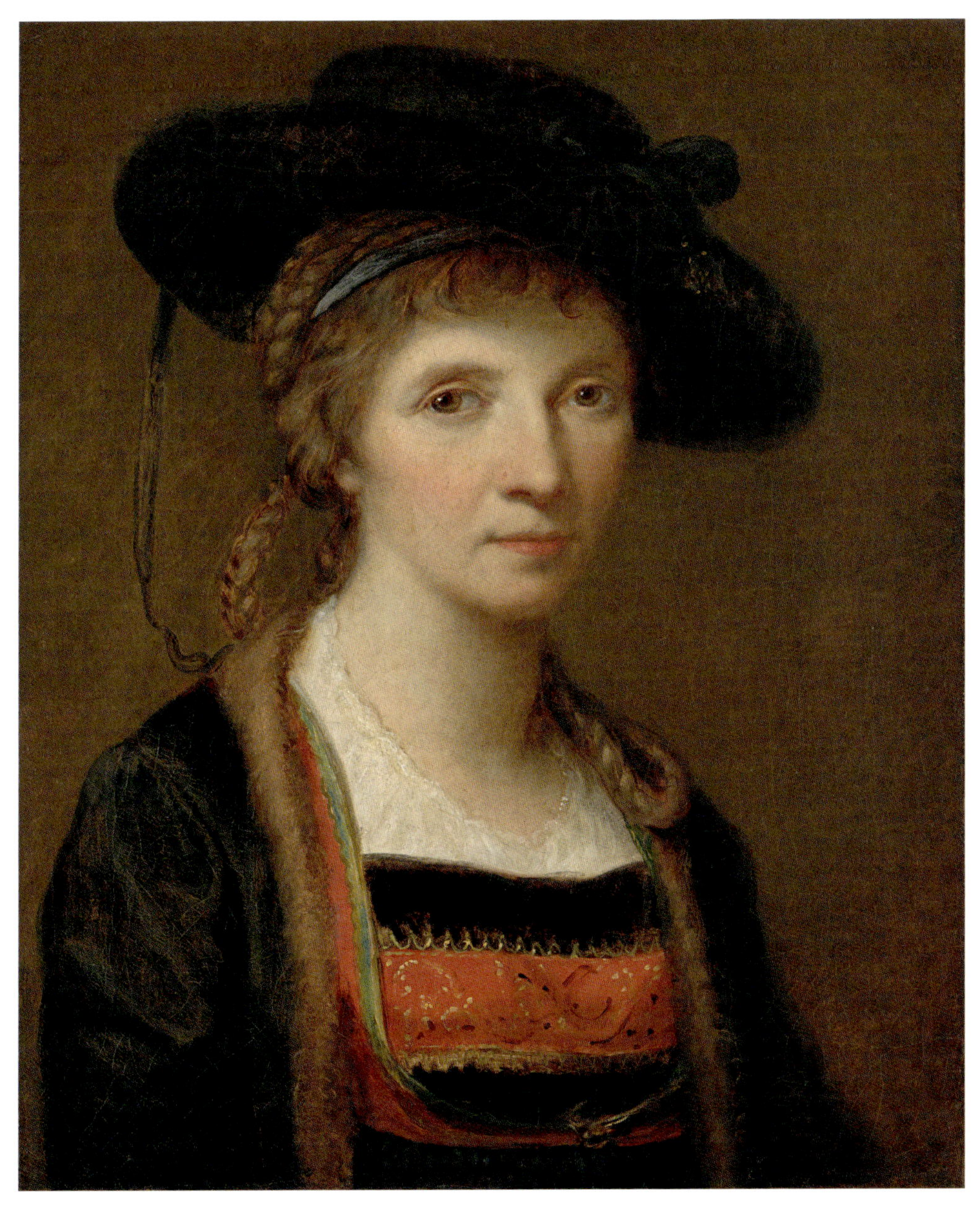

1
Self-portrait in the Traditional Costume of the Bregenz Forest, 1781
Oil on canvas, 61.4 × 49.2 cm
TLM, Ältere kunstgeschichtliche Sammlung,
Innsbruck, inv. Gem 301

2
Self-portrait with Stylus and Portfolio, 1784
Oil on canvas, 64.8 × 50.7 cm
Bayerische Staatsgemäldesammlungen Munich – Neue Pinakothek, inv. 1056

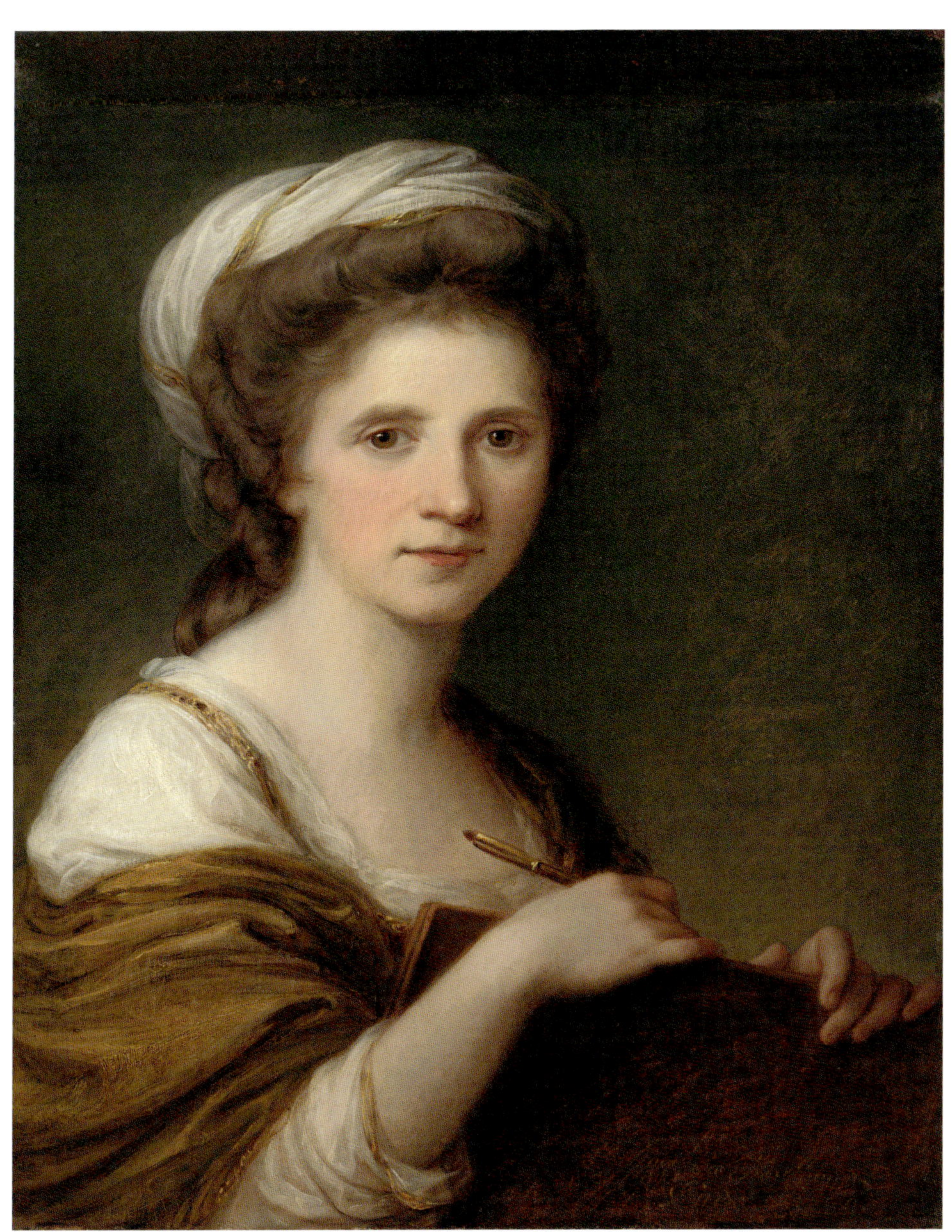

3
Self-portrait in all'antica Dress, 1787
Oil on canvas, 128 × 93.5 cm
Gallerie degli Uffizi, Florence, inv. 1890, no. 1928

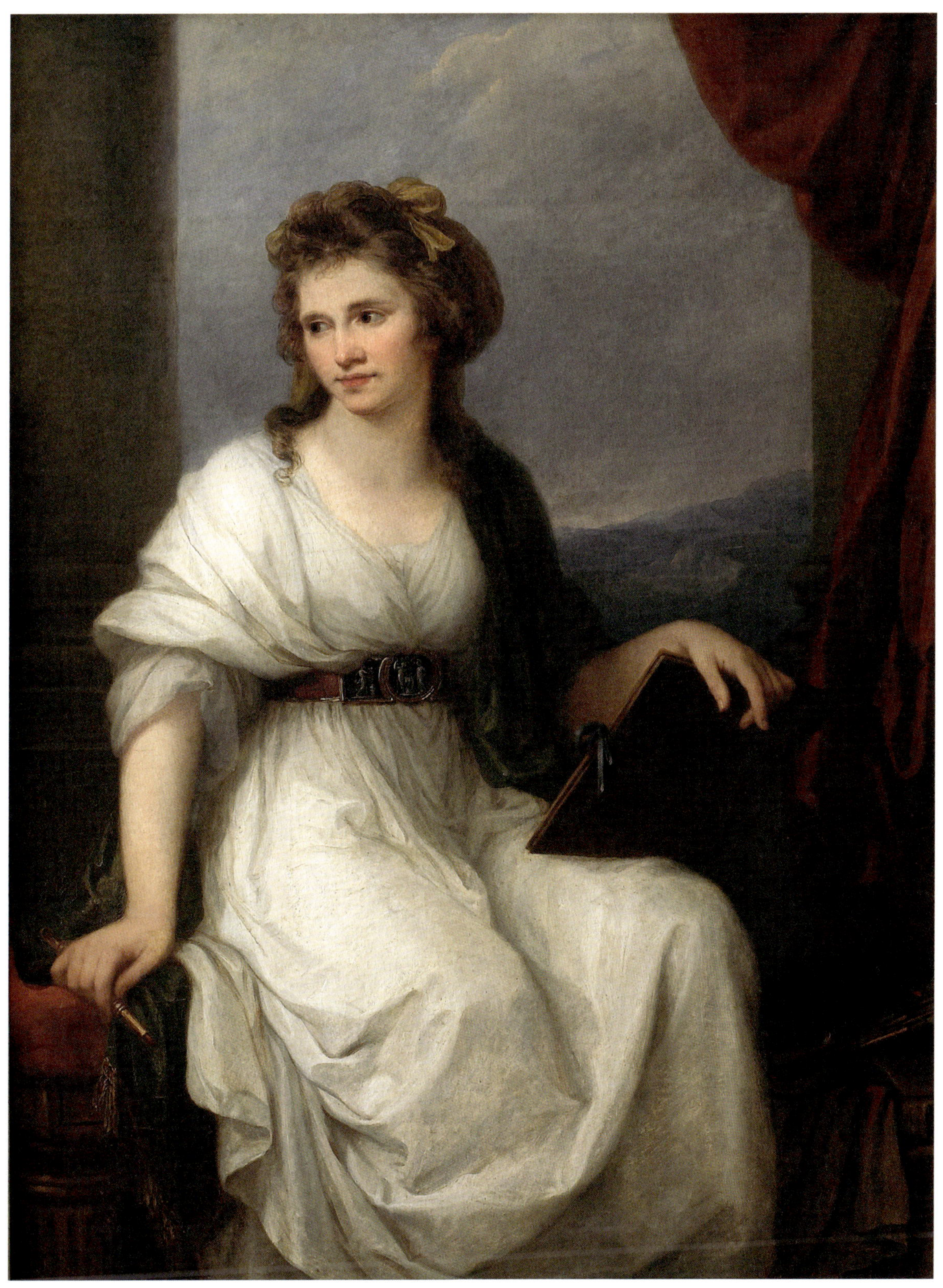

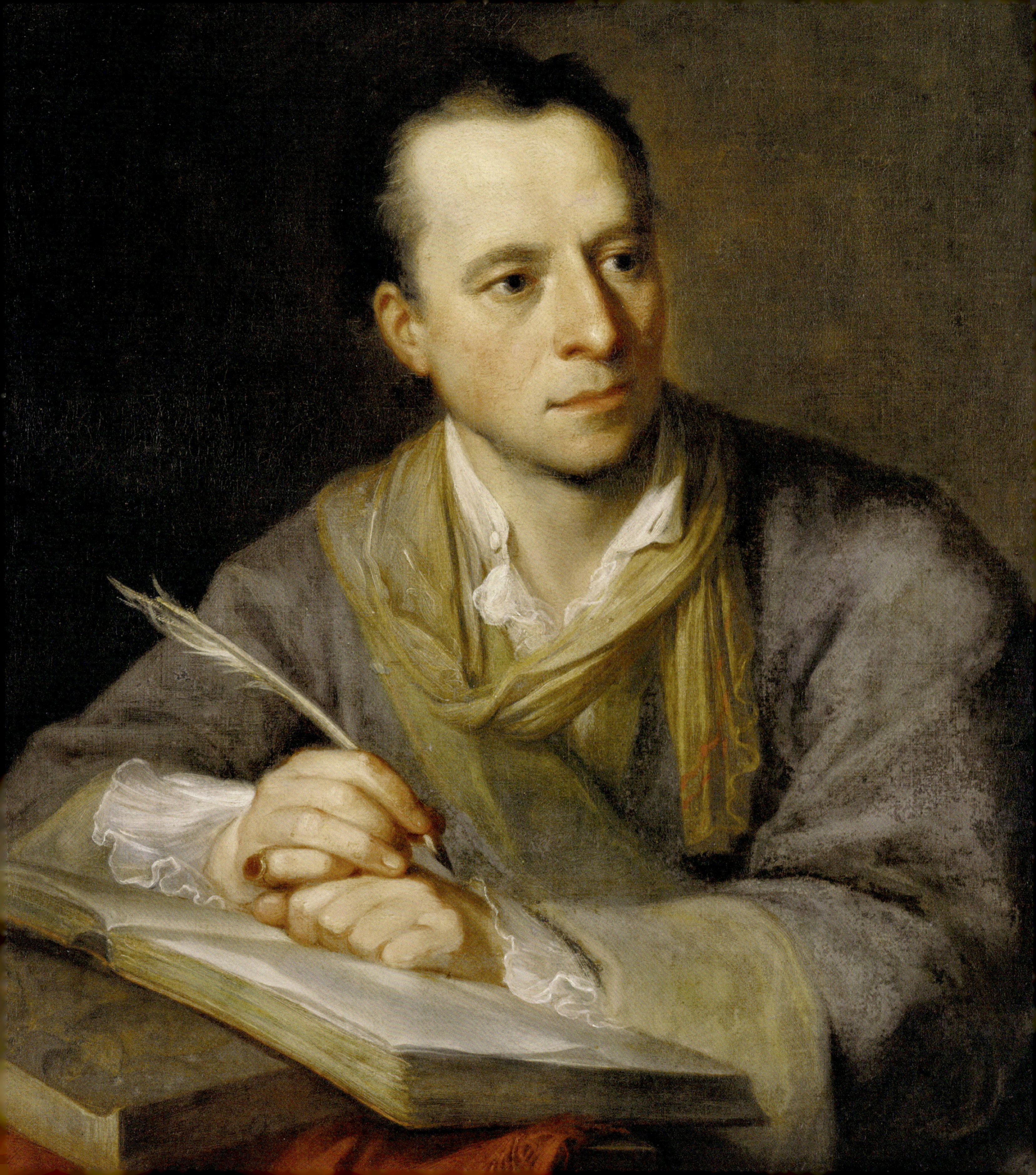

FROM ITALY TO ENGLAND

The seeds of Kauffman's success in England were sown long before her arrival. Visiting and living in several Italian cities during the late 1750s and early 1760s, she counted many British expatriates and visitors among her friends and early patrons. Their interest and support encouraged her move to London in 1766. Finding the capital a receptive environment, Kauffman rapidly established herself among the city's elite cultural and aristocratic circles and stayed for fifteen years.

Kauffman produced her first history paintings following her first visit to Rome in 1763. Works like *Penelope at Her Loom* (1764; cat. 4) demonstrate her precocious originality in focusing on a rarely portrayed figure from a popular text and in applying her knowledge of religious art to a classical theme. At the same time, the young artist secured numerous portrait commissions. These were mostly from men, and despite contemporary misgivings over women 'staring in men's faces', she successfully adopted an approach that emphasised informality and a sense of intimacy with the sitter.[1] Her understated portrayals offered a refreshing alternative to the more theatrical style of Rome's leading portraitist, Pompeo Batoni. Kauffman depicted the celebrated Neoclassical theorist Johann Joachim Winckelmann (1764; cat. 5), for example, seated at his desk deep in thought wearing casual attire. The small bas-relief of the Three Graces on which he leans is the only direct reference to his extensive knowledge of Classical art. The painting helped launch Kauffman's career internationally, her implied closeness to the eminent scholar enhancing her own reputation.[2]

Similarly, Kauffman's portrait of Britain's most famous actor and playwright, David Garrick (1764; cat. 6), served as her calling card in London when she sent it to exhibition in 1765. Garrick met and sat for Kauffman while visiting Naples with his wife, the Austrian dancer Eva Maria Veigel. The portrait makes no overt reference to his profession and shows Garrick in an unusual pose turning around in his chair to face the viewer as if offering a glimpse of the 'real' person behind the

Detail of cat. 5

roles.[3] Arriving in London the following year, Kauffman was already well known and travelled with Lady Bridget Wentworth Murray, wife of the British Resident in Venice, who provided a ready-made introduction to high society.[4] A striking feature of Kauffman's early years in London is the demand for portraits from women, especially after her commission to paint Queen Charlotte with her infant son George in 1767 (cat. 17).[5] Kauffman devised a novel set of motifs for her aristocratic female portraits that fostered an image of luxurious informality. Her sitters, seated in domestic interiors, wear loose Turkish-style dress and are often shown working at embroidery – presumably an allusion to the figure of Penelope from Homer's *Odyssey* (cat. 4) – or contemplating Classical sculpture. These portraits were part of the vogue for Turkish fashion stimulated by the travel accounts of Lady Mary Wortley Montagu and have been interpreted in terms of the gendering of orientalism. It has been argued that, as a woman artist, Kauffman was able to co-opt the aesthetics of the harem to create a cultural space for women away from the male gaze.[6] Kauffman's portraits, whether of men, women or family groups, were highly sought after in Britain and Ireland,[7] and – charging rates similar to those of artists like Reynolds – she had amassed the huge sum of £14,000 by the time she left London.[8]

Britain remained a challenging market for history painting yet Kauffman succeeded in gaining commissions in this genre. Mining an impressively eclectic range of historical and contemporary literature for inspiration, she created a distinctive repertoire of subjects, often highlighting female protagonists. *Cleopatra Adorning the Tomb of Mark Antony* of 1769–70 (cat. 8), for instance, was painted for her patron Brownlow Cecil and shown at the Royal Academy. As Bettina Baumgärtel has demonstrated, this upright canvas focuses on Cleopatra's mourning rather than her tumultuous life story, depicting the Egyptian queen dressed in modest but eye-catching white (as were many of the female heroines that Kauffman depicted during the 1770s).[9] Beyond classical literature, Kauffman portrayed scenes from later and contemporary sources including several paintings of *Rinaldo and Armida* (cats 9 and 10) from the Renaissance poet Torquato Tasso's *Jerusalem Delivered* (1581). Appropriately for her London audience, Kauffman also painted Shakespearean scenes and, more remarkably, obscure episodes from English history. *Eleanora Sucking the Venom Out of the Wound of Her Husband, King Edward I* (1776; cat. 11) depicts an anecdote highlighting the selfless heroism of Queen Eleanor of Castile who was said to have saved her husband's life by sucking venom from his wound when he was attacked with a poisoned dagger while on Crusade.[10] Several of these scenes proved hugely popular as engravings but it was Kauffman's emotive single-figure history paintings, like *Shakespeare's Tomb* (1772; cat. 12) and *Poor Maria* (1777; cat. 13), that really caught the public imagination, being copied in many forms and circulated all over Europe. Kauffman painted several versions of the latter, including one for Catherine the Great.[11]

4
Penelope at Her Loom, 1764
Oil on canvas, 172 × 122.2 cm
Brighton & Hove Museums, inv. FAH1975.33

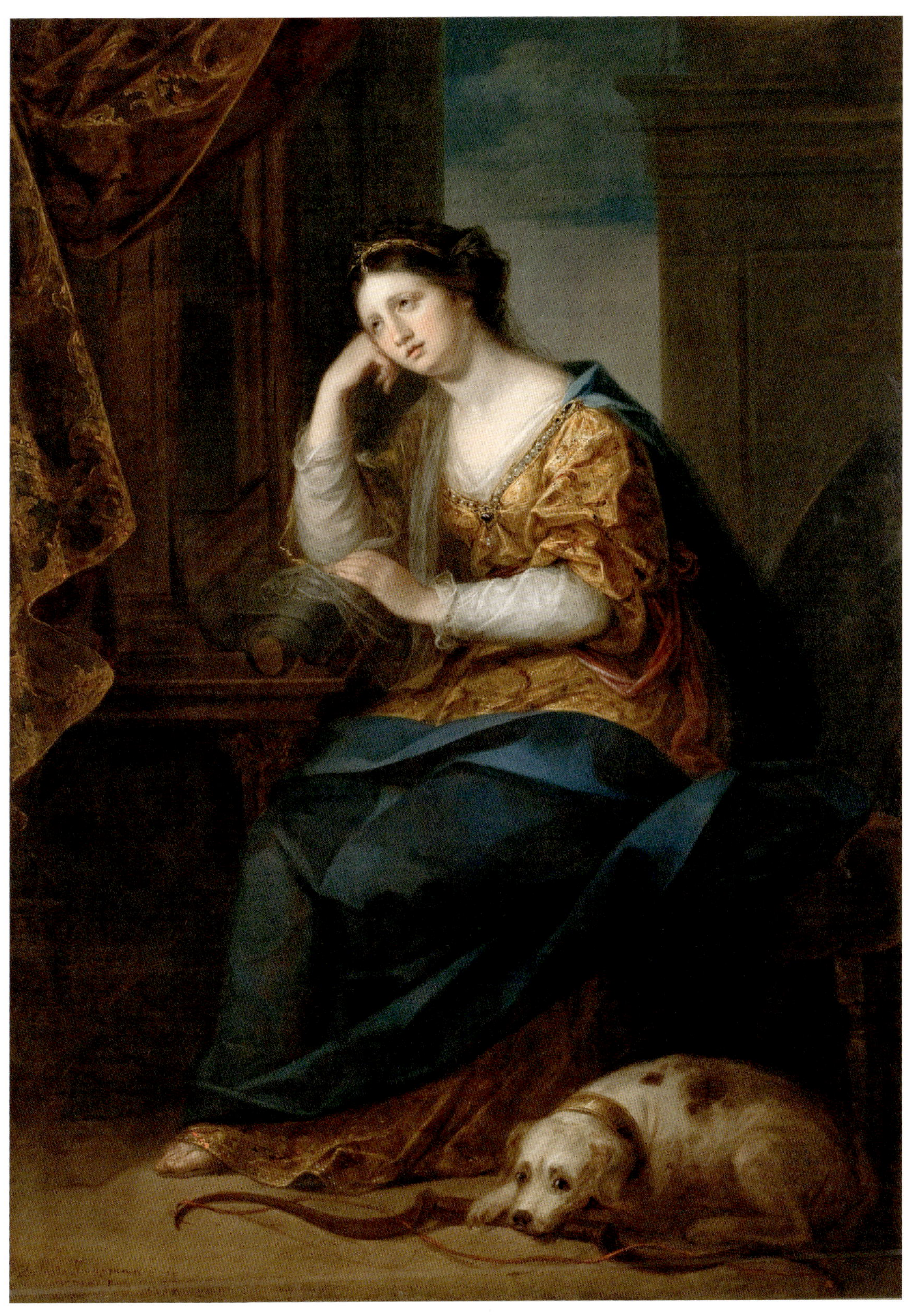

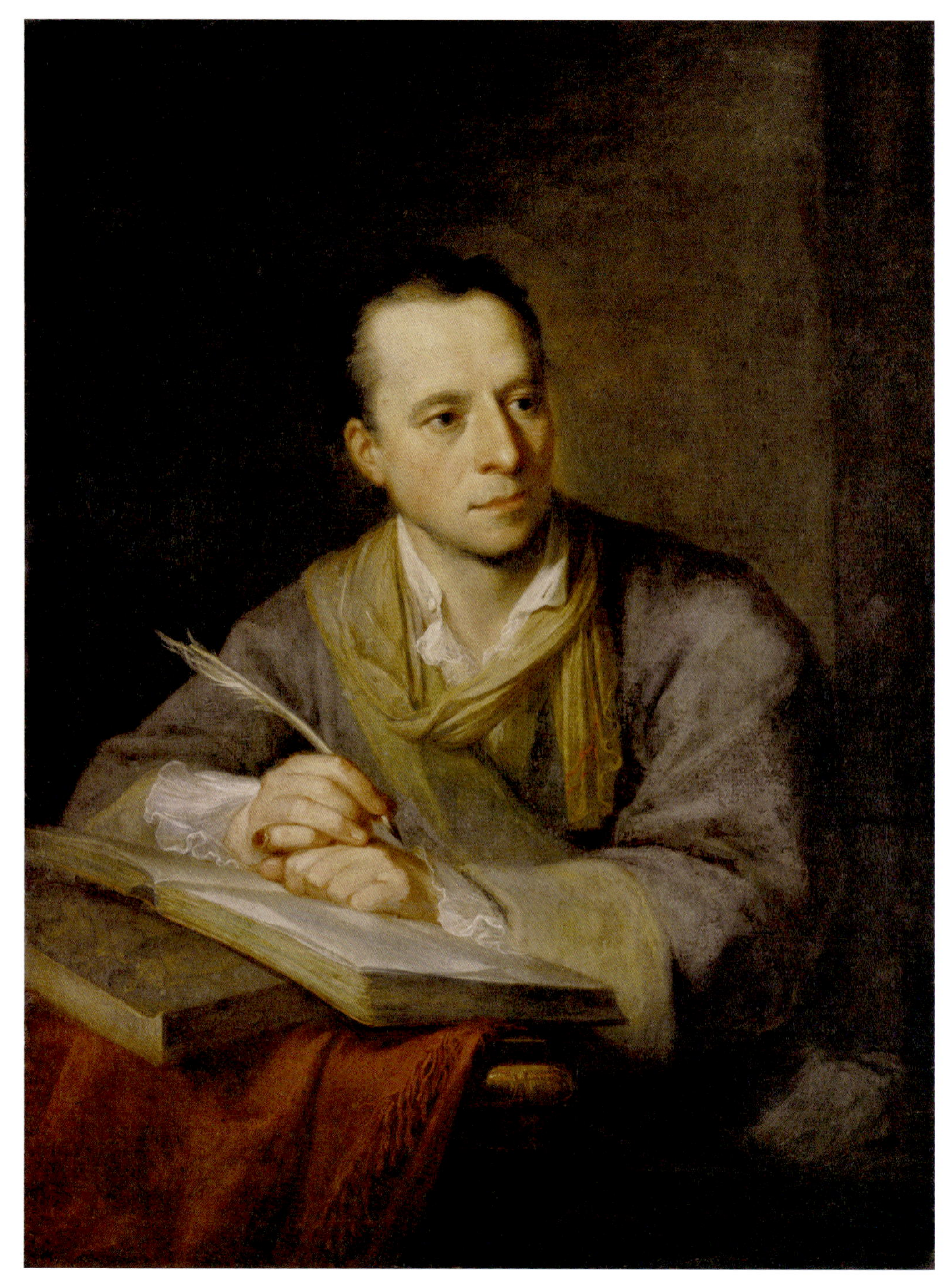

5
Portrait of Johann Joachim Winckelmann, 1764
Oil on canvas, 97 × 71 cm
Kunsthaus Zürich, Donated by Conrad Zeller, 1850, inv. 98

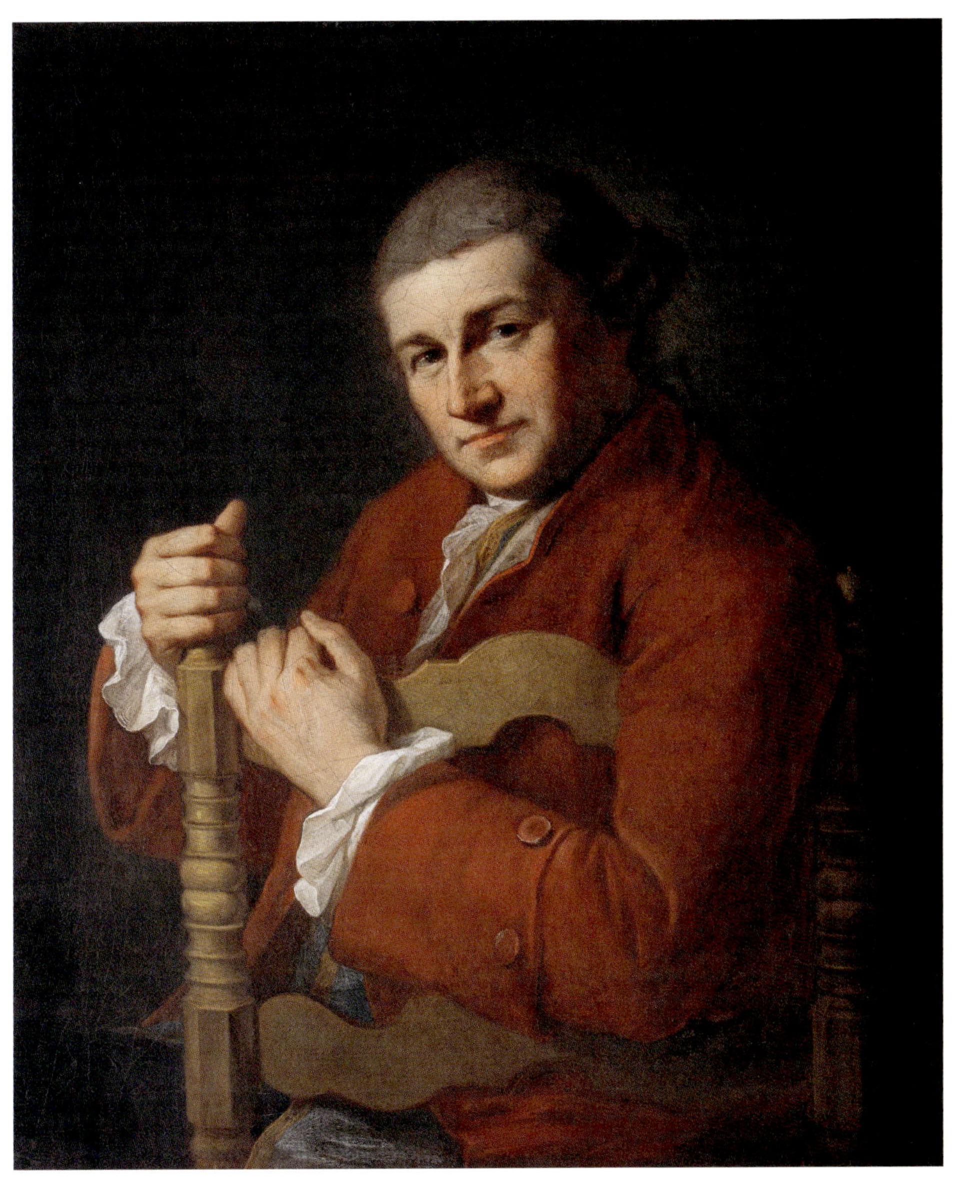

6
Portrait of David Garrick, 1764
Oil on canvas, 84.6 × 68.7 cm
The Burghley House Collection, inv. PIC176

7
Portrait of Martha Cocks in Turkish Dress with Embroidery Frame, 1772
Oil on canvas, 91 × 114.7 cm
Eastnor Castle Collection

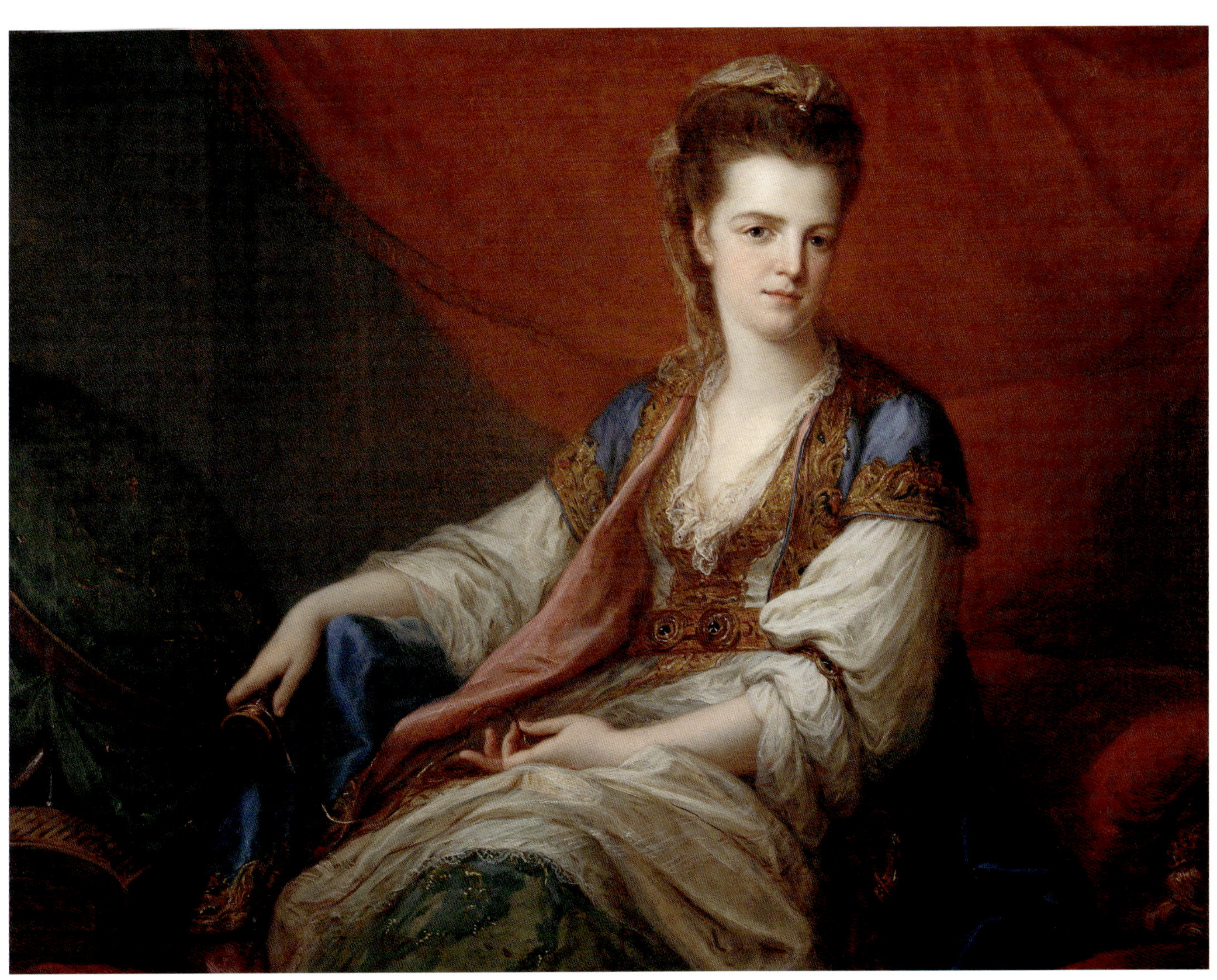

8
Cleopatra Adorning the Tomb of Mark Antony, c. 1769–70
Oil on canvas, 126.5 × 101.7 cm
The Burghley House Collection, inv. PIC286

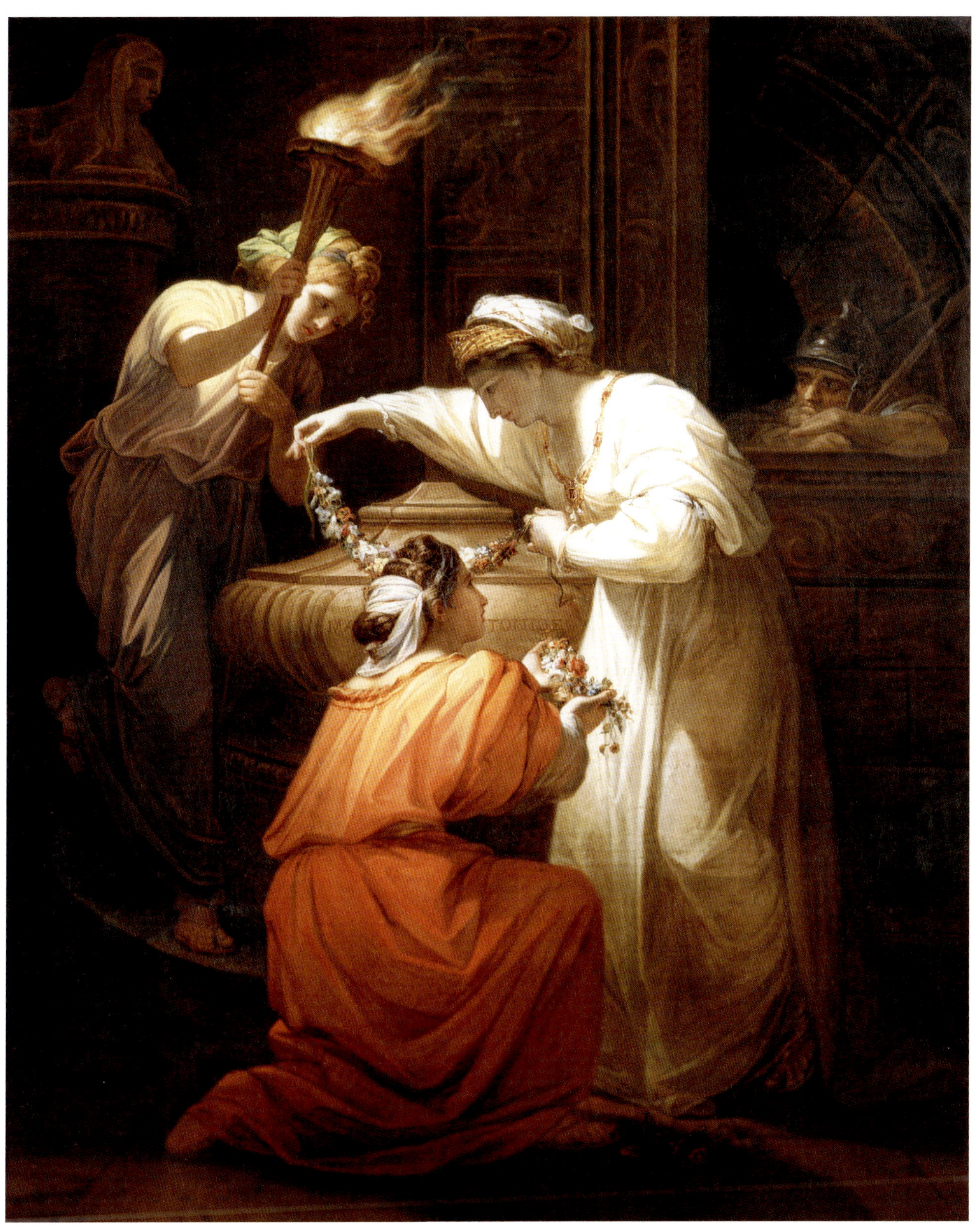

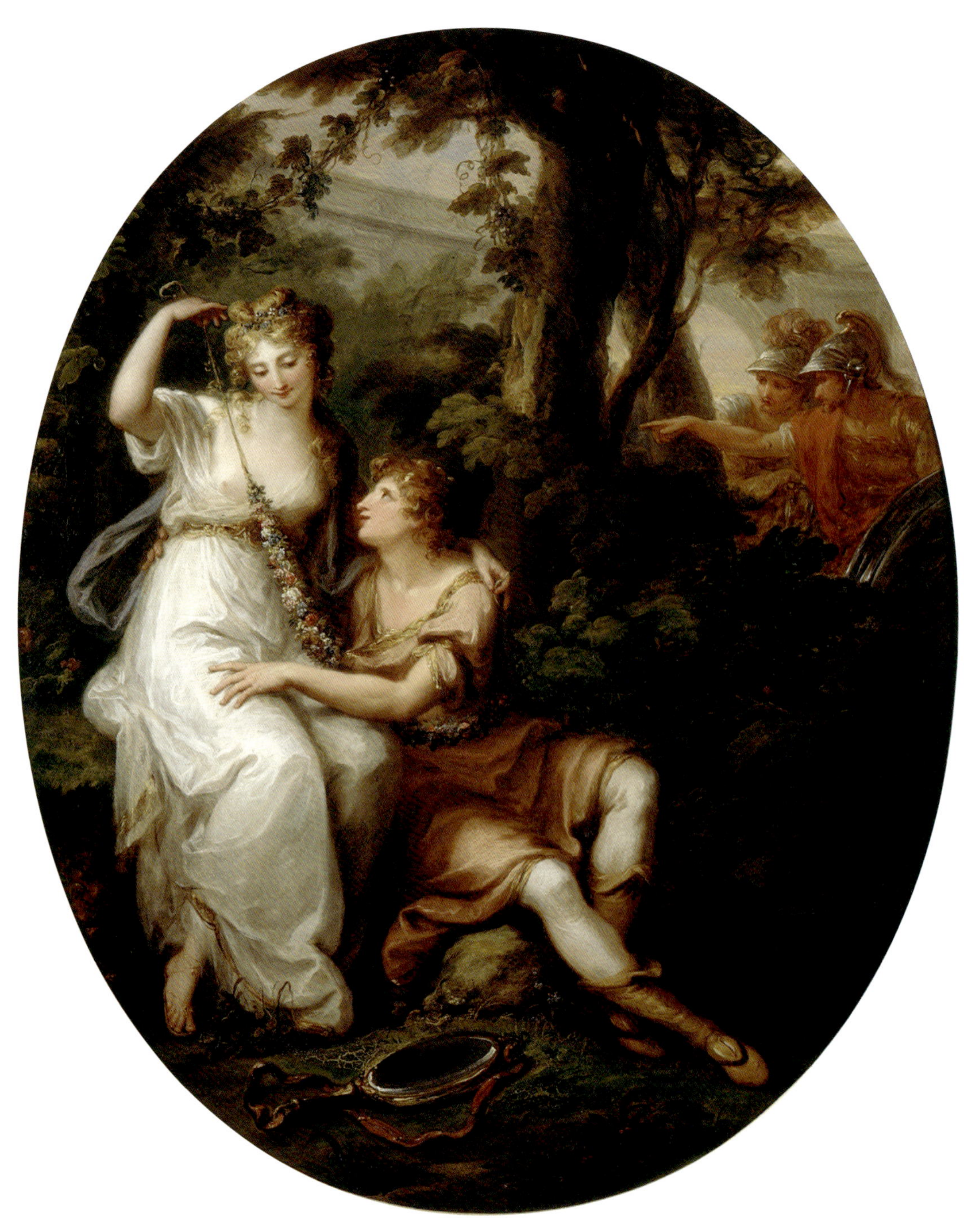

9
Rinaldo and Armida in the Magic Garden, c. 1772
Oil on canvas, 128.1 × 102.6 cm
English Heritage, Kenwood. The Ernest Edward Cook Bequest presented by the Art Fund, inv. 88029074

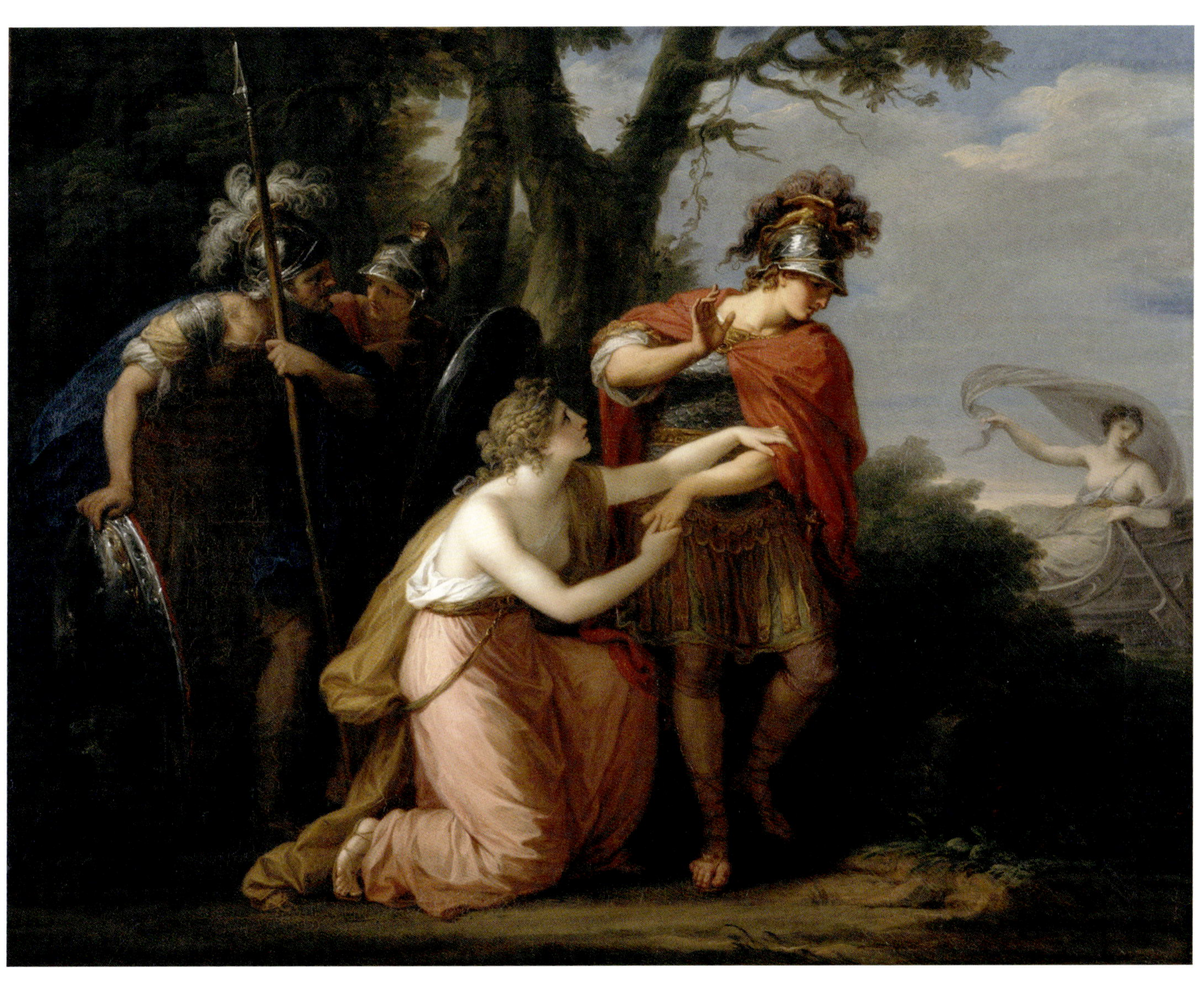

10
Armida Begs Rinaldo in Vain not to Leave Her, 1776
Oil on canvas, 102.1 × 127 cm
English Heritage, Kenwood, inv. 88029297

11
Eleanora Sucking the Venom Out of the Wound of Her Husband, King Edward I, 1776
Oil on canvas, 72.2 × 92.2 cm
Private collection, Vorarlberg

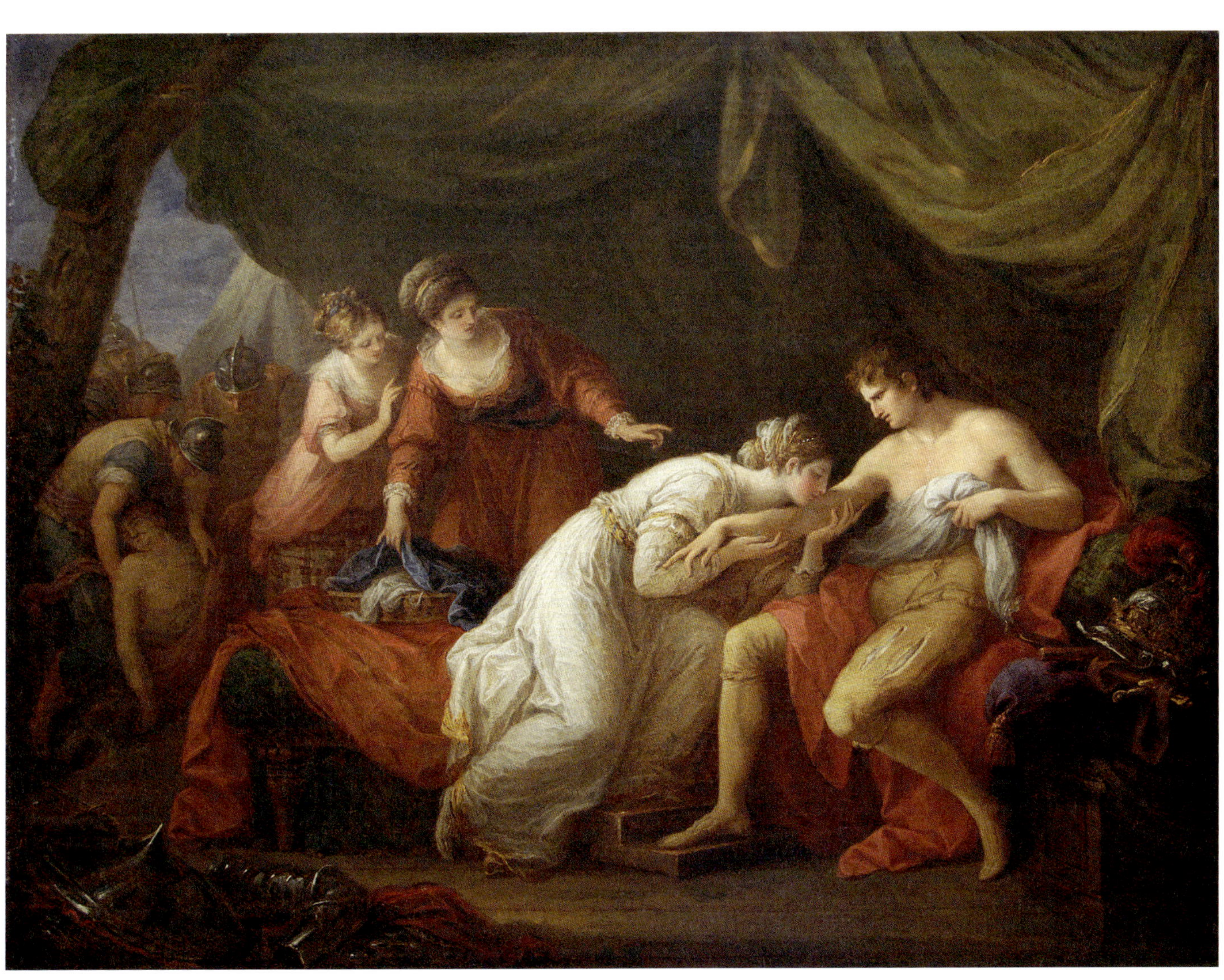

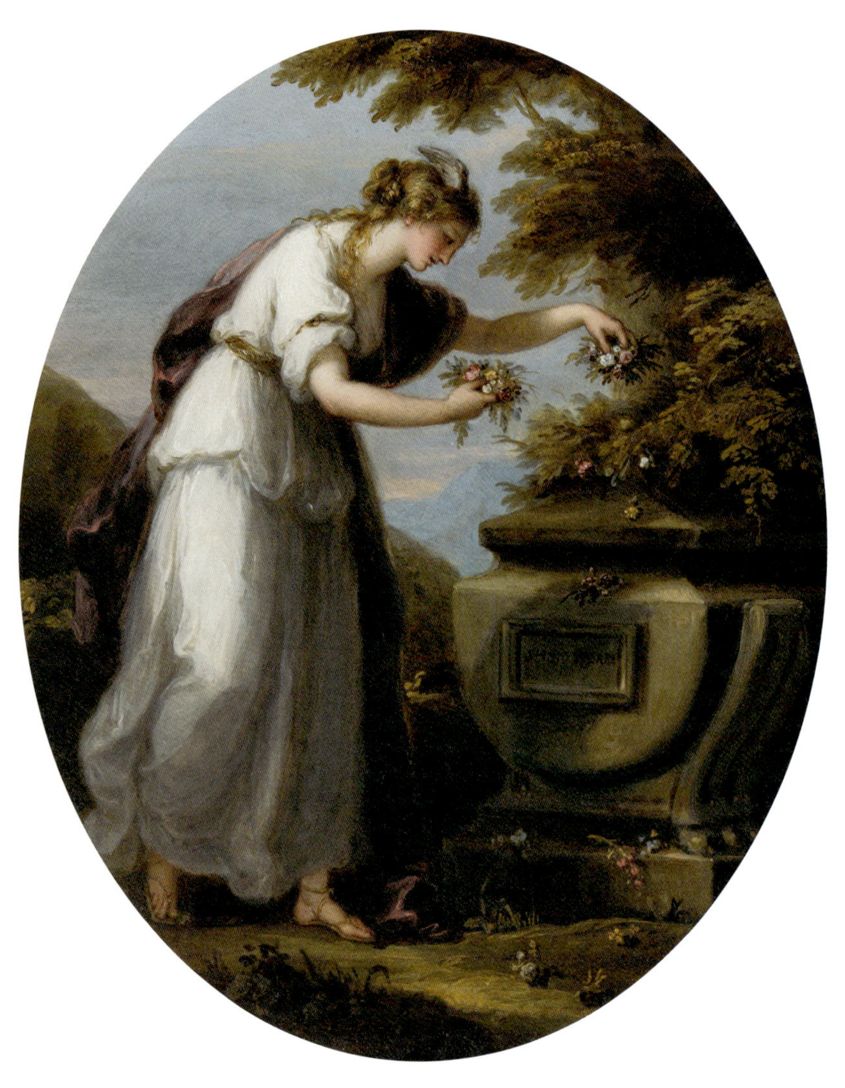

12
Shakespeare's Tomb, 1772
Oil on copper, 32.4 × 26 cm
The Burghley House Collection, inv. PIC230

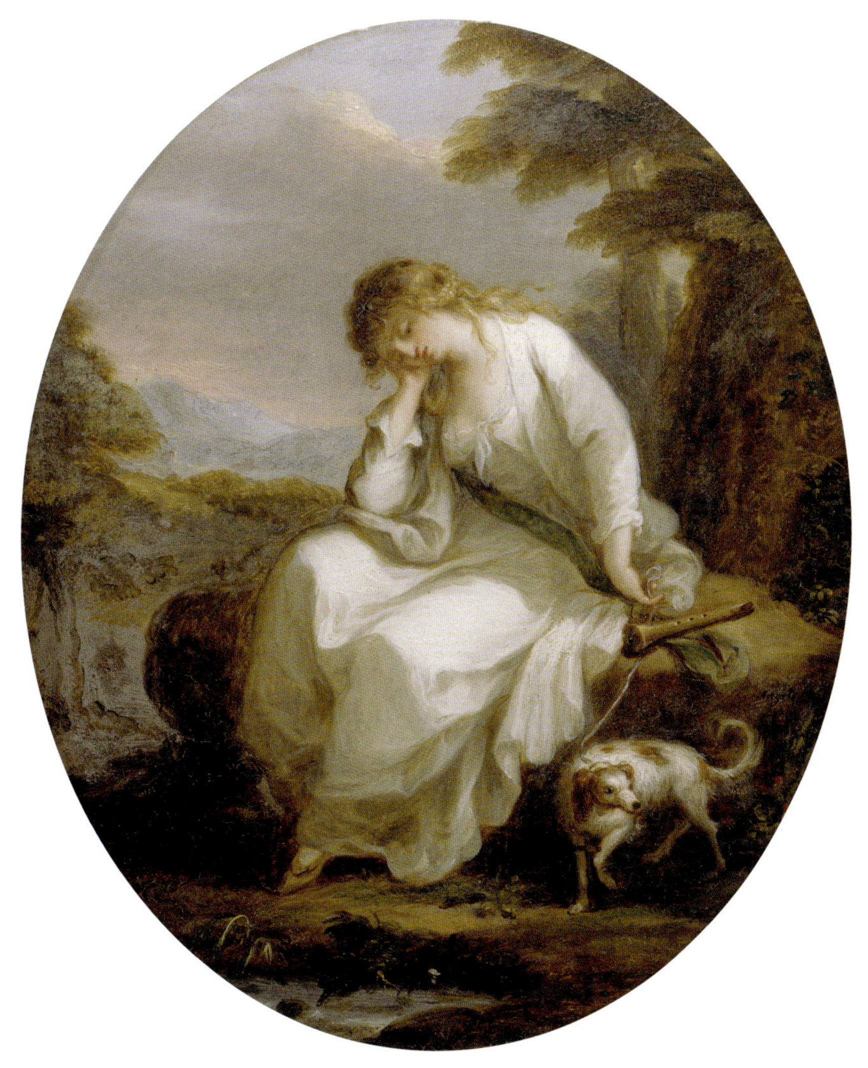

13
Poor Maria, 1777
Oil on copper, 31 × 22.9 cm
The Burghley House Collection, inv. PIC234

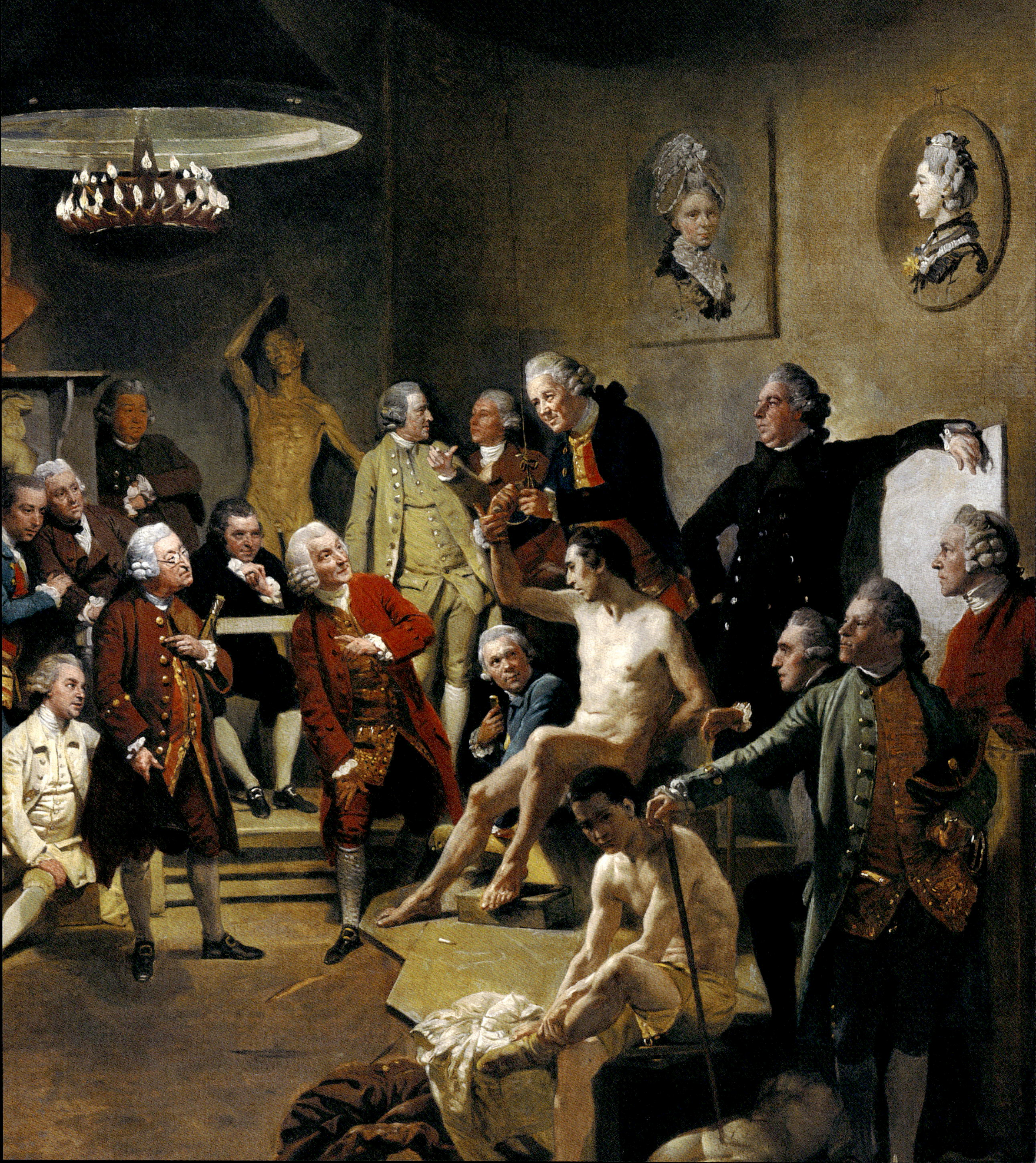

KAUFFMAN AND THE ROYAL ACADEMY

Founded in December 1768, the new Royal Academy of Arts in London sought to raise the status of professional artists in Britain and to encourage the production of artworks in the 'Grand Manner', emulating the elevated style of Renaissance and Classical art. Remarkably, given the exclusion of women from similar organisations in Britain at this date, Angelica Kauffman was among the 36 founding members of the institution along with one other woman, the painter Mary Moser. Kauffman was an ideal candidate for membership in many respects but her swift acceptance into the original inner circle of Academicians was assisted by crucial connections she forged during her first year in London.

Arriving in London in June 1766, Kauffman had already met Joshua Reynolds by the time she wrote to her father in July.[1] The two quickly became friends, leading to a rich social and artistic interaction which began with painting each other's portraits (see fig. 3 on p. 14 and cat. 16).[2] Kauffman portrayed her new friend informally, seated at his desk and looking towards the viewer. Reynolds is presented as both artist and theorist, surrounded by learned tomes with a bust of Michelangelo to one side and a blank canvas on the other.[3] Shortly afterwards, Kauffman secured an important commission to paint Queen Charlotte which also supported her inclusion at the new Royal Academy. Kauffman depicted the Queen raising the 'Genius of the Fine Arts' in the guise of her young son, the future George IV, as the sitter herself had specified (cat. 17).[4]

Kauffman and Moser were publicly celebrated as members of the new institution, and yet, as women, they held no official roles and the RA Schools were a male-only domain (cat. 14). At the prestigious annual exhibitions, Kauffman promoted her sophisticated history paintings, and selected portraits, which were received with great interest and, mostly, critical acclaim. The publication of prints after these works proved crucial to the growth of her reputation.[5] However, 'Angelica' was 'known by everybody' and, for a woman artist, such fame also attracted gossip and

Detail of cat. 14

mockery.[6] In 1775, her fellow Academician Nathaniel Hone (1718–1784) tried to exhibit a painting satirising both Reynolds and Kauffman at the Royal Academy (*The Pictorial Conjuror, Displaying the Whole Art of Optical Deception*, National Gallery of Ireland, Dublin); the oil sketch for the work is at Tate (see fig. 14, p. 31). A naked female figure in the background carrying a palette was thought to represent Kauffman herself and she was forced to assert herself robustly to ensure the painting's removal from the exhibition (cat. 38).[7]

A few years later, Kauffman was at the height of her success in England. In the 1779 exhibition, she not only showed seven of her own works but was also celebrated as a 'living muse' in Richard Samuel's group portrait *Portraits in the Characters of the Muses in the Temple of Apollo* (1778; cat. 19) which depicts Kauffman as the only artist alongside fellow 'bluestockings': eminent women writers, intellectuals and musicians.[8] Kauffman's greatest honour at the Royal Academy, though, was the commission for *The Elements of Art* (1780), four oval ceiling paintings depicting the foundations of the creative process according to academic art theory: *Invention* (see p. 80), *Design* (cat. 24), *Composition* (cat. 25) and *Colouring* (p. 81). Painted for the Academy's Council Room in its newly built apartments at Somerset House, these images break from tradition in personifying all four as women. Kauffman's works were singled out for praise, described in Joseph Baretti's account of the new rooms as 'executed with all that grace, elegance and accuracy which distinguish the best productions of this Extraordinary lady'.[9] In the portraits she produced at this time, Kauffman used similar imagery. In *Self-portrait in the Character of Design Listening to the Inspiration of Poetry* (1782; cat. 26), Bettina Baumgärtel has shown that Kauffman refers specifically to the concept of *disegno* – traditionally represented as a man – portraying herself with chalk and paper seated with the female personification of Poetry, presenting a collaborative approach of sisterly friendship and exchange between the two.[10]

Kauffman's *Self-portrait with Bust of Minerva* (*c*. 1780–84; cat. 15) seems to continue the artistic conversation with the Academy's President Joshua Reynolds. In 1780, he had painted his own grand self-portrait in academic robes for the new Council Room at Somerset House, reworking some of the motifs from Kauffman's 1767 portrayal of him including the bust of Michelangelo. Kauffman, in turn, presented herself with a bust of Minerva, goddess of wisdom and war, placed in a very similar position. Welcoming Kauffman back to Italy, the poet Ippolito Pindemonte wrote an epistle, perhaps referencing this portrait, describing Minerva leading the artist to Rome as a young woman and back again in later life to fulfil her potential.[11]

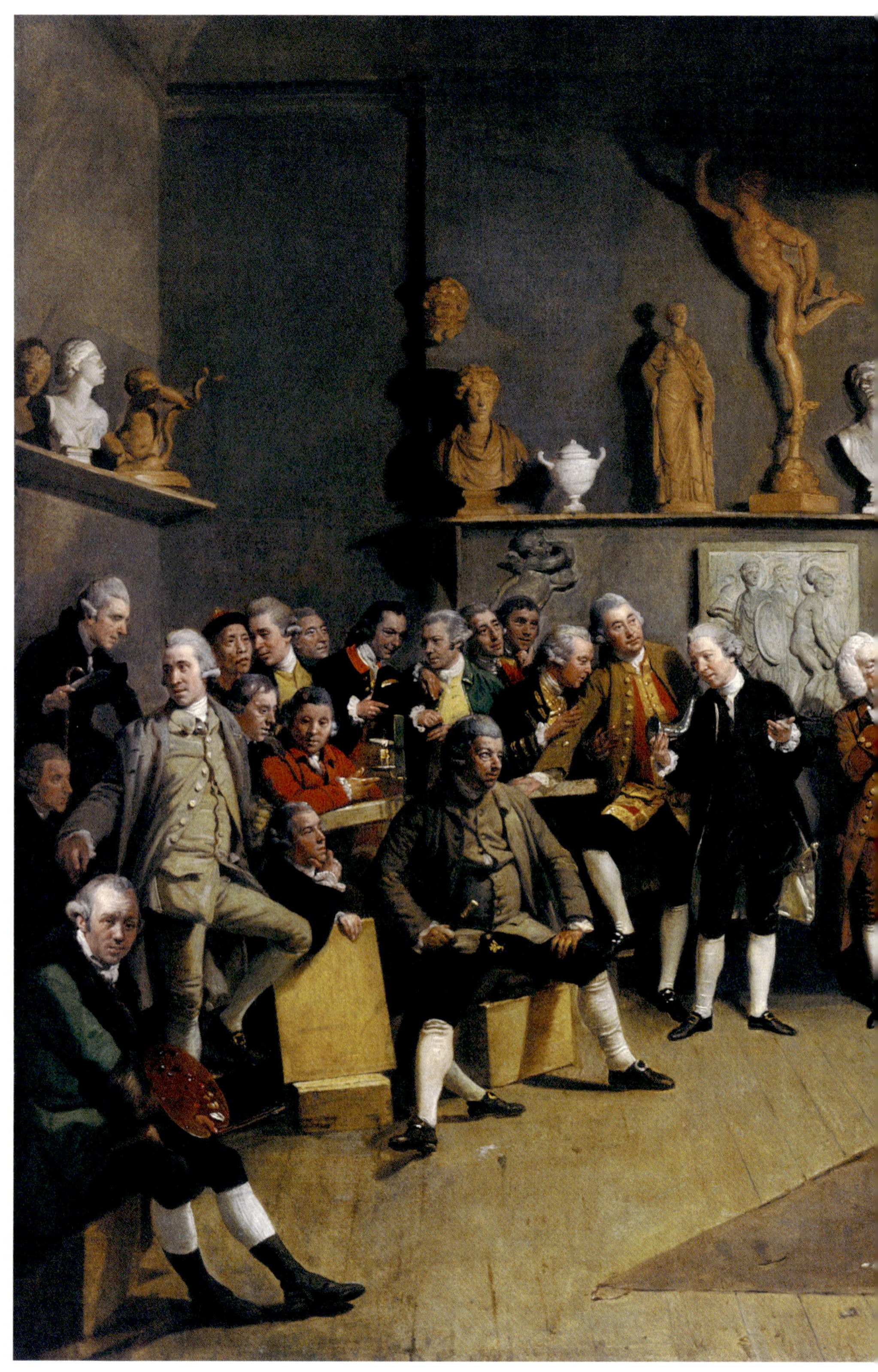

14
JOHAN ZOFFANY (1733–1810)
The Academicians of the Royal Academy, 1771–72
Oil on canvas, 101.1 × 147.5 cm
Royal Collection Trust / HM King Charles III, RCIN 400747

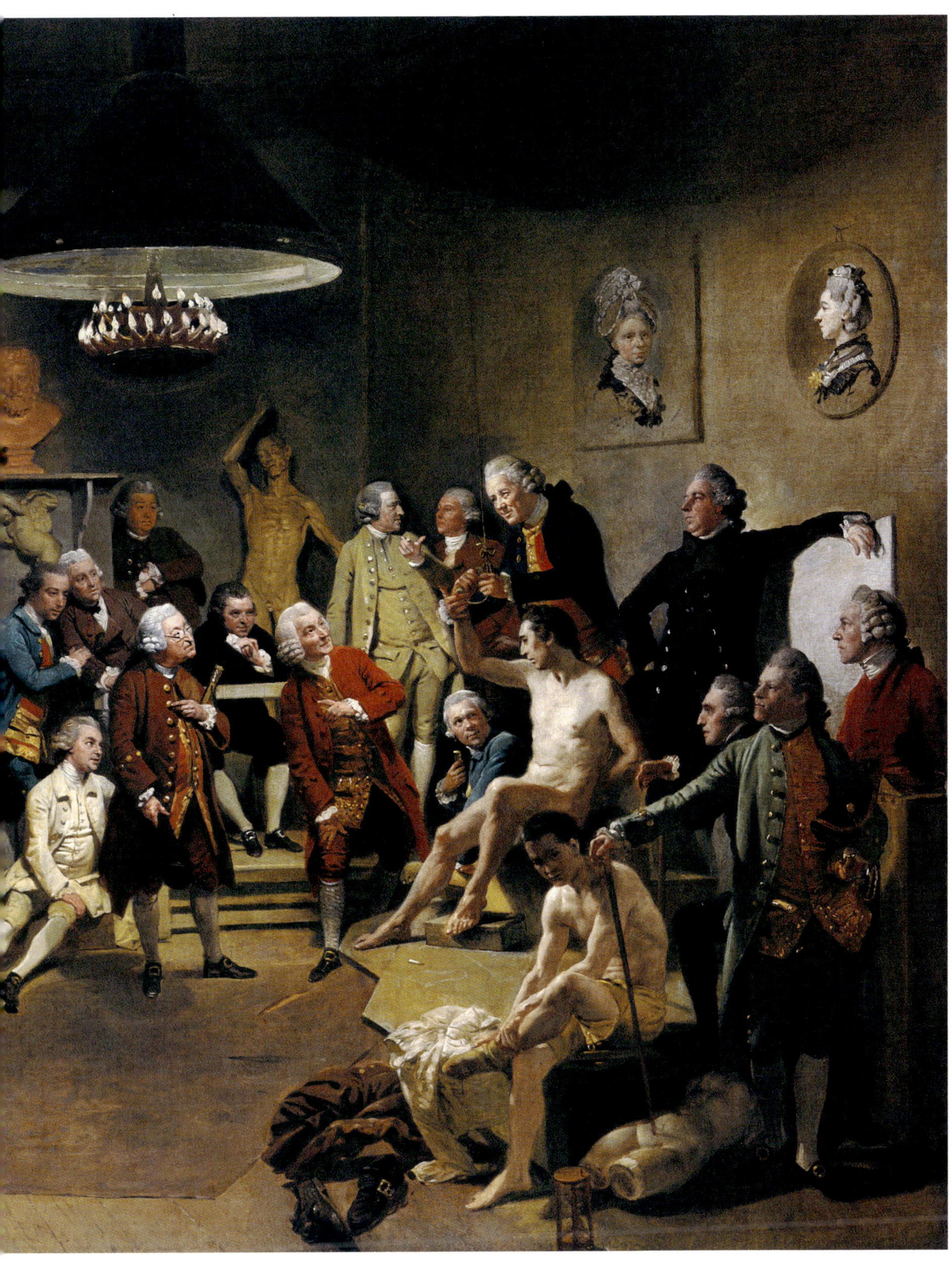

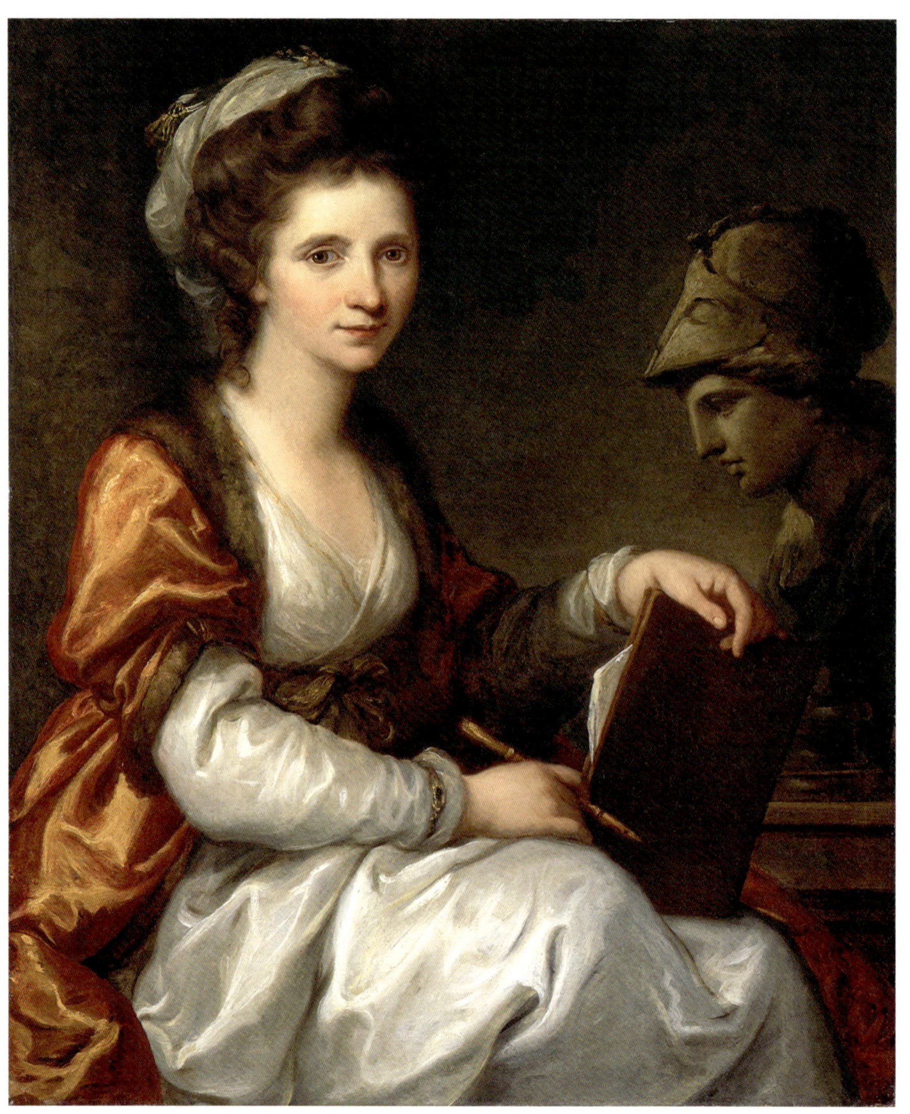

15
Self-portrait with Bust of Minerva, c. 1780–84
Oil on canvas, 93 × 76.5 cm
Grisons Museum of fine Arts, on deposit from the Gottfried Keller Foundation, Federal Office of Culture, Bern, inv. 321.000.1945

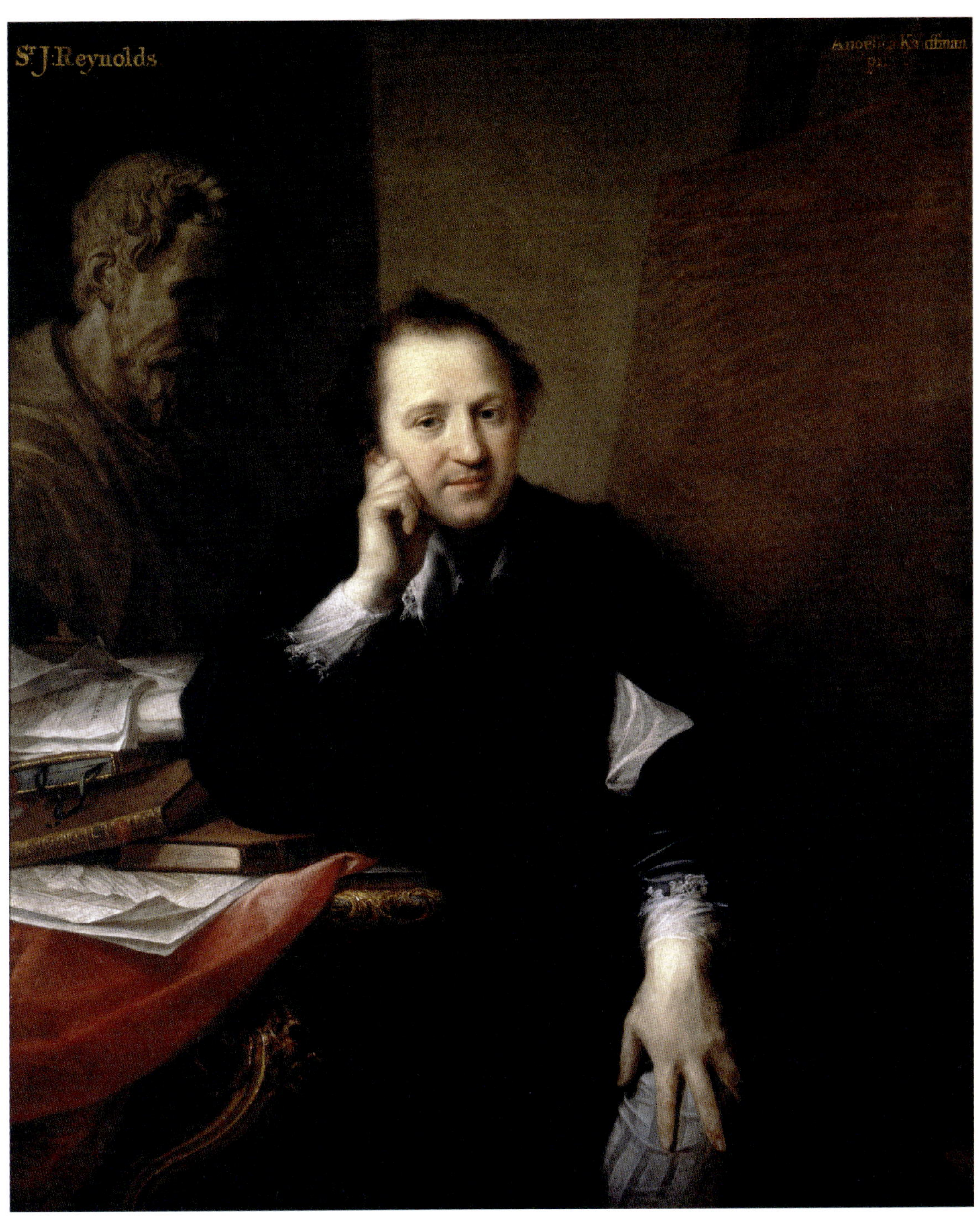

16

Portrait of Joshua Reynolds, 1767

Oil on canvas, 127 × 110.6 cm

National Trust Collections (Saltram House, The Morley Collection [accepted in lieu of tax by H.M. Treasury and transferred to the National Trust in 1957]), inv. NT 872180

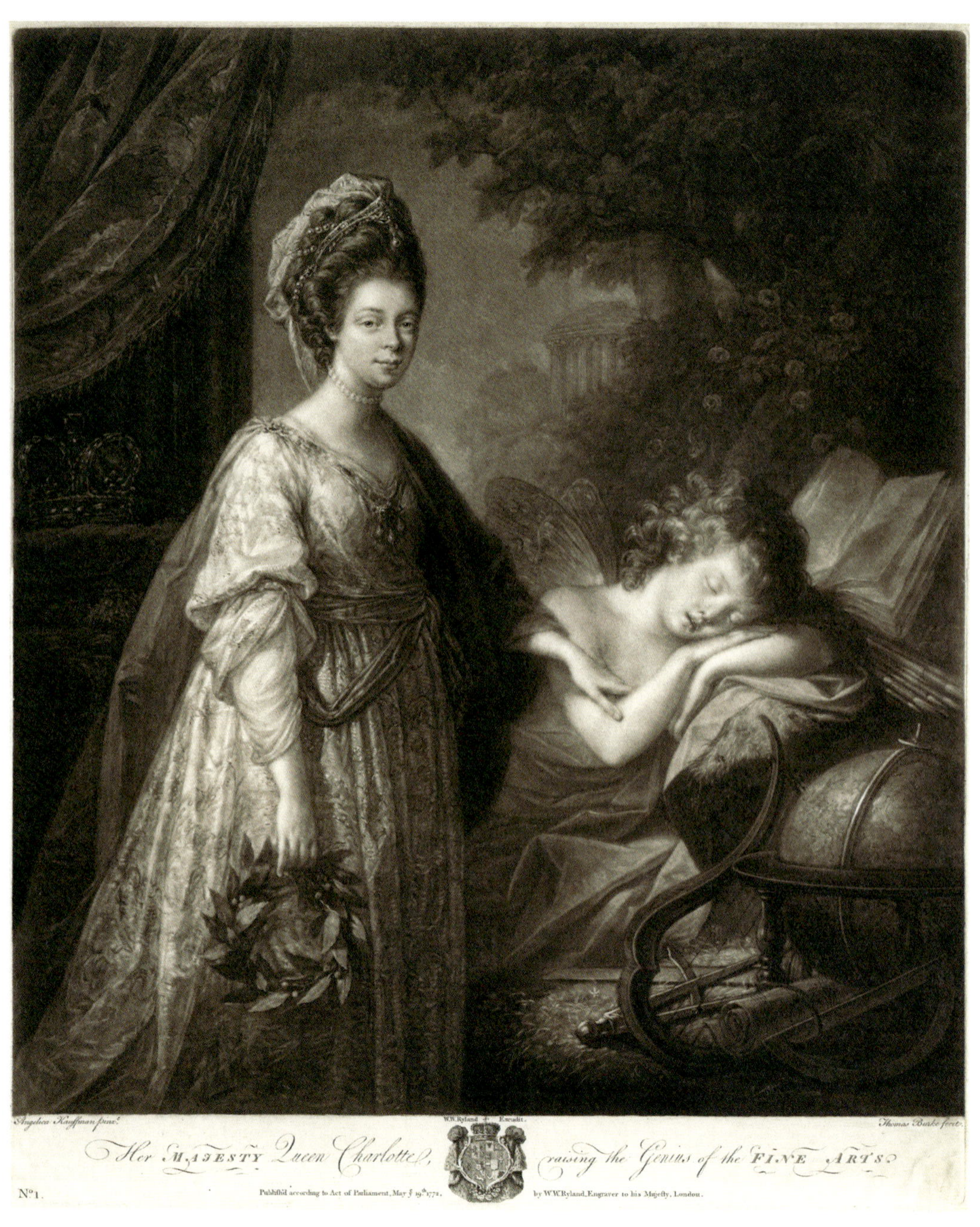

17
THOMAS BURKE (1741–1815), after ANGELICA KAUFFMAN
Her Majesty Queen Charlotte Raising the Genius of the Fine Arts, 1772
Mezzotint, 47.7 × 38.3 cm
Royal Academy of Arts, London, inv. 12/1595

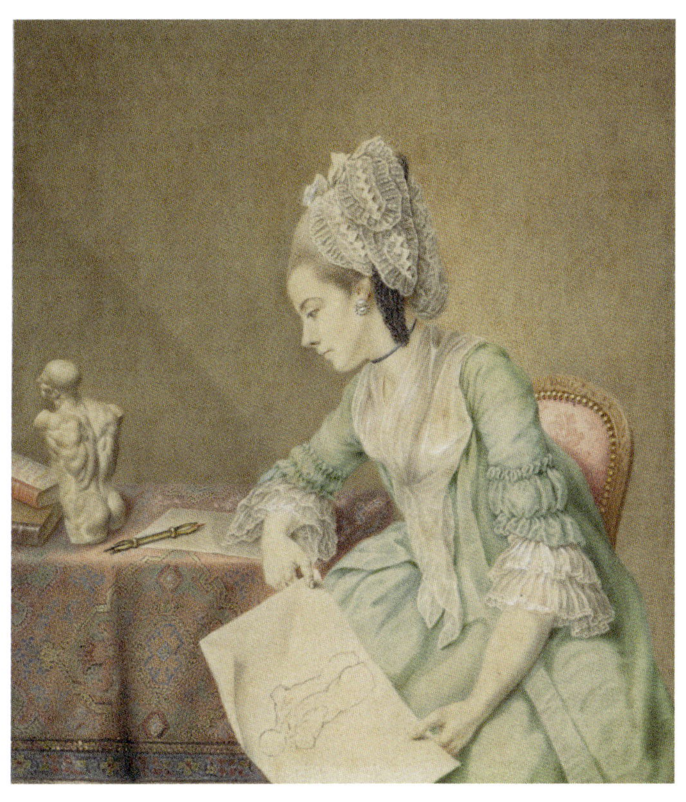

18
Attributed to NATHANIEL DANCE (1748–1827)
Portrait of Angelica Kauffmann, c. 1764–66
Watercolour on paper, 13.2 × 11.4 cm
National Galleries of Scotland. Lady Sybil Grant Bequest 1956, D 4772

19
RICHARD SAMUEL (active 1770–died 1787)
Portraits in the Characters of the Muses in the Temple of Apollo, 1778
Oil on canvas, 132.1 × 154.9 cm
Lent by the National Portrait Gallery, London. Acquired 1972, inv. NPG 4905

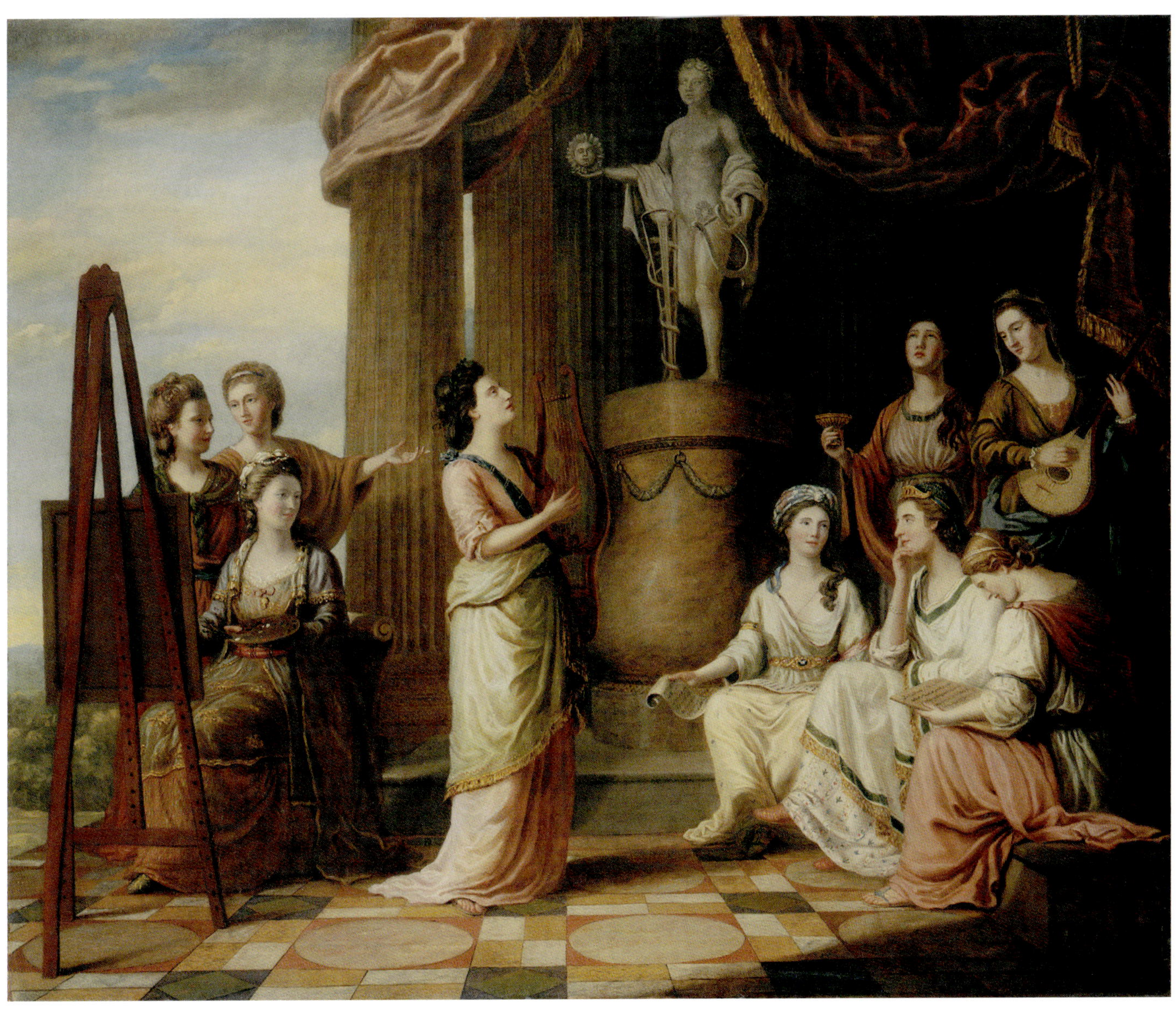

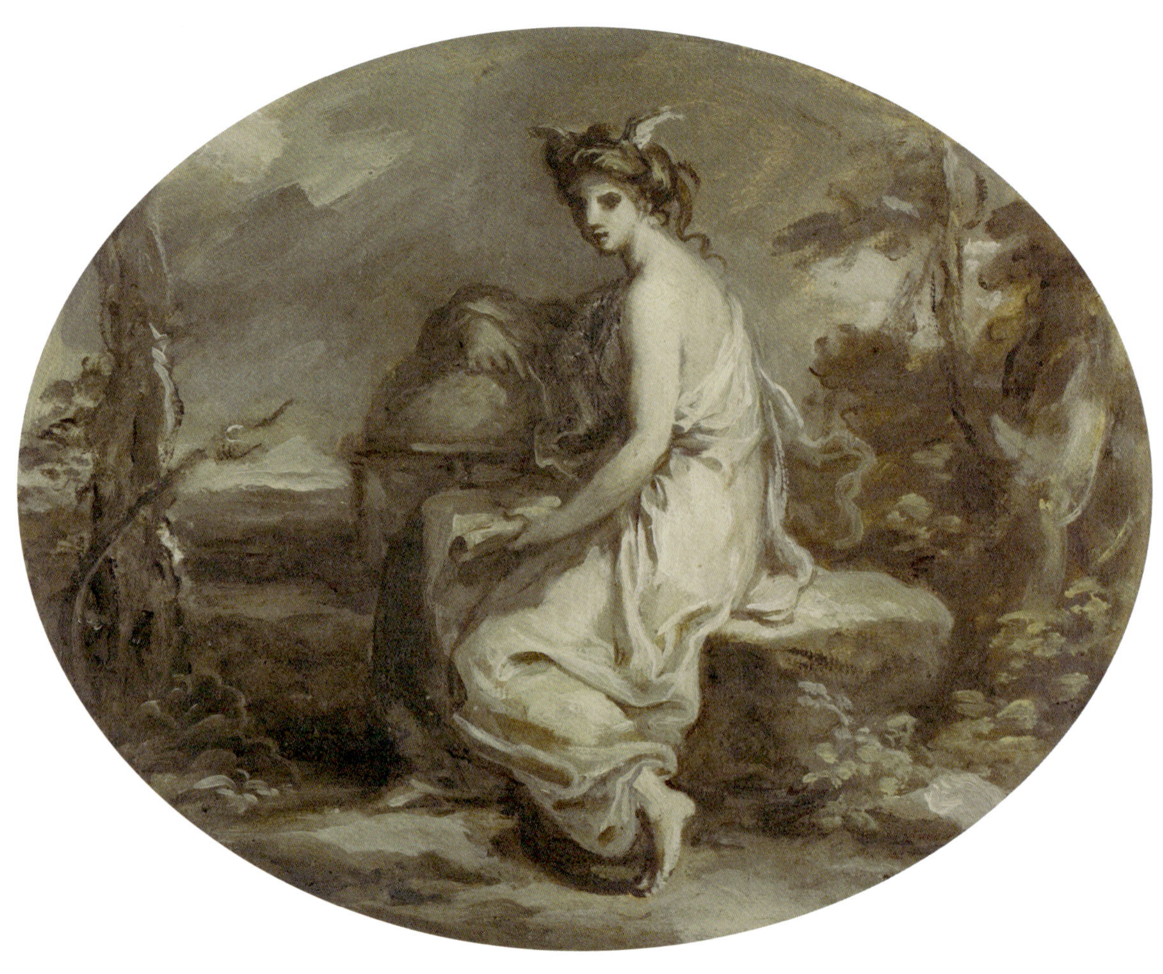

20
Invention, c. 1778–80
Oil on paper, 22.4 × 28 cm
Victoria and Albert Museum, London,
bequeathed by H.H. Harrod, inv. E.865-1948

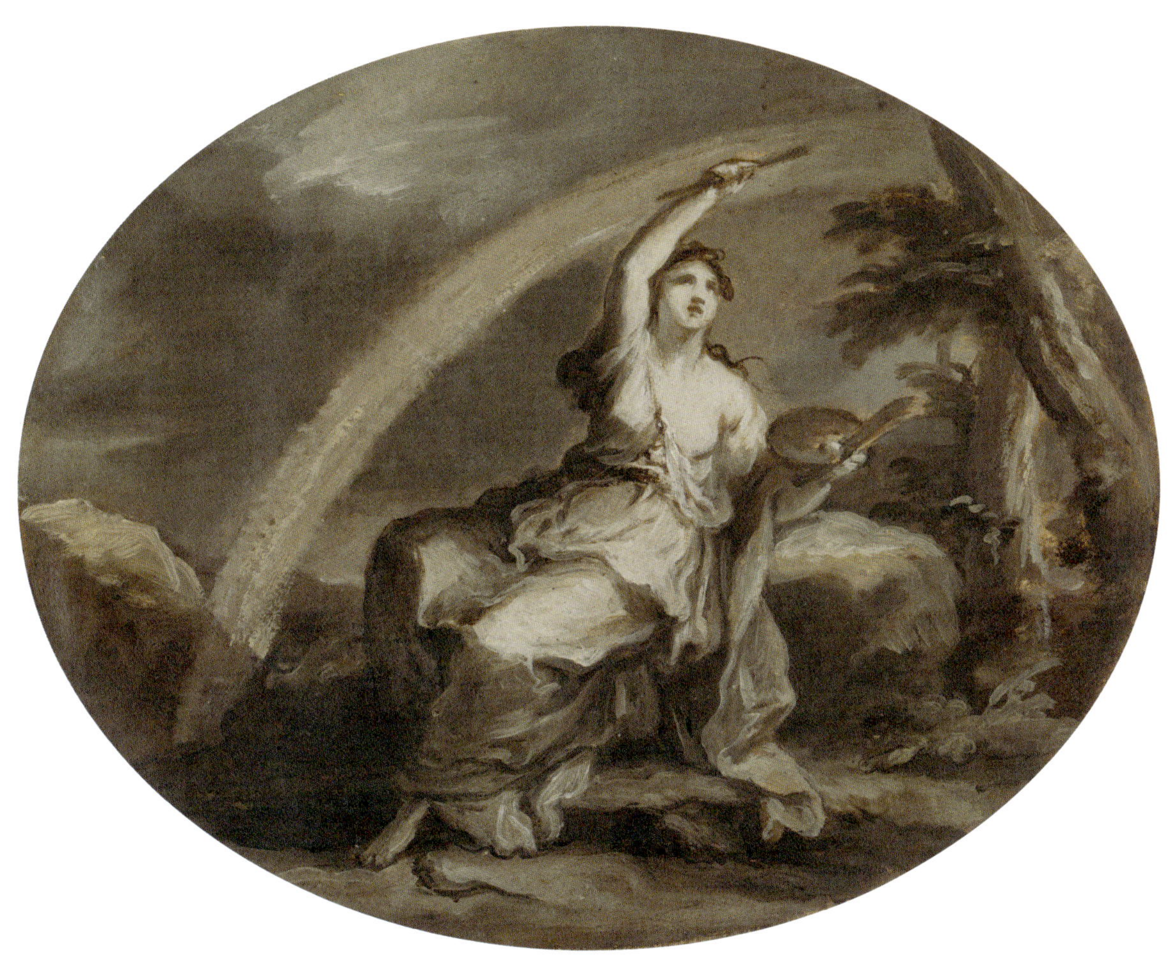

21
Colouring, c. 1778–80
Oil on paper, 22.4 × 28 cm
Victoria and Albert Museum, London,
bequeathed by H.H. Harrod, inv. E.863-1948

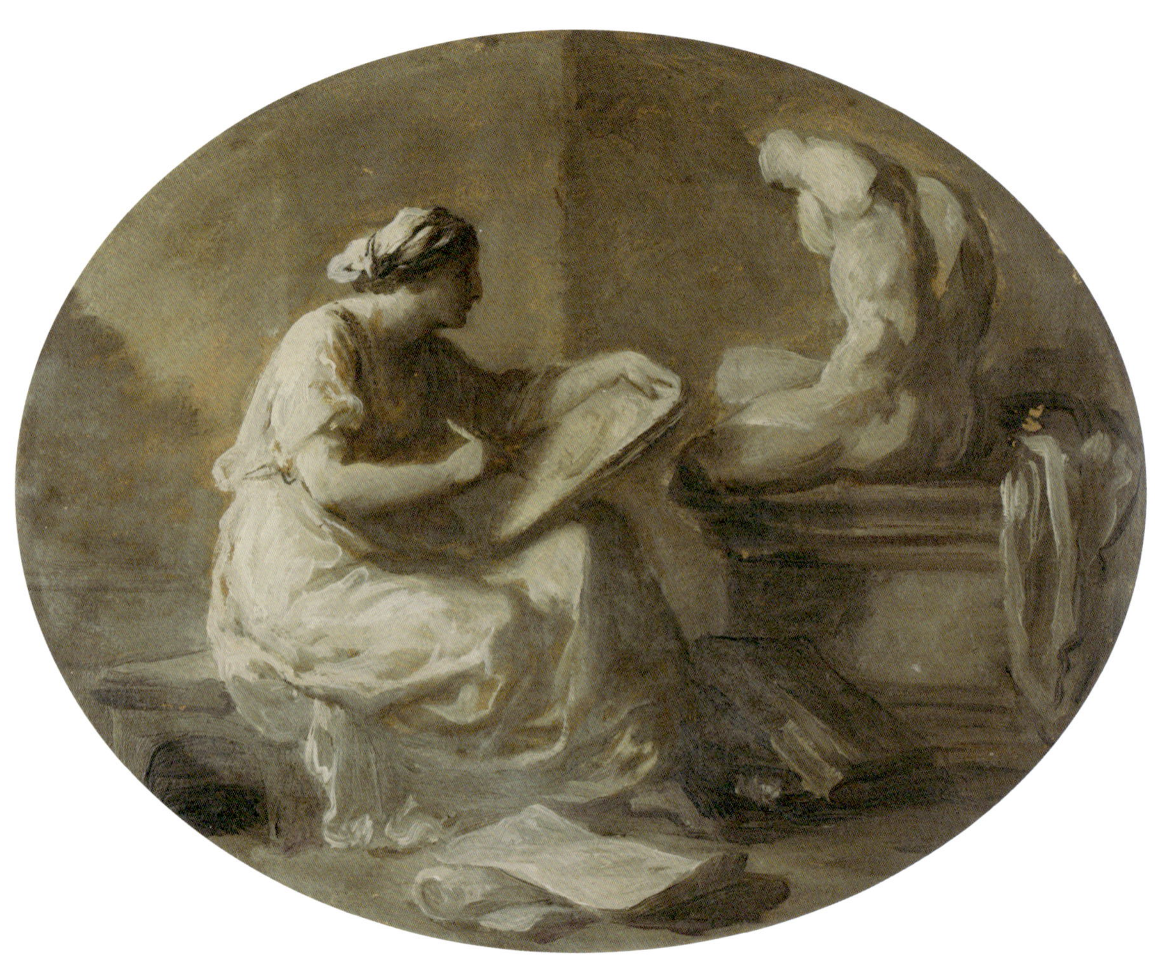

22
Design, c. 1778–80
Oil on paper, 22.4 × 28 cm
Victoria and Albert Museum, London, bequeathed by H.H. Harrod, inv. E.866-1948

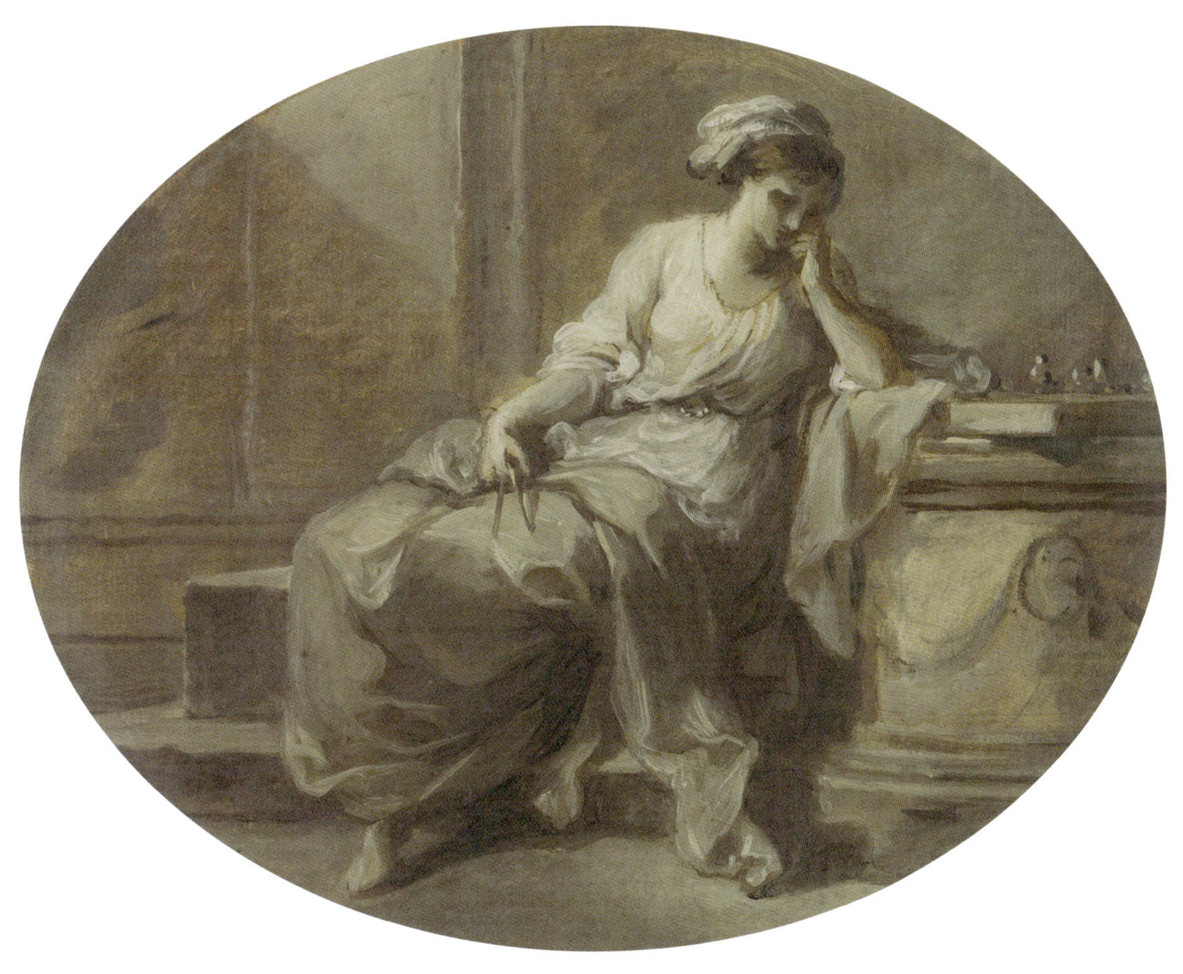

23
Composition, c. 1778–80
Oil on paper, 22.4 × 28 cm
Victoria and Albert Museum, London,
bequeathed by H.H. Harrod, inv. E.864-1948

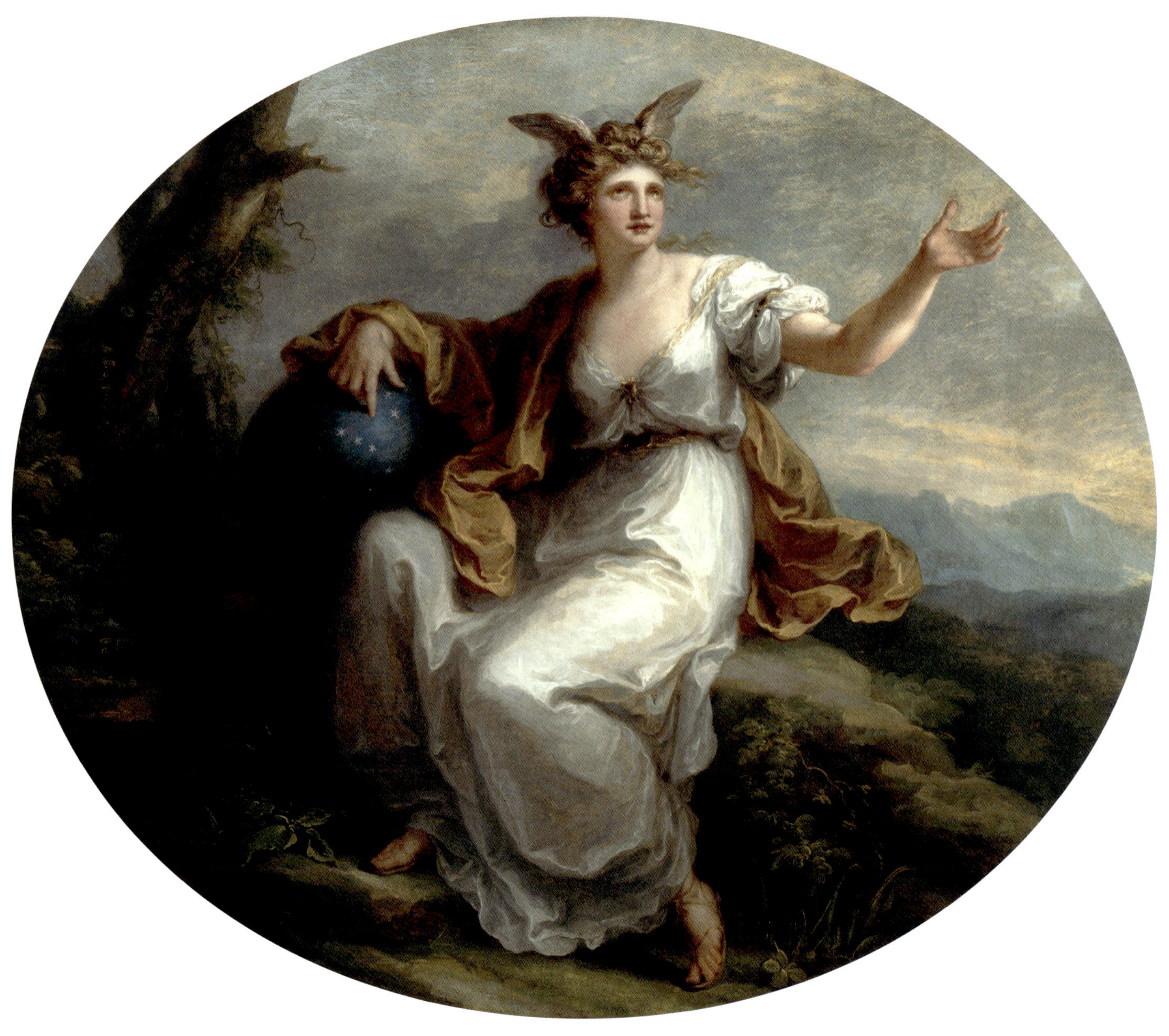

Invention, 1780 (NOT EXHIBITED)
Oil on canvas, 128.3 × 149 cm
Royal Academy of Arts, London, inv. 03/1128

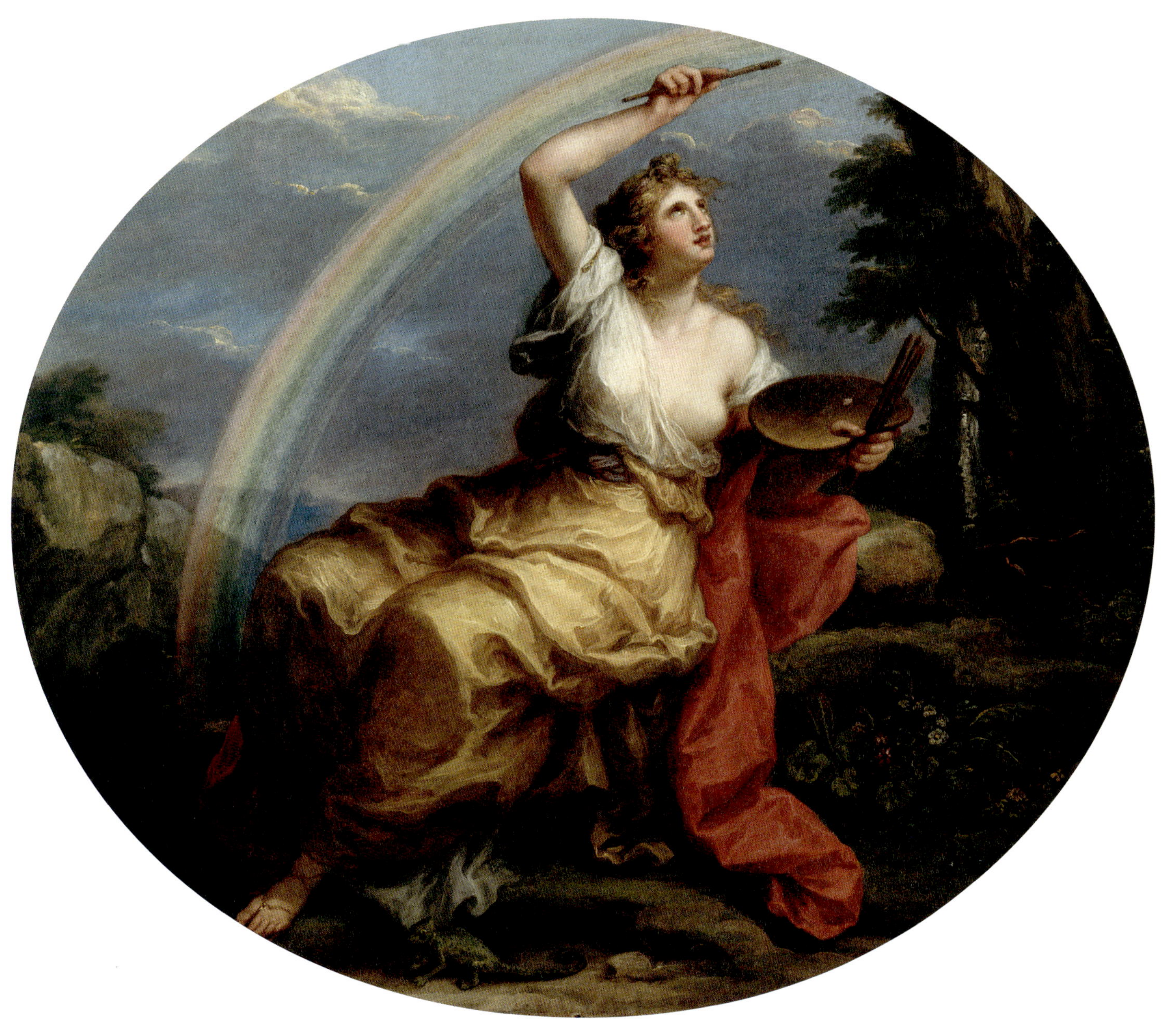

Colouring, 1780 (NOT EXHIBITED)
Oil on canvas, 128.3 × 149 cm
Royal Academy of Arts, London, inv. 03/1130

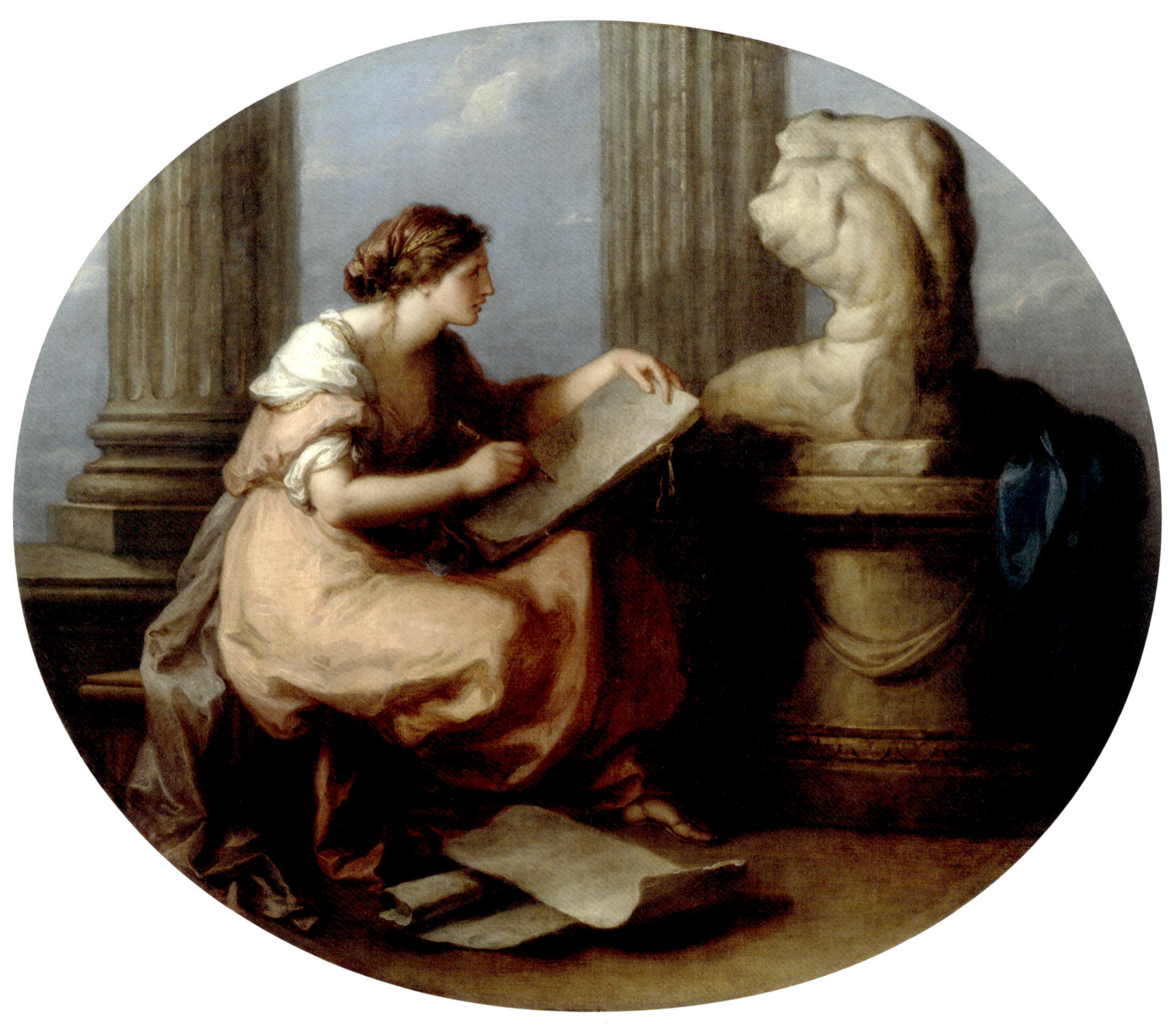

24
Design, 1780
Oil on canvas, 128.3 × 149 cm
Royal Academy of Arts, London, inv. 03/1129

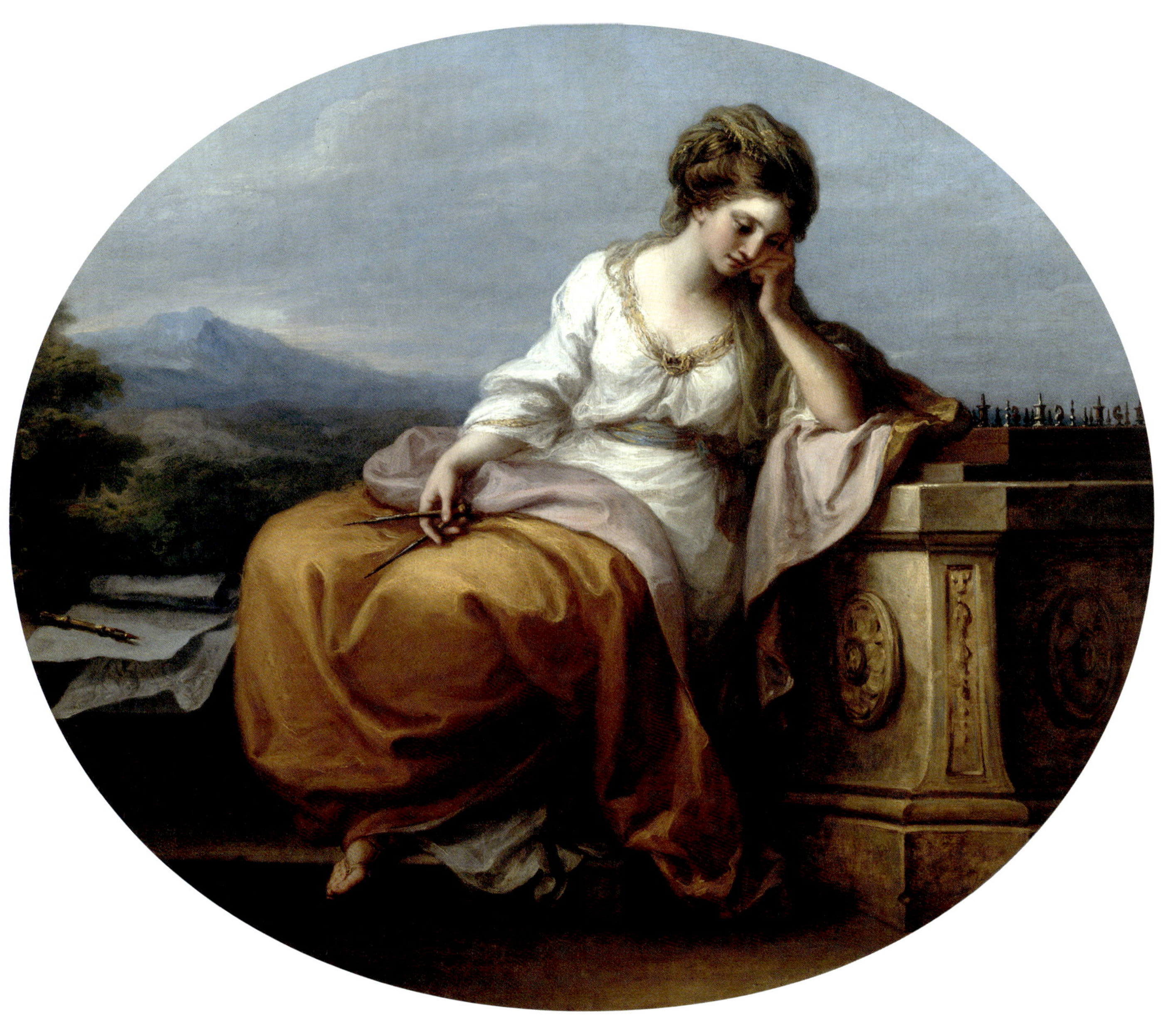

25
Composition, 1780
Oil on canvas, 128.3 × 149 cm
Royal Academy of Arts, London, inv. 03/1131

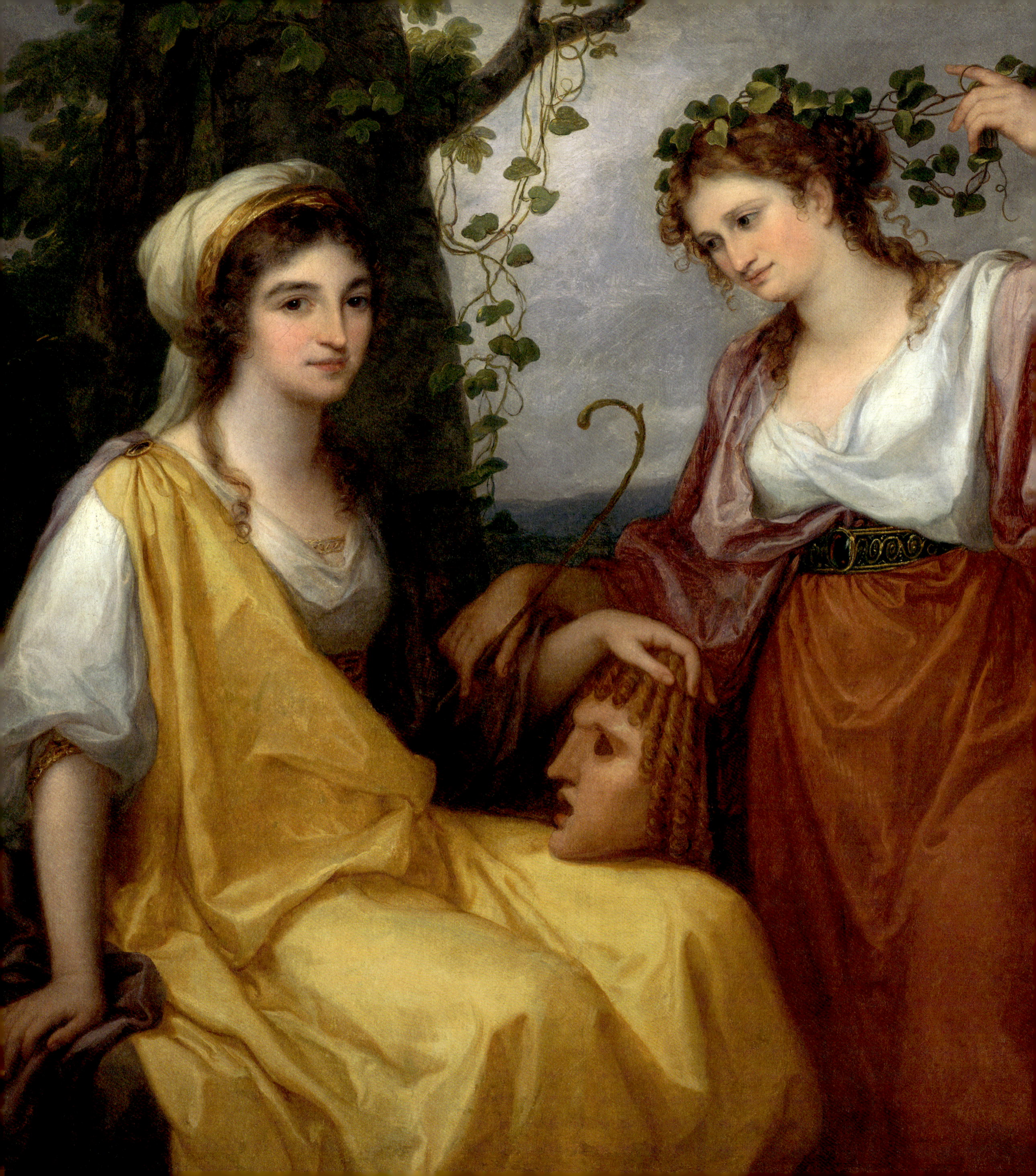

RETURN TO ROME

Having left Italy on the brink of success, Angelica Kauffman returned as an established artist at the height of her powers. Rome remained at the heart of the Grand Tour at this time, attracting communities of Italian and international artists, scholars and connoisseurs as well as wealthy aristocratic visitors drawn by its unrivalled architecture, ruins and collections of Classical and Renaissance art. One English traveller, John Forsyth, remarked in 1802: 'I have heard Angelica say that the water of Rome revived her powers, and gave her ideas.'[1] Kauffman certainly seems to have approached her work with renewed vigour and confidence in Rome, producing more ambitious images than ever before, and the period from 1782 until her death in 1807 represents the apogee of her career. Women – as sitters, subjects and patrons – became even more important to her work at this time.

Although Kauffman's move to Italy may have been partly motivated by lack of full support for history painting in England, her connections there remained important as she continued to send paintings to the Royal Academy and to receive commissions from British patrons.[2] The history paintings she produced in Rome build on similar themes to those which preoccupied her in England but they are generally more ambitious in tone, often featuring complex compositions. Her *Death of Alcestis* (1790; cat. 34) shown at the Royal Academy in 1791, is a radical work in which Kauffman extols traditional wifely virtues while co-opting the male heroic deathbed scene for her stoic female heroine.[3] *Ulysses on the Island of Circe* (1793; cat 35) was commissioned by the Rushout family and features on Kauffman's list of her 17 most important paintings. In this painting, the artist pays greater attention to the accurate depiction of 'all'antica' furnishings, which Bettina Baumgärtel has connected to both the works of Winckelmann and Bernard de Monfaucon's *Antiquity Explained and Represented in Sculptures* (1719).[4]

In England, Kauffman depicted few religious subjects but after her return to Rome, surrounded by the works of the Old Masters once again, she developed a

Detail of cat. 30

much stronger interest in such themes, favouring Biblical scenes in particular. These images proved popular in Rome and beyond, with Kauffman receiving a commission in 1790 from Pope Pius VI to paint the altar of the Swiss Chapel in Loreto. Her painting of *Christ and the Samaritan Woman* (1796; cat. 36) from the Gospel of St John (4: 1–38) was commissioned for a monastery but was later acquired by King Ludwig I of Bavaria. This painting and one of her last religious works, *David and Nathan* (1806–7; vorarlberg museum, Bregenz), were in her studio when she died and were carried in solemn procession at her funeral, which took place at the Basilica of Sant'Andrea delle Fratte in Rome. The ceremony was described in a letter translated by Joseph Bonomi which was read out to the Royal Academicians in London (cat. 39).[5]

Kauffman's practice as a portrait painter continued to thrive in Italy and she painted both for commissions and for her own pleasure. Even before arriving in Rome, she had already secured a commission for an ambitious large-scale family portrait from the Queen of Naples (fig. 7, p. 19) and she continued to portray many Grand Tourists. Kauffman painted numerous marriage portraits as well as pendant portraits of couples including the Anglo-Polish architect and theatrical set designer Michael Novosielski (1750–1795) (cat. 27) and his wife, the singer Regina Felicia Pasquali in 1791–92 (private collection). He is shown pointing to his design for the King's Theatre. She also painted Maria Hill and her husband Charles Brudenell-Bruce (1793–95; cats 28 and 29). The latter was so 'delited' with his wife's portrait that he commissioned his own, observing that Lord Berwick 'has had his done…in a Vandyck dress'.[6] Kauffman duly portrayed him in a similar costume imitating the paintings of Sir Anthony van Dyck, doyen of the swagger portrait.[7] This device allowed Kauffman to produce grander aristocratic portraits while retaining a sense of levity.

The most remarkable and pioneering of Kauffman's portraits during her years in Rome, however, are those of her female friends and fellow creatives. In her *Portraits of Domenica Morghen and Maddalena Volpato as Muses of Tragedy and Comedy* (1791; cat. 30) Kauffman painted her friends with the same allegorical approach she employed in portraying herself. Domenica Morghen and her sister-in-law Maddalena Volpato become the muses of Tragedy and Comedy holding their attributes of the tragic mask and Comedy's pedum, or crook.[8] Kauffman also cast Emma, Lady Hamilton, as Thalia, the Muse of Comedy, in her marriage portrait of 1791 (cat. 31). Hamilton was known for performing her 'attitudes' in imitation of Classical figures and posed for numerous artists including George Romney and Elisabeth Vigée Le Brun.[9] Kauffman subsequently produced two dramatic portraits of celebrated women poets who performed at her salons and with whom she must have felt particular affinity. The first depicts the *Impromptu Virtuoso Fortunata Sulgher Fantastici as Muse* (1792; Gallerie degli Uffizi, Florence), and sparked a fruitful artistic dialogue with both Fantastici and her daughter writing poems to Kauffman in response to the portrait.[10] The second presents the *Impromptu Virtuoso Teresa Bandettini Landucci as Muse* (1794; cat. 32) who, Kauffman noted in her Memoria, is painted 'in the gracious act of reciting, clad like a Muse in all'antica garb'. As Kauffman depicted herself, Fantastici and Landucci represent the powers of inspiration and creation combined.[11]

During the early 1790s, Kauffman turned her attention back to her own life and career, retrospectively immortalising the crucial choice she made as a young woman between music and art in her monumental *Self-portrait at the Crossroads Between the Arts of Music and Painting* (1794; cat. 33). Radically, Kauffman painted this scene from her own life on the same scale and level of ambition as a major history painting.[12] Moreover, she appropriated a male role, just as she had for many of her female heroines, presenting herself in the manner of Hercules choosing between Virtue and Vice to create a work that Bettina Baumgärtel has described as 'revolutionary'.[13] The composition also echoes the Three Graces and it is a testament to Kauffman's sophisticated handling and merging of visual references that the work was not considered hubristic. Her fellow Royal Academician James Barry, for one, responded to the painting's high ambitions: 'Some may say that this is great, since it was executed by a female; but I say, that whoever produced such a picture, in whatever age or whatever country, it is great, it is noble, it is sublime.'[14]

26
Self-portrait in the Character of Design Listening to the Inspiration of Poetry, 1782
Oil on canvas, diameter 61.2 cm
English Heritage, Kenwood. The Ernest Edward Cook Bequest presented by the Art Fund, inv. 88029077

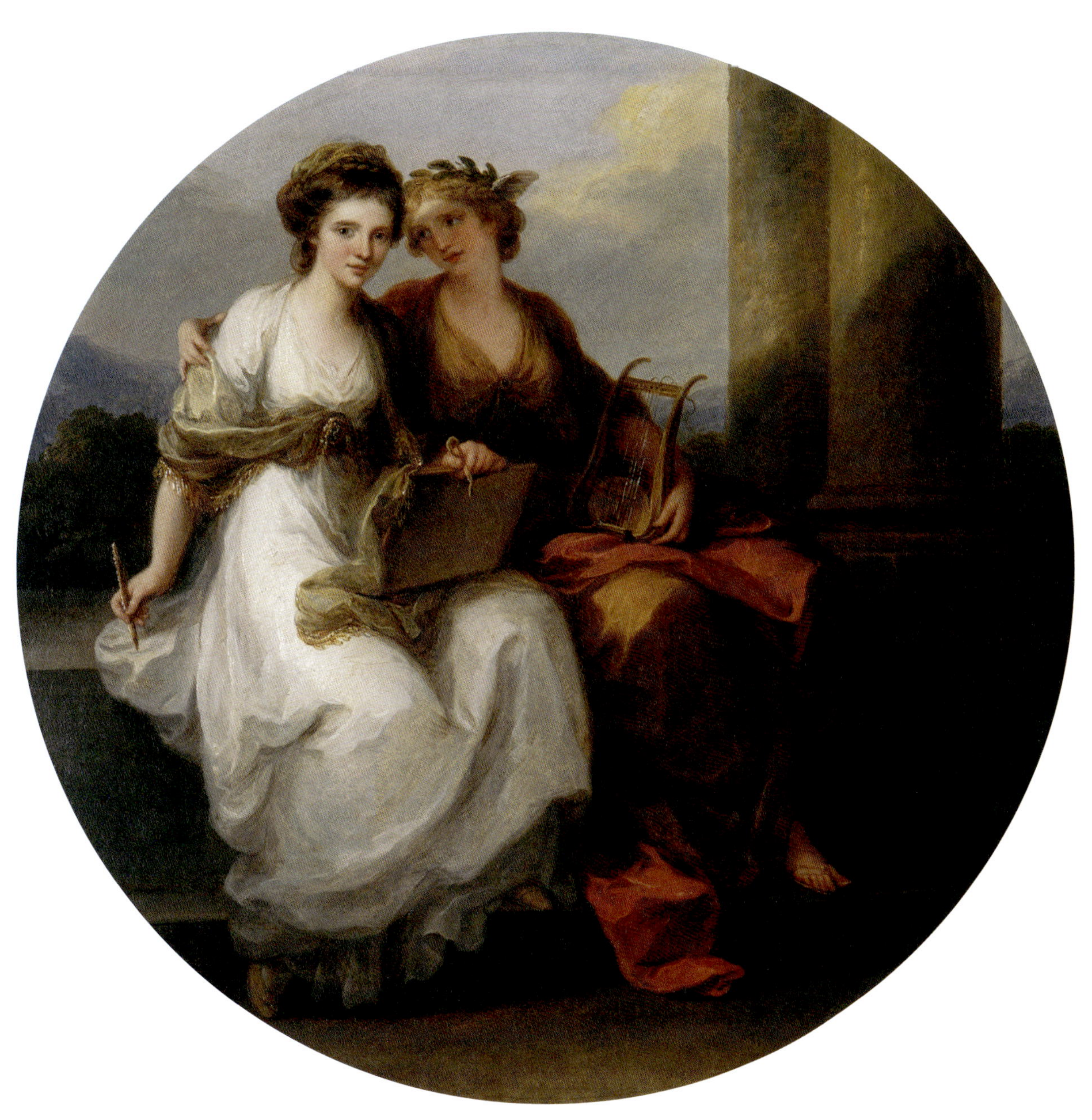

27
Michael Novosielski (1750–1795), 1791
Oil on canvas, 128 × 101.6 cm
National Galleries of Scotland. Bequest of Mrs Elizabeth Stewart 1879, inv. NG 651

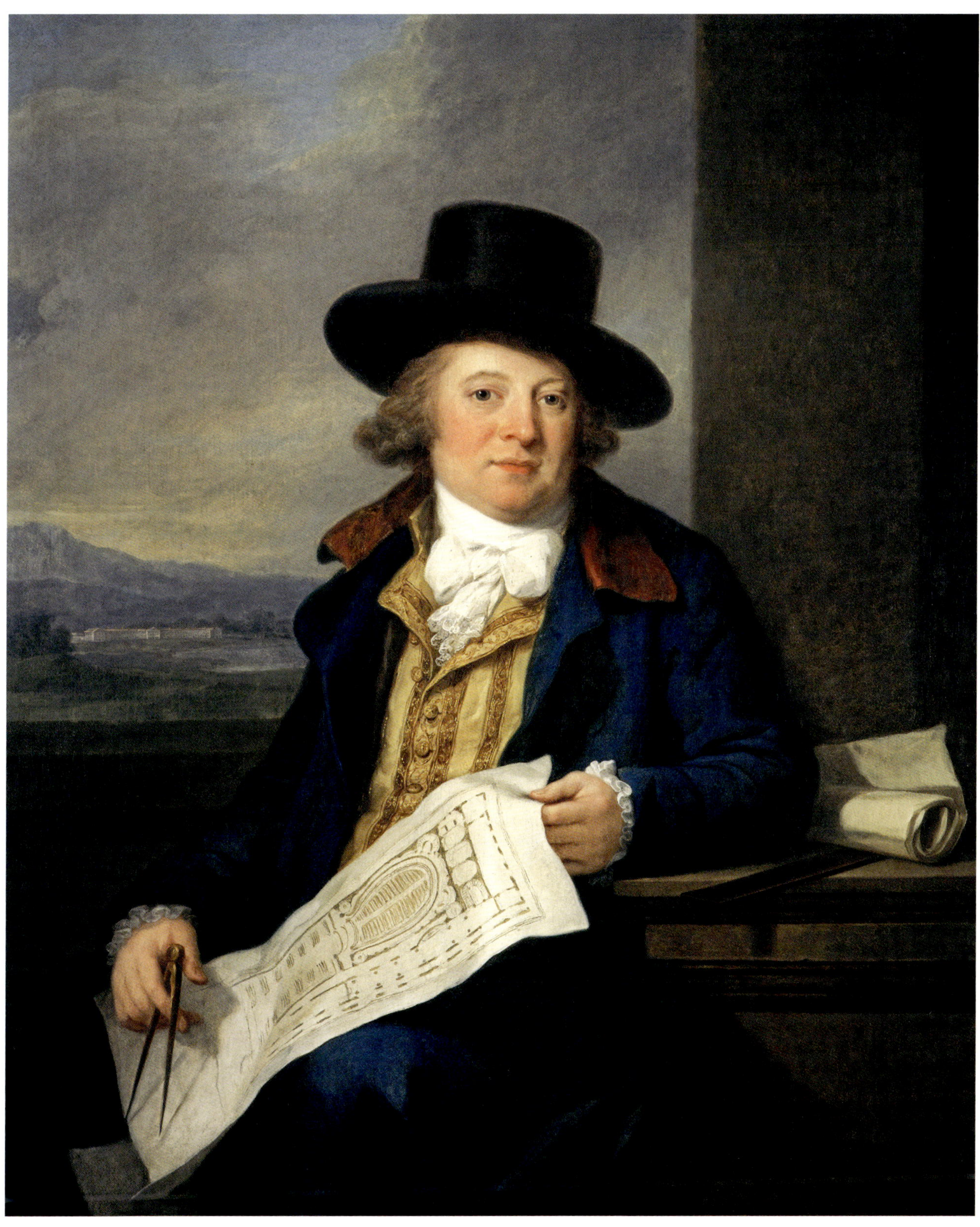

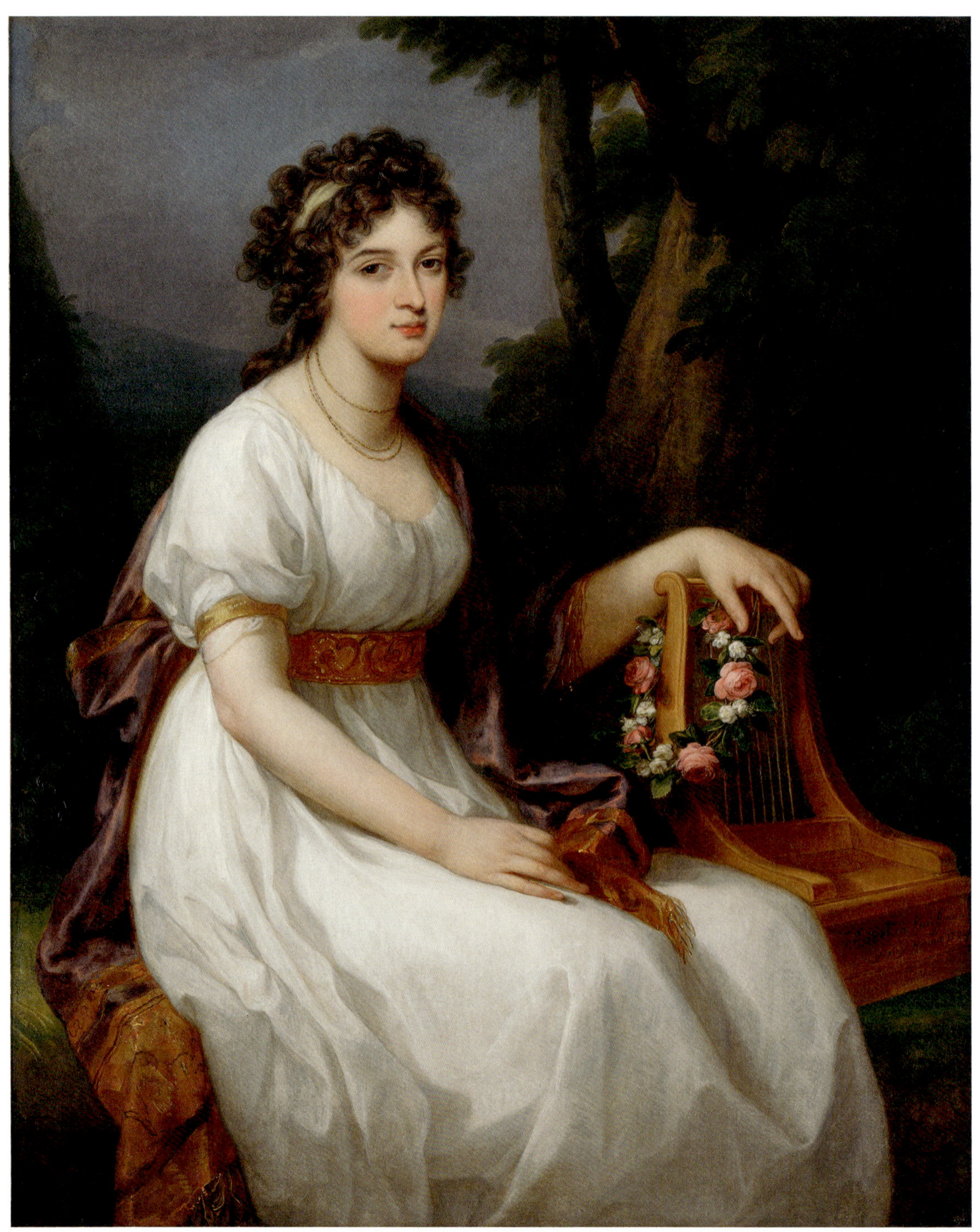

28
Portrait of Henrietta Maria Hill, later Brudenell-Bruce and Marchioness of Ailesbury, as the Muse Erato, 1792
Oil on canvas, 129.5 × 101.5 cm
Private collection

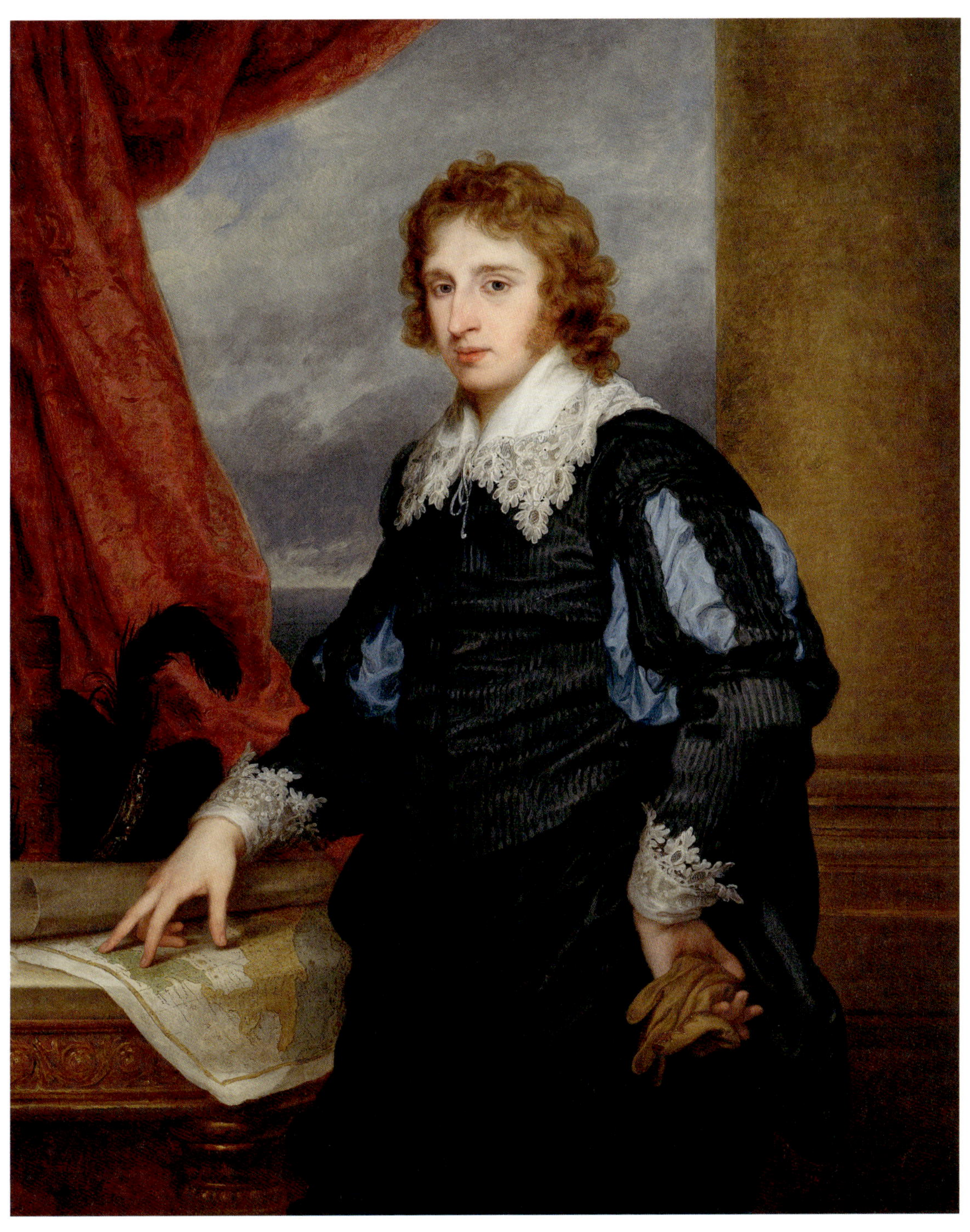

29
Portrait of Charles Brudenell-Bruce, later 1st Marquess of Ailesbury, 1795
Oil on canvas, 129.5 × 101.5 cm
Private collection

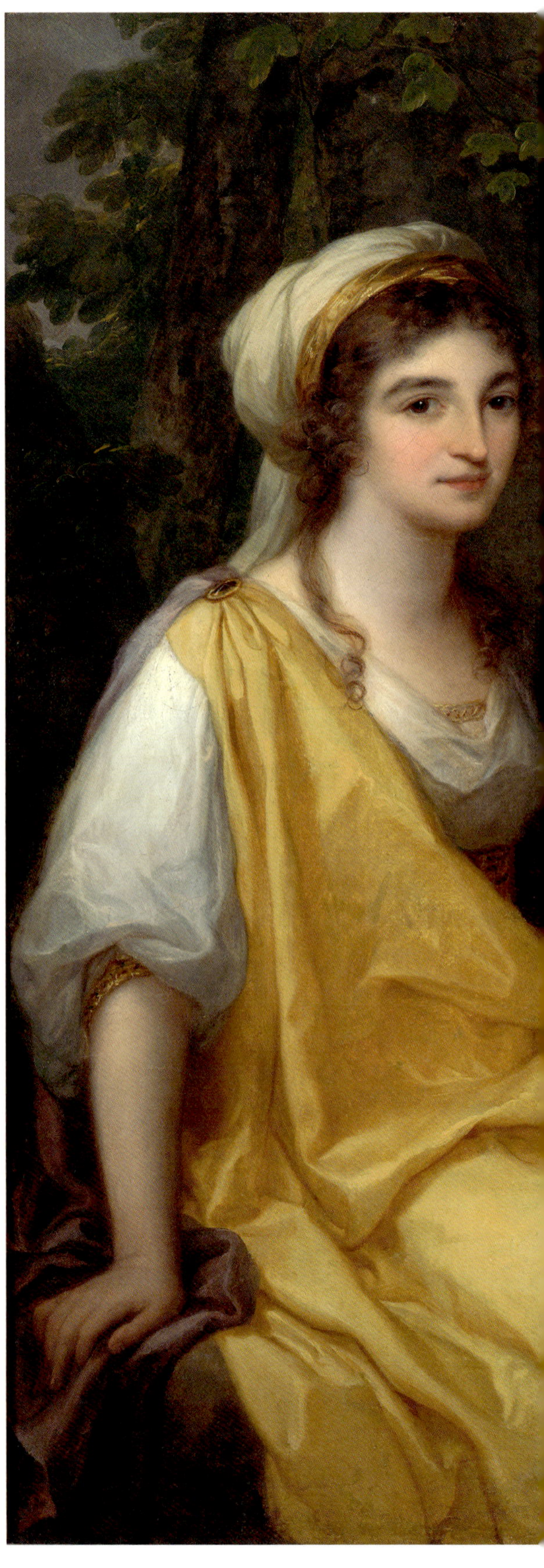

30
Portraits of Domenica Morghen and Maddalena Volpato as Muses of Tragedy and Comedy, 1791
Oil on canvas, 124.5 × 159.2 cm
National Museum in Warsaw, inv. M.Ob.1842 MNW

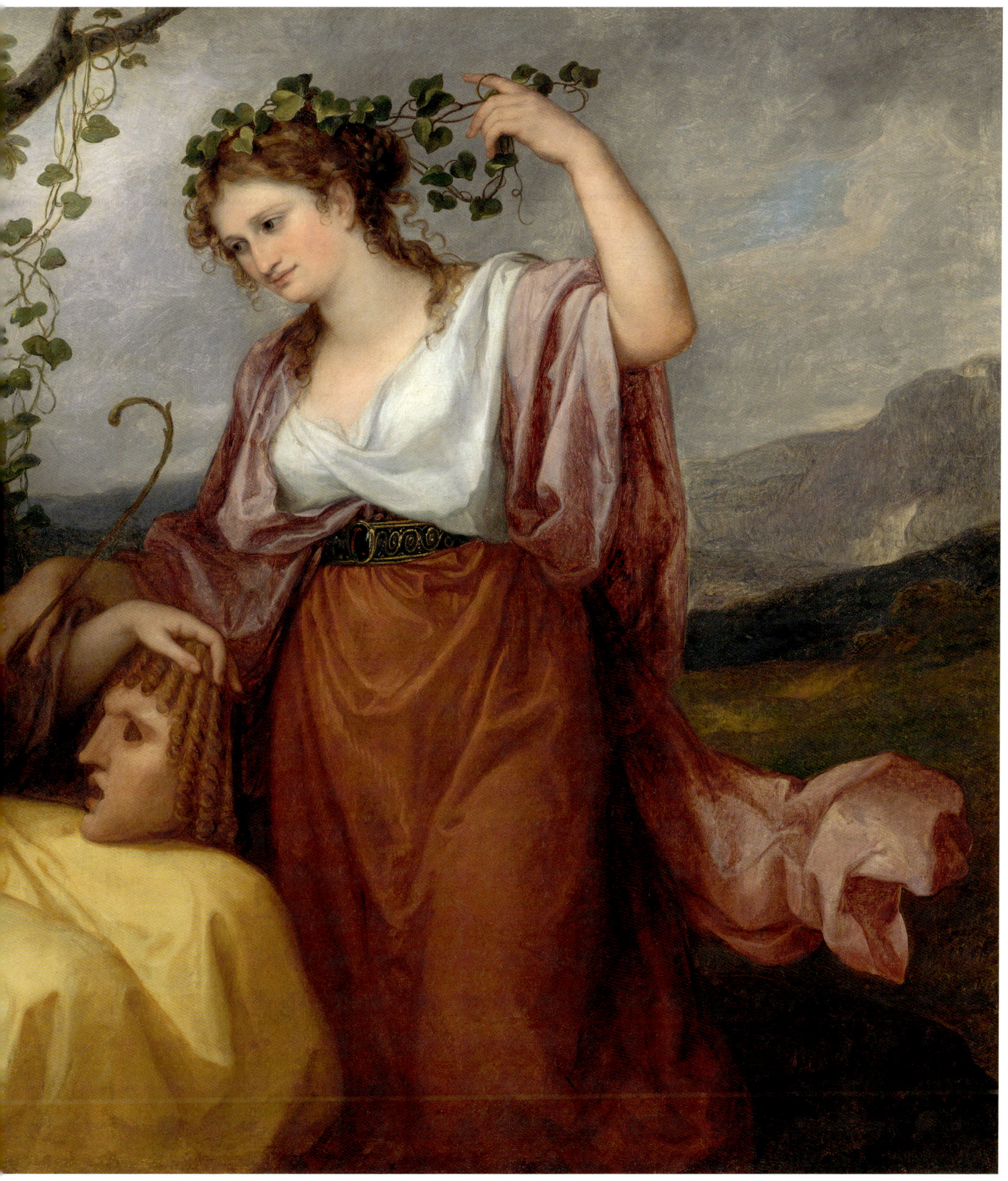

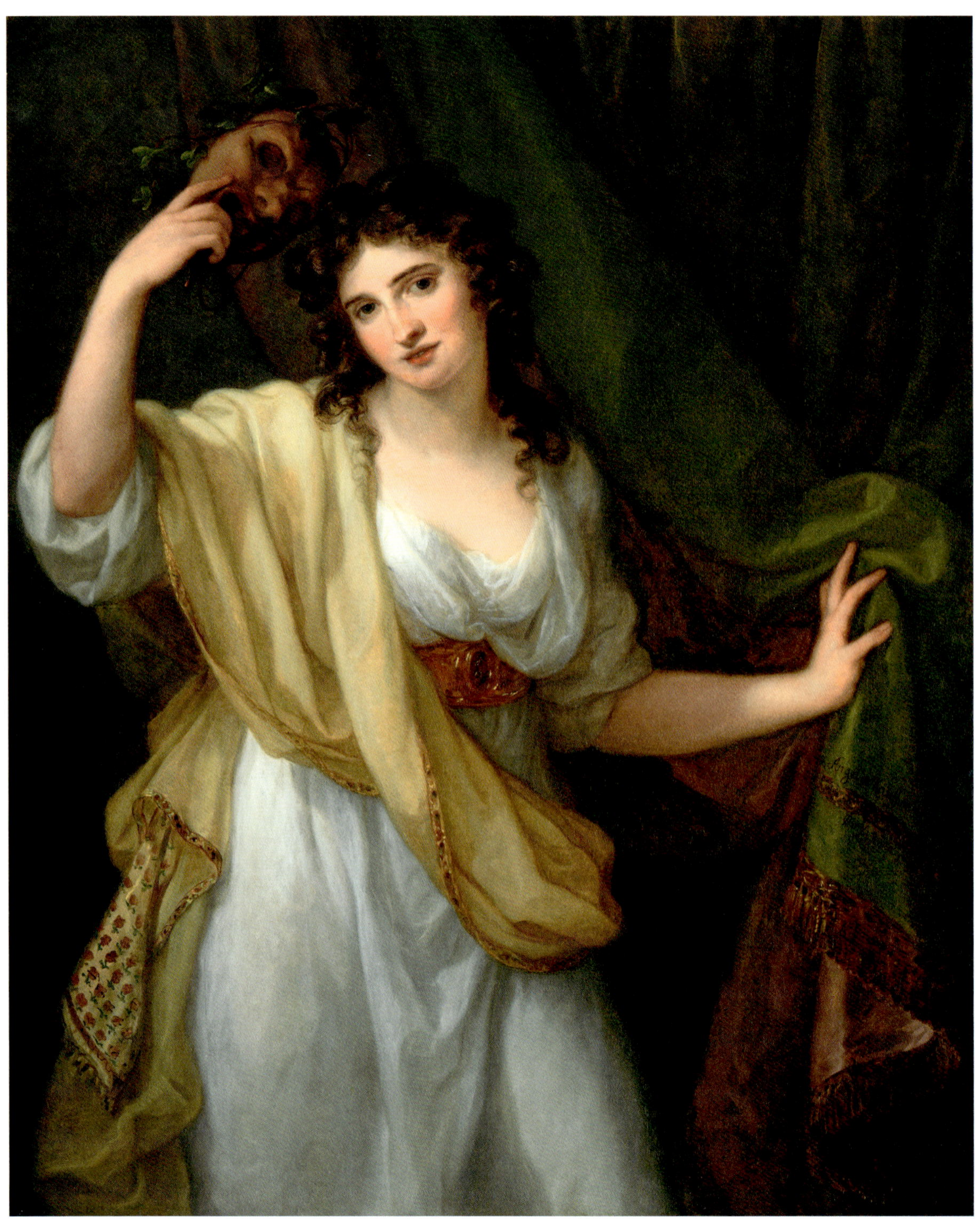

31
Portrait of Emma, Lady Hamilton, as Muse of Comedy, 1791
Oil on canvas, 127 × 101.6 cm
Private collection

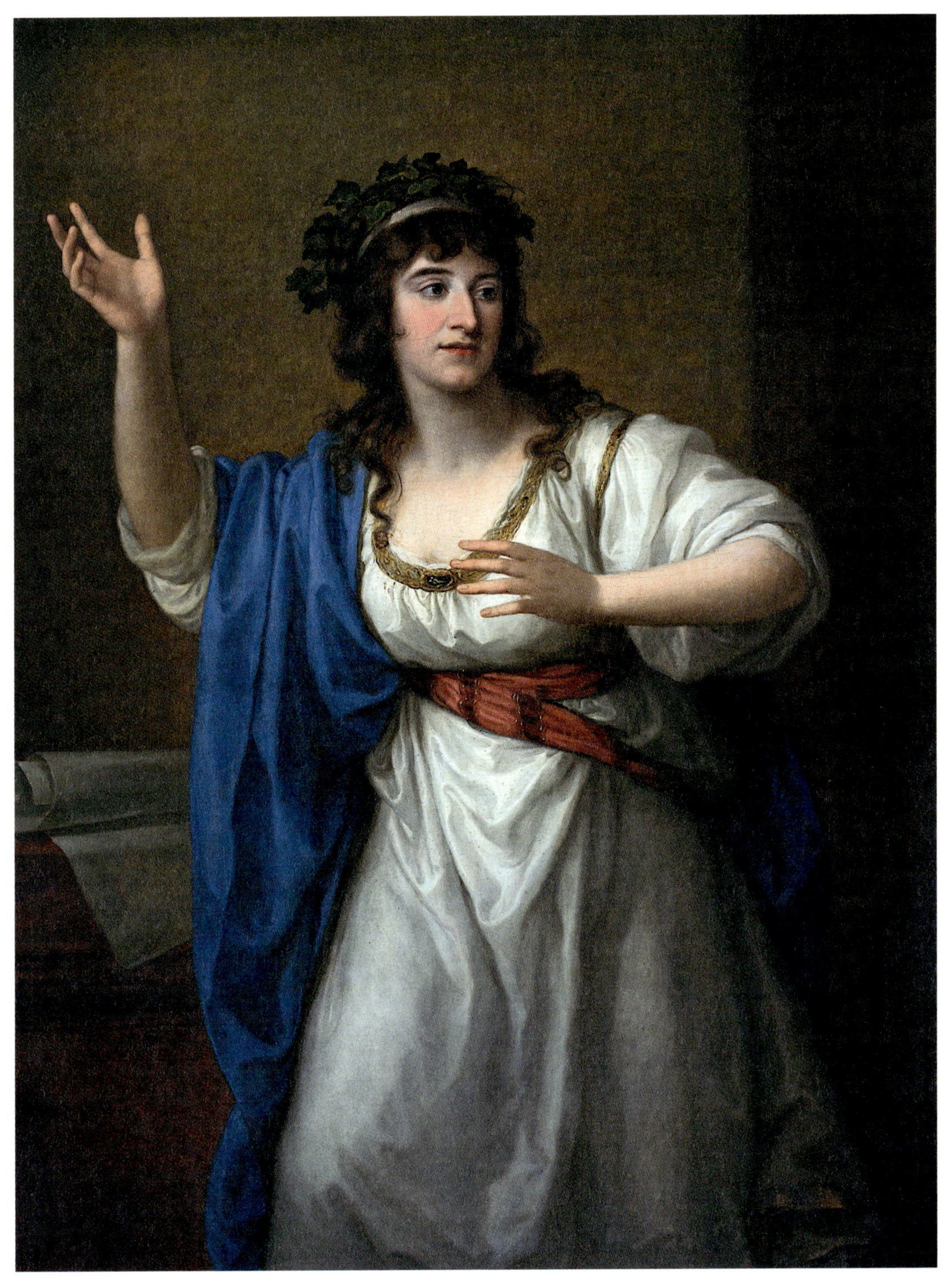

32
Portrait of the Impromptu Virtuoso Teresa Bandettini Landucci as Muse, 1794
Oil on canvas, 128.2 × 93.6 cm
Kunstpalast, Düsseldorf, inv. mkp M 2008-2

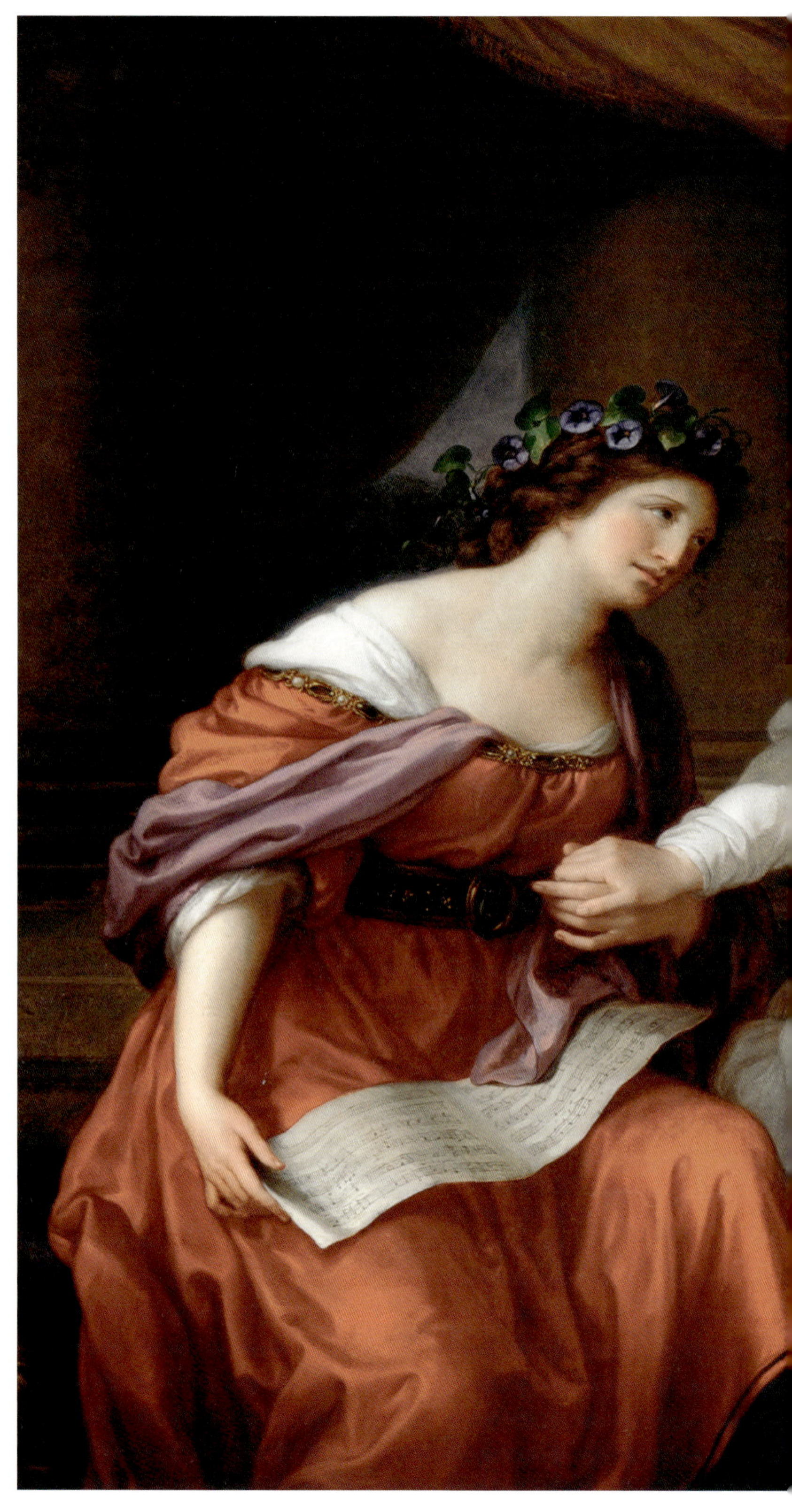

33
Self-portrait at the Crossroads Between the Arts of Music and Painting, 1794
Oil on canvas, 147.3 × 215.9 cm
National Trust Collections (Nostell Priory, The St Oswald Collection). Purchased by private treaty with the help of a grant from the Heritage Lottery Fund, 2002, inv. 960079

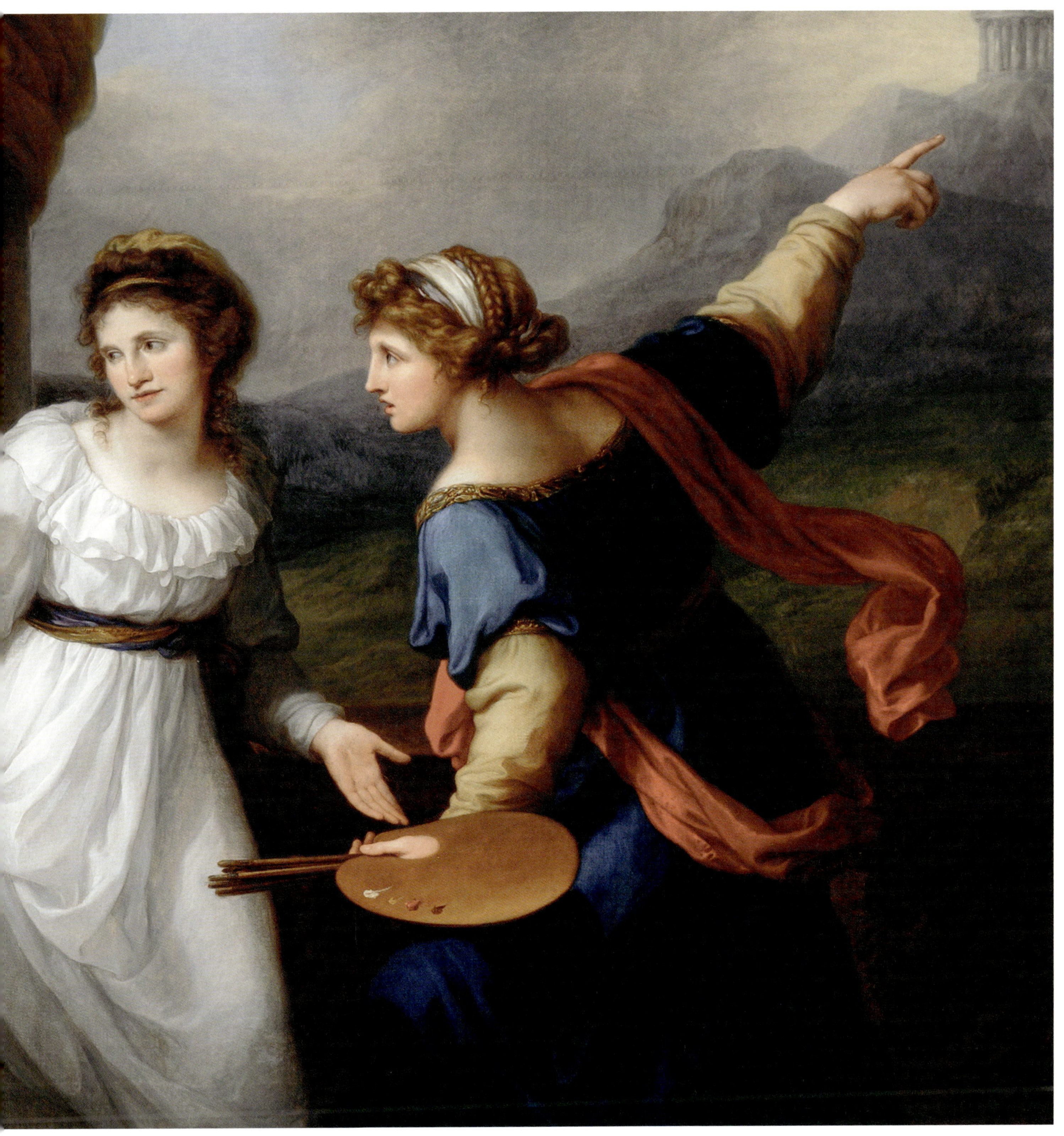

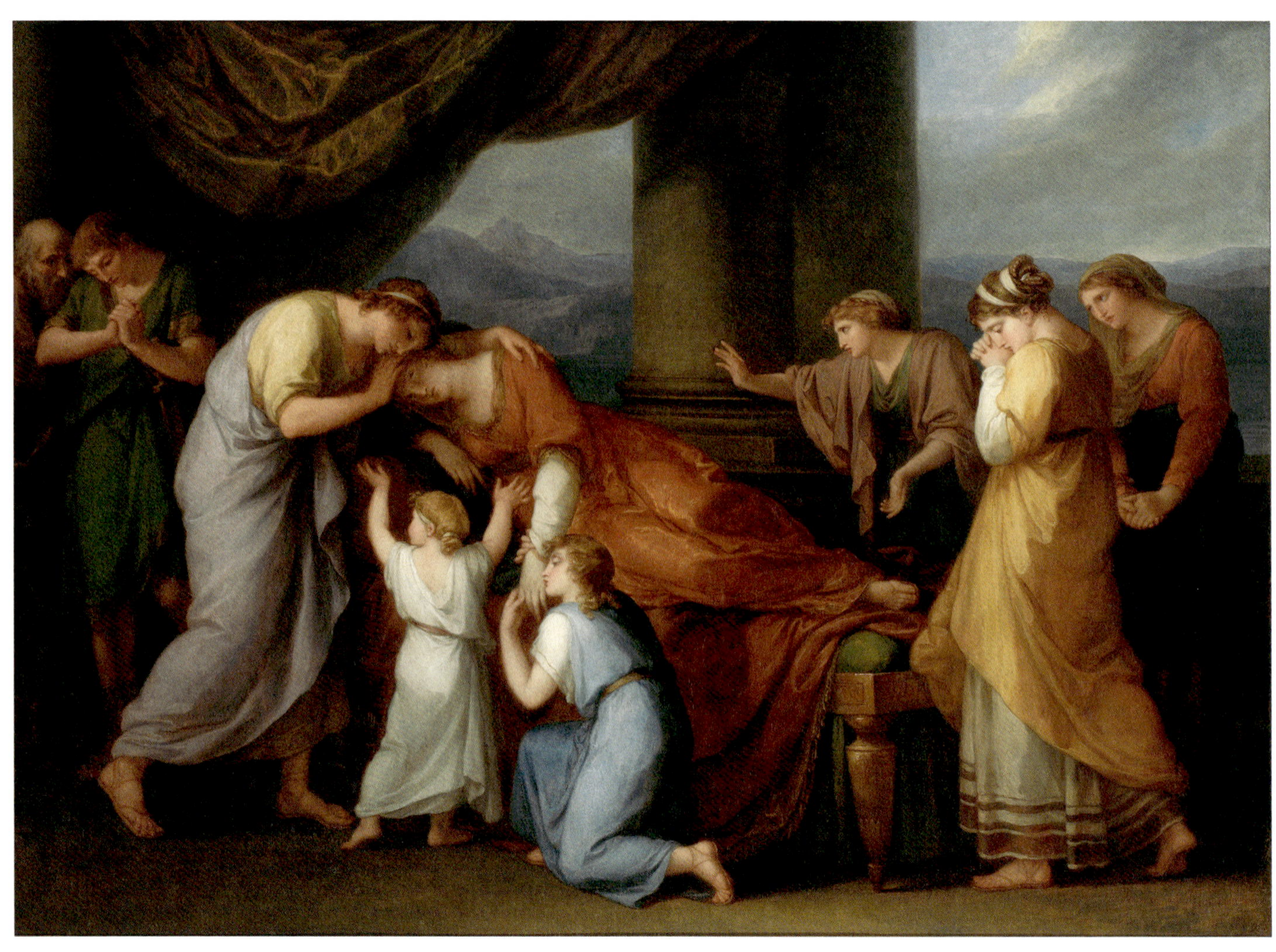

34
Death of Alcestis, 1790
Oil on canvas, 114 × 154 cm
vorarlberg museum, Bregenz,
inv. Gem 908

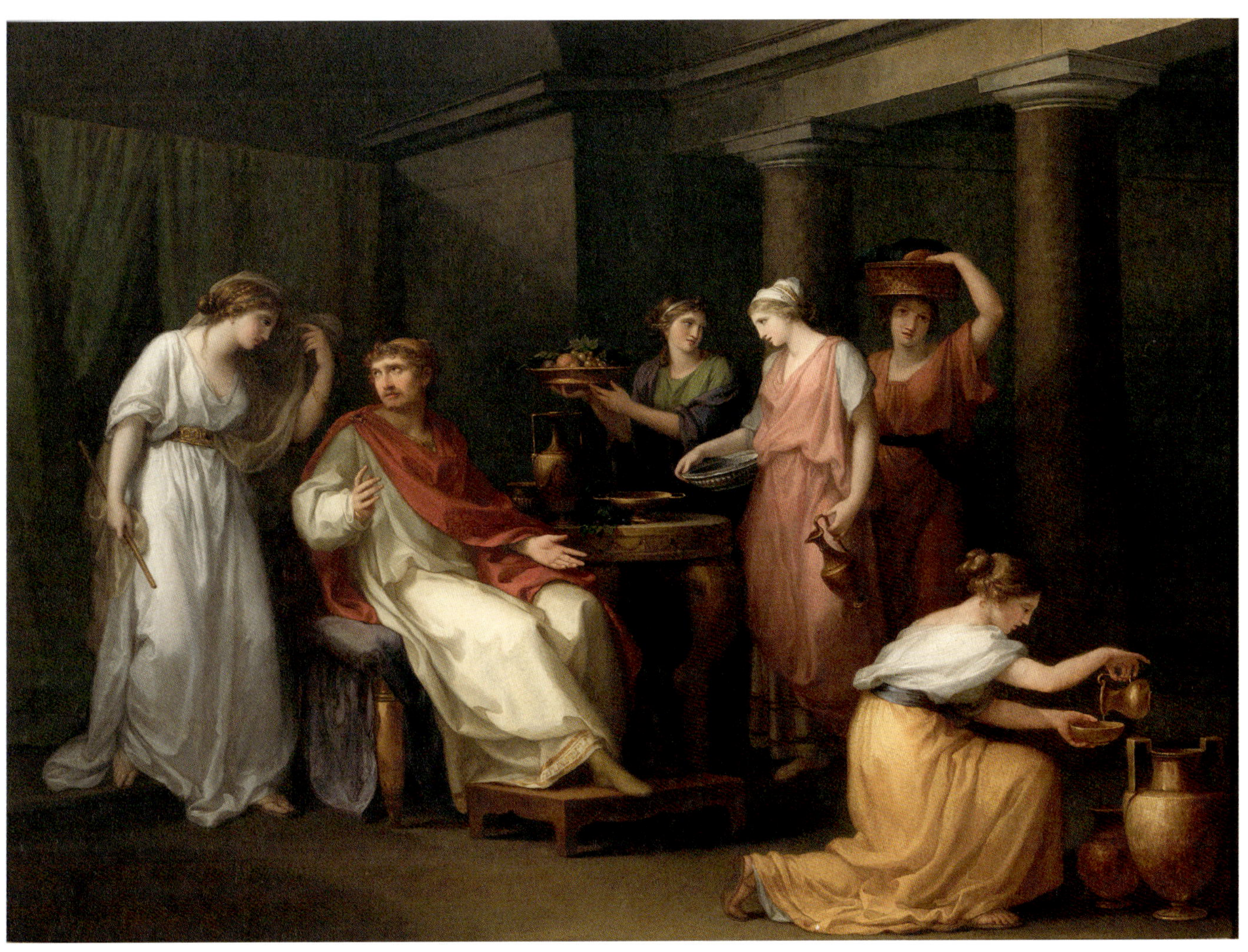

35
Ulysses on the Island of Circe, 1793
Oil on canvas, 115.5 × 155 cm
Loan from the Barrett Swiss Collection in memory of Nona Barrett

36

Christ and the Samaritan Woman, 1796

Oil on canvas, 123.5 × 158.5 cm

Bayerische Staatsgemäldesammlungen Munich – Neue Pinakothek, inv. 10634

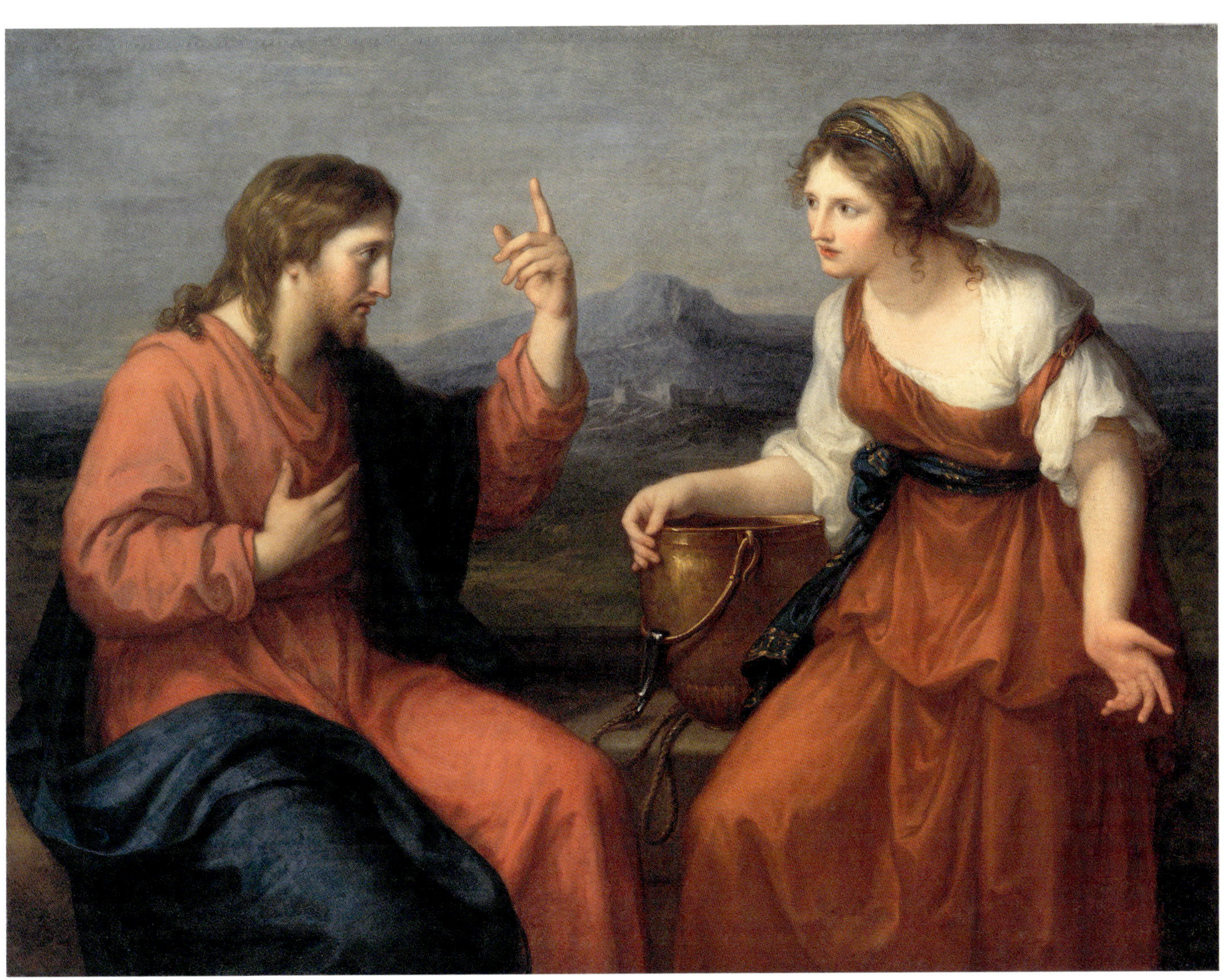

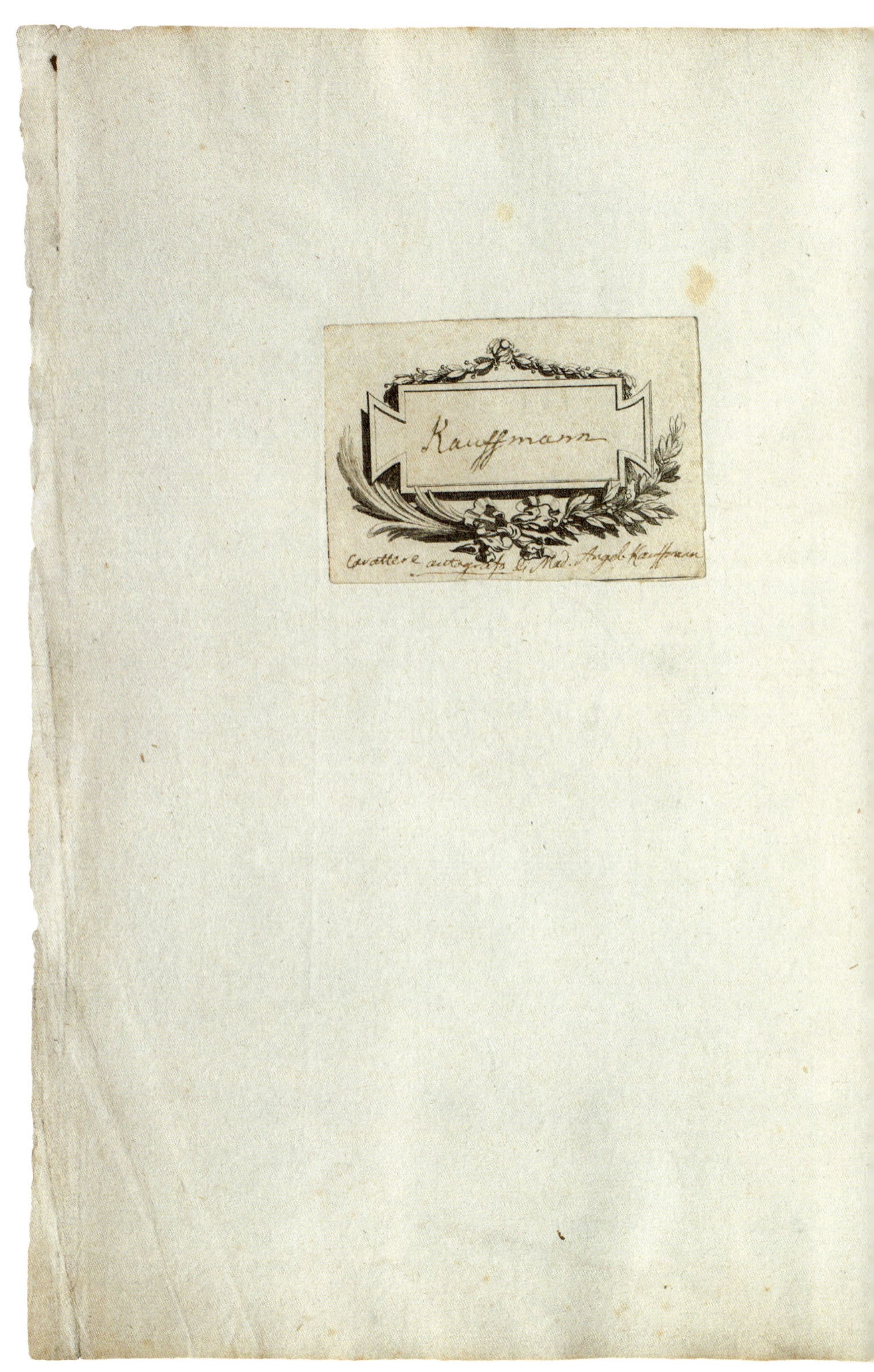

37
Memoria delle piture [*sic*]
fatte d' Angelica Kauffman,
December 1781–November 1795,
January 1796–November 1798
Royal Academy of Arts, London, inv. KAU/1

Memoria delle Pitture fatte d'Angelica Kauffman
dopo il suo ritorno d'Inghilterra che fù nell mese
d'otobre 1781. che si trovò a Venezia ——

Per Sua Altezza Imperiale
Gran Duca delle Russie

[margin: ...enezia ...embre 1781]

Un quadro di circa 3 piedi inglesi – rapresentante un
sogetto della storia d'inghilterra – Elleonora vicino all
punto di morte per il vellenno che suchio dalla ferita
che Edoardo Primo ricevette d'un traditore con arma avvele-
nata alla Guerra di Palestina — —— ——

per il sudetto Gran Duca [margin: ...aio 1781]

altro quadro simille all sudetto, rapres.te Elleonora ricupe-
ratta dall vellenno per via d'un antidotto, viene presentata
a Edoardo che la credeva gia morta, il momento quand
e sorpreso alla vista della Regina che le viene presentata
nell tempo che se ne stava nella più grande afflizione ——

quadro acquistato dall sudetto Gran Duca
della stessa Grandezza dipinto in inghilterra

Rapresenta la Morte di Leonardo da Vinci, allor che
vien visitatto da Francesco Primo di Francia che volse
vedere Leonardo purima che spirasse, lo abbraccia e Leonardo spira tra le Braccia dell monarca ——

Li 3. sudetti quadri furono pagati. Zecchini veneti. 460 . . .

per Mad.me Boyer a Londra

[margin: dipinto a ...enezia 1782 ...aggio]

Un circolo di p.di 2.2. rapres.te La Bellezza guidatta dalla
prudenza e coronatta dall Merito — pagatto Ghinee. 25. . .

per Mr Bowles a Londra

[margin: Venezia maggio 1782]

2. circoli di p.di 1.2. rappresentanti, Flora che mostra ad un
pittore il modo di dipingere li fiori – un amorino che
tiene de fiori ed il pittore nella più grande attenzione.
l'altro rapresenta Ganimede avendo giocatto a dadi con
cupido la vinse tutti li suoi dadi sta piangendo dinan-
zi cercane che sta in atto di sgridare Ganimede ——
Li due per Ghinee —— —— —— 50

a Mr Strange Residente d'inghilterra
a Venezia

Una Testa di Bella donna agiustatta in carattere Maga
pagatta Ghinee —— 15

a Giuseppe Zucchi a Venezia

due ovalletti con sue maggi figurine di donna
regallatto dalla pittrice all sudetto ——

RAA/SEC/1/7 6

Gentlemen:

I have had the honour of a visite from Sir Will. Chambers – the purpose of which was to reconcile me to submite to the exhibition of a Picture which gave me offence, however I may admire the dignity of the gentlemen who are superior to the malignity of the author, I should have held their conduct much more in admiration, if they had taken into consideration a Respect to the sex· which it is their glory to support.
If they fear the loss – of an academician who pays no respect to that sex – I hope I may enjoy the liberty of leaving to them the pleasure of that academician and withdrawing one object who never willingly deserved his or their Ridicule.
I beg leave to present my Respects to the Society and hope they will always – regard their own honour — I have but one request to make, to send home my Pictures. If that is to be exhibited:

I am gentlemen

Golden Square
Tuesday morn

your most obedient Servant
Angelica Kauffman.

38
Letter from Angelica Kauffman to the Council of the Royal Academy, April 1775
Royal Academy of Arts, London, inv. RAA/SEC/1/7

Gentlemen, two days past I received this letter
From Mr. Bonomi

"Dear Sir"

This Morning I received a letter from my Correspondent in Rome D. M. A. Borsi, concerning the death of Mrs Angelica Kauffman, which I shall transcribe word for word.

a The letter to Mr Bonomi from Rome 7th November 1807

Dear Sir,

What for some time I foresaw, after about twenty days confinement in bed, with the greatest tranquility of spirit, always present to herself, having twice received the blessed Sacrament & two days before Extreme-Unction, perfectly resigned, Courageously met the Death of the Righteous on thursday last 5th Inst. at half past two in the afternoon, the great Woman, the always illustrious, holy & most pious Mrs Angelica Kauffman. I shudder in acquainting you with such unfortunate news, knowing the grief that it will cause to you, & to Mrs Bonomi. I shall now relate the particulars of her Illness, & funeral. During her severe illness all her numerous friends, did what they could to restore her, & every one was grieved in the apprehension of loosing her, You may easily believe more than I can express how much their grief encreased at her Death, I only therefore shall mention, that they vied with each other, in endeavouring to perform their last Duties in the most decorous obsequies; celebrated this morning in the Church of S. Andrea delle Fratte, conducted by Canova, & other virtuosi friends. The Church was Decorated as is customary for Nobles; at 10 O'clock in the morning the Corpse was accompanied to the Church by two very numerous Brotherhoods, 50 Capuchins & Priests. The Bier was carried by some of the Brotherhood, but the four Corners of the Pall, by four Young Ladies properly dressed for the occasion, the four tassels were held by the four first Gentlemen of the Academy, these were followed by the rest of the Academicians & Virtuosi who carried in triumph two of her Pictures; & every one with a large waxe taper lighted" ——

This Sir is the melancholy account I thought it my Duty to transmit to you as President of the R. Academy. Be pleased, You & Mrs West to accept my and Mrs Bonomi's united Compliments & I have the honor to be,

Dear Sir,

Your obedient humble Servant
Joseph Bonomi

76 Gt Titchfield Street
Monday Afternoon Dec. 21st 1807

39
Letter from Joseph Bonomi to Benjamin West, with annotations by Benjamin West, 21 December 1807
Royal Academy of Arts, London, inv. RAA/SEC/1/28

CHRONOLOGY

BETTINA BAUMGÄRTEL

30 October 1741
Born in Chur, Switzerland, the only child of Johann Joseph Kauffman and Cleophea Lutz.

1750
Draws her first portraits in pastel, aged nine.

1752
The family moves to Como in northern Italy, then governed by Austria; her father works for the Counts of Salis.

c. 1753
Paints her first self-portrait as a singer.

1754–57
First visit to Italy, performs as a singer, paints portraits and makes copies after Old Masters paintings.

1757
Death of the artist's mother.

Father and daughter paint frescoes in the parish church of the Holy Trinity at Schwarzenberg, her only works in fresco.

c. 1758/59–1765
Second visit to Italy.

1761–62
Studies the works of Correggio in Parma, and of Guido Reni and Annibale Carracci in Bologna.

June 1762–
In Florence she is given a studio in the Medici collection. She makes copies after Guercino, Raphael, Rembrandt and other artists, and befriends the young American artist Benjamin West, a later President of the Royal Academy.

October 1762
Honorary membership of the Accademia Clementina di Bologna; elected a member of Florence's Accademia delle Arti del Disegno. Meets British Grand Tourists and paints numerous portraits; makes her first etchings under the guidance of Johann Friedrich Reiffenstein, a lifelong friend.

1763–
First visit to Rome, paints her first large-scale history paintings (cat. 4) and studies antiquities.

1763–64
Visits Naples and copies works in the Capodimonte Museum.

April 1764
Returns to Rome, and paints her portrait of the archaeologist Johann Joachim Winckelmann (cat. 5).

May 1765
Full membership of Rome's Accademia di San Luca; paints *Hope* (fig. 13) as her reception piece.

Her portrait of David Garrick (cat. 6) is exhibited at the Free Society of Artists in London to great acclaim.

July 1765
Travels via Bologna to Venice, without her father, and then on to London with Lady Bridget Wentworth, wife of John Murray, British Resident in Venice, leaving in spring 1766.

June 1766
Arrives in London and opens a studio, first at Suffolk Street, Charing Cross, later at Golden Square in Soho.

1766–67
Receives a commission from the Queen Mother for the *Portrait of Augusta, Duchess of Brunswick-Lüneburg (1737–1813) with Her Son Prince Charles George Augustus (1766–1806)* (fig. 10). Joshua Reynolds, later first President of the Royal Academy, promotes her; they paint each other's portraits (cat. 16 and fig. 3).

Spring 1767
Her father arrives in London.

November 1767
Secretly marries Count Frederick de Horn, who turns out to be an impostor and a fortune hunter. The marriage is annulled in February 1768.

1768
Shows history paintings at the exhibition of the Free Society of Artists in London.

10 December 1768
Founding member of the Royal Academy of Arts. She and Mary Moser remain the only female Royal Academicians until the twentieth century.

1769
Shows history paintings at the opening exhibition of the Royal Academy.

1770
She is one of the first artists to paint scenes from ancient and medieval British history (cat. 11).

Summer 1771
Six-month trip to Ireland; paints numerous portraits of the Irish gentry.

1772–
Produces etchings, some in collaboration with her future brother-in-law Giuseppe Carlo Zucchi.

1773
Selected to decorate the interior of St Paul's Cathedral alongside Joshua Reynolds, Nathaniel Dance and James Barry; the project is never realised.

1775
Objects to Nathaniel Hone's painting *The Pictorial Conjuror, Displaying the Whole Art of Optical Deception*, a satire on Reynolds and herself. Succeeds in having it removed from the exhibition at the Royal Academy.

1776–
Her oils are reproduced by Matthew Boulton as 'mechanical paintings' used in numerous interior decorations.

1780
Completes the prestigious commission for four ceiling paintings, *Invention*, *Design*, *Composition* and *Colouring* (pp. 80–81 and cats 24 and 25), for Somerset House, the new home of the Royal Academy.

14 July 1781
Marries the Venetian painter Antonio Zucchi.

July 1781
Leaves London and travels via Flanders and Schwarzenberg to Venice, where she meets the future Tsar Paul I of Russia and his wife Sophie Dorothea of Württemberg.

1781–98
Antonio Zucchi begins to keep a book of Kauffman's work and income, *Memoria delle piture fatte* (cat. 37), which was continued up to 1798 by the artist herself.

1782
Death of her father.

Honorary membership of the Accademia di Venezia.

May 1782
Opens a studio in Rome next to the Spanish Steps. Her salon becomes a meeting place for famous travellers to Rome.

Summers of 1782–85
Invited by Carolina of Austria, Queen of Naples, to her court to paint a monumental portrait of the royal family (fig. 7).

1785–
Paints portraits of members of European royal and princely houses.

Stanislaus III Poniatowski of Poland, the Austrian Emperor Joseph II and Catherine the Great, Empress of Russia, acquire large-format history paintings (fig. 6).

1785–86
Giovanni Gherardo de Rossi publishes the first in-depth biography of Kauffman in the journal *Memorie per le Belle Arti*.

1786–88
Becomes a close friend of the Weimar circle of artists, including Johann Wolfgang von Goethe, Johann Gottfried Herder and the Duchess Anna Amalia of Saxe-Weimar-Eisenach; paints their portraits when in Rome.

1789
Her self-portrait (cat. 3) for the Grand Duke of Tuscany's famous gallery of self-portraits at the Uffizi, Florence, is hung next to that of Michelangelo (today attributed to Jacopino del Conte).

Invited by the publisher John Boydell to contribute to his Shakespeare Gallery in Pall Mall, London.

1791
Receives her first and only commission from Pope Pius VI, to paint an altarpiece for the Swiss Chapel of the Santa Basilica, Loreto.

Starts her major *Self-portrait at the Crossroads Between the Arts of Music and Painting* (cat. 33) and various role portraits of her artist friends such as *Portrait of Emma, Lady Hamilton, as Muse of Comedy* (cat. 31)

December 1795
Death of her husband Antonio Zucchi.

1797
Exhibits her last picture at the Royal Academy.

1798
French troops occupy Rome; her studio is spared from looting.

c. 1801
Paints her last self-portrait.

1802
Gives *The Coronation of the Virgin* to the parish church of Schwarzenberg in Vorarlberg as an altarpiece.

1805
Receives her last major portrait commission from Crown Prince Ludwig I of Bavaria.

1806
Completes her last altarpiece, the *Birth of St John the Baptist*, for Count Francesco Martinengo da Barco.

5 November 1807
Dies in Rome after a short illness.
The Accademia di San Luca organises a magnificent funeral ceremony, in which Kauffman's last major paintings, *David and Nathan* and *Christ and the Samaritan Woman* (cat. 36), are carried behind her coffin. A huge crowd attends the burial service at Sant'Andrea delle Fratte.

See also the Angelica Kauffman Research Project (https://www.angelika-kauffmann.de/en/chronology/), whose chronology has been online since May 2013.

LIST OF WORKS EXHIBITED

1
***Self-portrait in the Traditional Costume of the Bregenz Forest*, 1781**
Oil on canvas, 61.4 × 49.2 cm
TLM, Ältere kunstgeschichtliche Sammlung, Innsbruck, inv. Gem 301

Select bibliography: Sickler and Reinhart 1810; Baumgärtel 1990, p. 266; Baumgärtel, in Düsseldorf 1998, p. 232, cat. 109; Ammann 2012, pp. 143, 149–52; Baumgärtel, in Düsseldorf 2020, pp. 50–51, cat. 6.

2
***Self-portrait with Stylus and Portfolio*, 1784**
Oil on canvas, 64.8 × 50.7 cm
Bayerische Staatsgemäldesammlungen Munich – Neue Pinakothek, inv. 1056

Select bibliography: Munich 1978, cat. 1056; Baumgärtel, in Constance 1992, cat. 3; Baumgärtel, in Düsseldorf 1998, p. 233, cat. 110; Baumgärtel, in Stendal 2016, p. 8, fig. 1, p. 25, cat. I.1.

3
***Self-portrait in all'antica Dress*, 1787**
Oil on canvas, 128 × 93.5 cm
Gallerie degli Uffizi, Florence, inv. 1890, no. 1928

Select bibliography: Kauffman Memoria, pt. 1, p. 23; Prinz 1971, pp. 218–19, doc. nos 186–89; Webster, in Florence 1971, pp. 58–59, cat. 58, illus.; Rice and Eisenberg 1991, pp. 124–26, figs 1–3; Baumgärtel 1998b, p. 224; Baumgärtel, in Düsseldorf 1998, p. 228, fig. 121; Rosenthal 2006, pp. 265, 268–69, figs 153, 155 (*Muse of Painting*); Casciu, in Florence 2006, p. 159, under cat. 82; Bezzini, in Florence 2010, pp. 316–17, cat. 172, no. 7; Facchin 2010, pp. 198–200, 204, 209; Florence Uffizi 2010, p. 68, cat.21; Baumgärtel 2017, pp. 360–78, fig. 1 (with older sources); Baumgärtel, in Dessau 2018, p. 51, cat. 5; Düsseldorf 2020, pp. 56–57, cat. 9.

4
***Penelope at Her Loom*, 1764**
Oil on canvas, 172 × 122.2 cm
Brighton & Hove Museums, inv. FAH1975.33

Select bibliography: Brighton 1992, p. 29, fig 12; London 2007, p. 8, fig. 2; Baumgärtel, in Düsseldorf 2020, pp. 12-13, fig. 3.

5
***Portrait of Johann Joachim Winckelmann*, 1764**
Oil on canvas, 97 × 71 cm
Kunsthaus Zürich, Donated by Conrad Zeller, 1850, inv. 98

Select bibliography: Justi 1898, pp. 64–66, p. 263; Schulz 1962, pp. 119, 151, 167, fig. 148; Tutsch 1995, pp. 169–75; Baumgärtel, in Düsseldorf 1998, pp. 128–30, 133, cats 21 and 24; Baumgärtel 2016a, pp. 180–81, 185–86; Baumgärtel 2016c, pp. 64–84, fig. 68, cat. II.1–15; Baumgärtel, in Dessau 2018, pp. 103–05, cats 32–33, 51; Baumgärtel, in Düsseldorf 2020, pp. 60–61, cat. 10.

6
***Portrait of David Garrick*, 1764**
Oil on canvas, 84.6 × 68.7 cm
The Burghley House Collection, inv. PIC176

Select bibliography: Clayton 1876, p. 286, no. 6; Shawe-Taylor, in Nottingham and Edinburgh 1987, p. 41, fig. 33; Rosenthal 1996, pp. 101–02, 139–48, 146, 190; Baumgärtel, in Düsseldorf 1998, pp. 25, 216, fig. 8; Rosenthal 2006, pp. 59–60, fig. 25; London 2007, pp. 11–12, fig. 4; Baumgärtel, in Düsseldorf 2020, pp. 65–67, cat. 13.

7
***Portrait of Martha Cocks in Turkish Dress with Embroidery Frame*, 1772**
Oil on canvas, 91 × 114.7 cm
Eastnor Castle Collection

Select bibliography: Worcester 1882, p. 70, cat. 385; Eastnor Castle 1889, p. 25, and other edns; Baumgärtel, in Düsseldorf 2020, pp. 118–19, cat. 44.

8
***Cleopatra Adorning the Tomb of Mark Antony*, c. 1769–70**
Oil on canvas, 126.5 × 101.7 cm
The Burghley House Collection, inv. PIC286

Select bibliography: London RA 1770, p. 15, cat. 118; Los Angeles 1976, p. 177, cat. 48; Baumgärtel, in Düsseldorf 1998, pp. 27–28, 140, 347, fig. 10, cats 190–93; London 2001b, pp. 342–43, cat. 363; Baumgärtel 2004, pp. 239–40, cat. 52 (with older lit.); Baumgärtel, in Düsseldorf 2020, pp. 72–73, cat. 16.

9
***Rinaldo and Armida in the Magic Garden*, c. 1772**
Oil on canvas, 128.1 × 102.6 cm
English Heritage, Kenwood. The Ernest Edward Cook Bequest presented by the Art Fund, inv. 88029074

Select bibliography: London Phillips 1879, no. 831; Manners and Williamson 1924, p. 206 (erron. titled *Damon and Musidora*); London Christie 1939, p. 14, lot 67 (erron. titled *Damon and Musidora*); Kenwood 1955, p. 99, cat. 367; Baumgärtel, in Düsseldorf 1998, p. 419 under cat. 258; Bryant, in Kenwood 2003, pp. 136–39, cat. 27; Baumgärtel, in Düsseldorf 2020, pp. 84–85, cat. 22.

10
***Armida Begs Rinaldo in Vain not to Leave Her*, 1776**
Oil on canvas, 102.1 × 127 cm
English Heritage, Kenwood, inv. 88029297

Select bibliography: London RA 1776, p. 15, cat. 158; Munich 1979, cat. 139; Baumgärtel, in Constance 1992, pp. 161–62, cat. 24; Baumgärtel, in Düsseldorf 1998, p. 419, cat. 258.

11
***Eleanora Sucking the Venom Out of the Wound of Her Husband, King Edward I*, 1776**
Oil on canvas, 72.2 × 92.2 cm
Private collection, Vorarlberg

Select bibliography: London RA 1776, p. 15, cat. 155 (*Rapin's History*, vol. 3, p. 179); Zucchi 1999, p. 29; De Rossi 1811, p. 54; Baumgärtel 1987, p. 369, cat. 4b, fig. 38; Brighton 1992, pp. 62-63, fig. 43; Baumgärtel, in Düsseldorf 1998, pp. 176–77, cat. 61; Porto 2001, pp. 206–07, cats 95 and 96; Baumgärtel, in Dessau 2018, pp. 115–16, cat. 41; Baumgärtel, in Düsseldorf 2020, pp. 78–79; Hirtenfelder, in Schwarzenberg 2023, p. 15, fig. 9.

12
***Shakespeare's Tomb*, 1772**
Oil on copper, 32.4 × 26 cm
The Burghley House Collection, inv. PIC230

Select bibliography: Zucchi 1999, no. 43; Burghley House 1815, p. 68 (*Fame*); Waagen 1838, p. 487 (*Fama*); Brinton 1903, p. 33 (*Fancy Scattering Flowers*); Manners and Williamson 1924, pp. 127, 182, 188; Walch 1968, p. 243, cat. 30; Baumgärtel, in Constance 1992, pp. 159–60, cat. 23; Baumgärtel, in Düsseldorf 1998, p. 221, cat. 102; Baumgärtel, in Düsseldorf 1998, p. 72; Baumgärtel, in Düsseldorf 2020, pp. 80, 82, cat. 20.

13
***Poor Maria*, 1777**
Oil on copper, 31 × 22.9 cm
The Burghley House Collection, inv. PIC234

Select bibliography: Moser 1809, p. 254; Burghley House 1815, p. 68; Manners and Williamson 1924, pp. 182, 205, 237; Gordon 1974, pp. 53–6, fig. 9; Baumgärtel, in Constance 1992, pp. 164–65, cat. 28; Baumgärtel 1987, vol. 2, cats 62–64, 70, figs 45, 326, 327; Baumgärtel 1989a, p. 328; Baumgärtel 1990, pp. 232–43, fig. 45; Walch, Baumgärtel and Alexander, in Düsseldorf 1998, pp. 28, 39, 72, 76, 413, cat. 255; Baumgärtel, in Düsseldorf 2020, pp. 81, 83, cat. 21.

14
JOHAN ZOFFANY (1733–1810)
***The Academicians of the Royal Academy*, 1771–72**
Oil on canvas, 101.1 × 147.5 cm
Royal Collection Trust / HM King Charles III, RCIN 400747

Select bibliography: London RA 1772, p. 25, cat. 290; Millar, in Royal Collection 1969, cat. 1210; Treadwell 2009, pp. 172–83, 192, 256, 281, 363, 397; Webster 2011, pp. 252–61; Stevens, in New Haven 2011, pp. 218–21, cat. 44; Spies-Gans 2022, pp. 19–21, fig. 2.

15
***Self-portrait with Bust of Minerva*, c. 1780–84**
Oil on canvas, 93 × 76.5 cm
Grisons Museum of fine Arts, on deposit from the Gottfried Keller Foundation, Federal Office of Culture, Bern, inv. 321.000.1945

Select bibliography: Baumgärtel 1990, p. 117; Baumgärtel, in Constance 1992, pp. 141–42, cat. 1, fig. 1; Baumgärtel, in Bremen 1993, pp. 84–85, cat. 8; Baumgärtel, in Düsseldorf 1998, pp. 230–31, cat. 108; Rosenthal 2006, pp. 246–47, fig. 139; Baumgärtel, in Düsseldorf 2020, pp. 54–55, cat. 8 (dat. *c.* 1784).

16
***Portrait of Joshua Reynolds*, 1767**
Oil on canvas, 127 × 110.6 cm
National Trust Collections (Saltram House, The Morley Collection [accepted in lieu of tax by H.M. Treasury and transferred to the National Trust in 1957]), inv. NT 872180

Select bibliography: Manners and Williamson 1924, pp. 20, 24, 26, 200; Kenwood 1955, p. 15, cat. 18; Dodd, in Saltram 1981 and 1990, no. 89T, fig. Id; Penny, in London RA 1986, pp. 339–40, no. 169; Shawe-Taylor, in Nottingham 1987, p. 28, no. 23; Baumgärtel 1987, vol. 2, p. 449, no. 179, fig. 98; Brighton 1992, pp. 31, 38, fig. 14; Rosenthal 1996, pp. 176, 182–86, figs 1, 43, 48; Baumgärtel, in Düsseldorf 1998, pp. 188–89, no. 71; Mannings 2000, p. 592, no. R 20; Rosenthal 2006, pp. 76–121, fig. 46; Baumgärtel, in Düsseldorf 2020, pp. 96–97, cat. 29.

17
THOMAS BURKE (1741–1815),
after ANGELICA KAUFFMAN
***Her Majesty Queen Charlotte Raising the Genius of the Fine Arts*, 1772**
Mezzotint, 47.7 × 38.3 cm
Royal Academy of Arts, London, inv.12/1595

Select bibliography: Smith 1878–83, vol. 1, p. 133, no. 1; Alexander 1992b, p. 144, fig. 117, list no. 6; Baumgärtel, in Düsseldorf 1998, pp. 159–60, cat. 51; Baumgärtel, in Stendal 2016, pp. 27–28, cat. I.5.

18
Attributed to NATHANIEL DANCE (1748–1827)
***Portrait of Angelica Kauffmann*, c. 1764–66**
Watercolour on paper, 13.2 × 11.4 cm
National Galleries of Scotland. Lady Sybil Grant Bequest 1956, inv. D 4772

Selected bibliography: Baumgärtel 1987, vol. 2, p. 513, cat. 326, fig. 50; Baumgärtel 1990, pp. 60–63, fig. 6; Baumgärtel 1998a, p.18, fig. 3; Rosenthal 2006, pp. 229–30, fig. 125; Sloan, in Edinburgh 2008, pp. 132–33, cat. 81 (attributed to).

19
RICHARD SAMUEL
(active 1770–died 1787)
***Portraits in the Characters of the Muses in the Temple of Apollo*, 1778**
Oil on canvas, 132.1 × 154.9 cm
Lent by the National Portrait Gallery, London. Acquired 1972, inv. NPG 4905

Select bibliography: London RA 1779, p. 21, cat. 282; Rosenthal 1996, pp. 233–34, fig. 67; Düsseldorf 1998, pp. 240–41, fig. 126; Peltz, in London 2008, pp. 56–89, p. 60.

20
***Invention*, c. 1778–80**
Oil on paper, 22.4 × 28 cm
Victoria and Albert Museum, London, bequeathed by H.H. Harrod, inv. E.865-1948

21
***Colouring*, c. 1778–80**
Oil on paper, 22.4 × 28 cm
Victoria and Albert Museum, London, bequeathed by H.H. Harrod, inv. E.863-1948

22
***Design*, c. 1778–80**
Oil on paper, 22.4 × 28 cm
Victoria and Albert Museum, London, bequeathed by H.H. Harrod, inv. E.866-1948

23
***Composition*, c. 1778–80**
Oil on paper, 22.4 × 28 cm
Victoria and Albert Museum, London, bequeathed by H.H. Harrod, inv. E.864-1948

24
***Design*, 1780**
Oil on canvas, 128.3 × 149 cm
Royal Academy of Arts, London, inv. 03/1129

25
***Composition*, 1780**
Oil on canvas, 128.3 × 149 cm
Royal Academy of Arts, London, inv. 03/1131

Select bibliography: Manners and Williamson 1924, pp. 130, 206, fig. p. 120 (*Genius, Design, Composition, Painting*); Walch 1968, cats 111–14 (*Design, Composition, Genius, Colouring*); Bregenz 1968, p. 73, cats 67a–d, figs 39–42 (*Invention, Design, Composition and Painting*); Hutchison 1968, pp. 48, 66–67, fig. 24b; Greer 1980, fig. 81 (*Disegno*); Baumgärtel 1987, vol. 2, cats 265 a–d, figs 49 a–d; Baumgärtel 1990, pp. 55–63, fig. 5 (*Design*); Postle, in Nottingham 1991, pp. 60–61, cat. 34 (*Design, Composition, Genius, Painting*); Brighton 1992, figs 51–57 (as grisaille without *Colouring*, confusion between the oil painting and bozzetto); Walch, in Düsseldorf 1998, pp. 69–72; Baumgärtel, in Düsseldorf 1998, p. 194, cats 75–78 (bozzetti); Baumgärtel, in Dessau 2018, pp. 112–13, cats 37–40; Baumgärtel, in Düsseldorf 2020, pp. 102–109, cats 34–41.

26
***Self-portrait in the Character of Design Listening to the Inspiration of Poetry*, 1782**
Oil on canvas, diameter 61.2 cm
English Heritage, Kenwood. The Ernest Edward Cook Bequest presented by the Art Fund, inv. 88029077

Select bibliography: Kauffman Memoria, pt. 1, p. 5 (1782); Shawe-Taylor 1982, p. 525, fig. 41; Baumgärtel 1987, vol. 2, p. 423, cat. 114, figs 198, 272; Baumgärtel 1990, pp. 197–204, cat. 114, figs 198, 272 (as *Disegno*); Rosenthal 1996, pp. 330–31, figs 128, 129 (date 1783); Baumgärtel, in Düsseldorf 1998, pp. 35, 224–25, 238–39, 242, cat. 112; Kenwood 2003, pp. 142–45, cat. 29; Ingamells, in London 2004, p. 299 (dat. 1782); Rosenthal 2006, pp. 244–46, figs 137, 138; Baumgärtel 2017, p. 375; Baumgärtel, in Düsseldorf 2020, pp. 52–53, cat. 7.

27
***Michael Novosielski (1750–1795)*, 1791**
Oil on canvas, 128 × 101.6 cm
National Galleries of Scotland. Bequest of Mrs Elizabeth Stewart 1879, inv. NG 651

Select bibliography: Edinburgh 1980, p. 72, fig. 651; Edinburgh 2001, pp. 76–77, cat. 33; London 2007, pp. 15, 39–40, fig. 7.

28
***Portrait of Henrietta Maria Hill, later Brudenell-Bruce and Marchioness of Ailesbury, as the Muse Erato*, 1792**
Oil on canvas, 129.5 × 101.5 cm
Private collection

29
***Portrait of Charles Brudenell-Bruce, later 1st Marquess of Ailesbury*, 1795**
Oil on canvas, 129.5 × 101.5 cm
Private collection

Select bibliography: Kauffman Memoria, pt. 1, pp. 40, 46; Manners and Williamson 1924, pp. 92, 94, 164, 166, 177; Rosenthal 1996, p. 121 (dat. 1793); Ingamells 1997, pp. 143–44 (dat. June 1793, letters from Revd Brand); Knight 1998, p. 71; Jones 2018, pp. 34, 36, fig. 7; Baumgärtel, in Düsseldorf 2020, pp. 126–39, cats 48 and 49 (dat. 1795).

30
***Portraits of Domenica Morghen and Maddalena Volpato as Muses of Tragedy and Comedy*, 1791**
Oil on canvas, 124.5 × 159.2 cm
National Museum in Warsaw, inv. M.Ob.1842 MNW

Select bibliography: Kauffman Memoria, pt. 1, p. 37, no. 199 (*c.* April 1792); Manners and Williamson 1924, p. 162; Warsaw 1938, pp. 151–52, 181, cat. 263, fig. 150 (as *Allegory*); Pawłowska 1967, pp. 76–78, fig. 4; Szymanski 1968, p. 48, fig. 3; Pawłowska 1969, pp. 118, 120, fig. 27; Baumgärtel 1987, vol. 2, pp. 464–65, cat. 214, fig. 220; Baumgärtel, in Düsseldorf 1998, pp. 264–65, cat. 133; Meyer, in Milan 2002, pp. 201, 465; Fossataro 2006, p. 50, fig. 2; Mazzocca, in Monza 2015, pp. 104, 136; Baumgärtel, in Düsseldorf 2020, pp. 167–69, cat. 67.

31
***Portrait of Emma, Lady Hamilton, as Muse of Comedy*, 1791**
Oil on canvas, 127 × 101.6 cm
Private collection

Select bibliography: Kauffman Memoria, pt. 1, p. 36 (1791); De Rossi 1811, pp. 78–79; Morrison 1893, p. 117; Manners and Williamson 1924, after pp. 82, 86–87, 161, 210, 235, 240; Pawłowska 1967, pp. 78–79, fig. 6; Baumgärtel 1990, pp. 149–52, fig. 30; Baumgärtel 1992b, pp. 21–43; London 1996, p. 272, cat. 171 (deemed lost); Rosenthal 1996, pp. 232, 234, 243–44, fig. 77 (deemed lost), p. 245, fig. 78; Pointon 1997, pp. 201–02; Baumgärtel, in Düsseldorf 1998, pp. 240, 262–63, fig. 131; Ittershagen 1999, pp. 73, 208–11, 258 (deemed lost); Rosenthal 2006, pp. 154–55, 183–87, fig. 95; Baumgärtel 2017, p. 365; Baumgärtel, in Düsseldorf 2020, pp. 170–71, cat. 68.

32
***Portrait of the Impromptu Virtuoso Teresa Bandettini Landucci as Muse*, 1794**
Oil on canvas, 128.2 × 93.6 cm
Kunstpalast, Düsseldorf, inv. mkp M 2008-2

Select bibliography: Kauffmann Memoria, pt. 1, p. 43, no. 222 (March 1794, 1st version); Brun 1800, pp. 231–33; De Rossi 1871, p. 76; Fachini 1824, p. 229; Bandettini 1837, p. 93; Giornale Arcadico 1837, pp. 233–53; Rosini 1847, pp. 101–02, 111; Chur 1941, portrait 1, no. 20 (as Maddalena Riggi); Baumgärtel 1987, vol. 1, pp. 288–93 ('attitude portrait'), vol. 2, p. 436, cat. 147, fig. 292; Baumgärtel 1989a, pp. 336–39; Baumgärtel 1990, pp. 205–08, 338; Baumgärtel, in Constance 1992, pp. 152–54, cat. 16; Baumgärtel 1992b, pp. 21–43; Baumgärtel 1998b, pp. 238–41, 321; Rosenthal 2006, pp. 182–83, fig. 94; Facchin 2010, p. 203 (erron. as priv. coll.); Baumgärtel 2009, pl. 5; Baumgärtel 2011, p. 117; Lissoni, in Milan 2015, pp. 48–49, cat. 10 (1st version); Holubec, in Düsseldorf 2020, pp. 30–35; Baumgärtel, in Düsseldorf 2020, pp. 176–77, cat. 71.

33
***Self-portrait at the Crossroads Between the Arts of Music and Painting*, 1794**
Oil on canvas, 147.3 × 215.9 cm
National Trust Collections (Nostell Priory, The St Oswald Collection). Purchased by private treaty with the help of a grant of the Heritage Lottery Fund, 2002, inv. 960079

Select bibliography: Moser 1809, p. 259; De Rossi 1811, pp. 16–17; Kenwood 1955, pp. 13–14, cat. 14; Parker and Pollock 1981, pp. 21–22, 89–90, fig. 50; Baumgärtel 1987, vol. 2, pp. 273, 424, 489, 521, cats 115, 116, 373, figs 156–58; Roworth 1988, pp. 217–18, fig. 21.3; Baumgärtel 1990, pp. 131–75, 273, 306–08, 373, figs 26–28; Baumgärtel 1992a, pp. 21–43; Baumgärtel, in Constance 1992, p. 152; Baumgärtel, in Bremen 1993, fig. 2; Baumgärtel 1996, p. 31; Rosenthal 1996, pp. 340–41, 353, fig. 136; Baumgärtel, in Düsseldorf 1998, pp. 224–25, 234–47, cat. 111; Roworth 2004, pp. 915, 918; Rosenthal 2006, pp. 271– 81, fig. 156 (dat. 1794–96); Holubec 2008, pp. 101, 105–06, figs 1, 5a, 5b; Peltz, in London 2008, pp. 82–84, fig.; Baumgärtel 2016a, pp. 173–74; Baumgärtel 2017, p. 377; Baumgärtel, in Düsseldorf 2020, pp. 40–41, 43, cat. 2; Hirtenfelder, in Schwarzenberg 2023, pp. 26–28, fig. 16.

34
***Death of Alcestis*, 1790**
Oil on canvas, 114 × 154 cm
vorarlberg museum, Bregenz, inv. Gem 908

Select bibliography: Kauffman Memoria, pt. 1, p. 30 (1790), pt. 4, p. 68, no. 8; London RA 1791, p. 8, cat. 214; Zucchi Indice 1804, no. 17; De Rossi 1811, p. 81; Gerard 1893, p. 371; Graves 1905, vol. 2, no. 214; Manners and Williamson 1924, pp. 157, 173, 238; Baumgärtel, in Constance 1992, cat. 36, fig. 16; Baumgärtel, in Düsseldorf 1998, pp. 98–99, cat. 238; Baumgärtel, in Düsseldorf 2020, pp. 144–45, cat. 56.

35
***Ulysses on the Island of Circe*, 1793**
Oil on canvas, 115.5 × 155 cm
Loan from the Barrett Swiss Collection in memory of Nona Barrett

Select bibliography: Kauffman Memoria, pt. 1, p. 40 (1793); pt. 2, p. 52 (1796); pt. 4, p. 66; Zucchi Indice 1804, no. 6; Manners and Williamson 1924, pp. 93, 98, 163, 168, 172, 232; Baumgärtel, in Constance 1992, p. 173, cat. 37, fig. 17; Baumgärtel, in Bremen 1993, pp. 89–91, cat. 12; Baumgärtel, in Düsseldorf 1998, pp. 369–70, cat. 215; Baumgärtel, in Düsseldorf 2020, pp. 146–47, cat. 57.

36
***Christ and the Samaritan Woman*, 1796**
Oil on canvas, 123.5 × 158.5 cm
Bayerische Staatsgemäldesammlungen Munich – Neue Pinakothek, inv. 10634

Select bibliography: Munich 1978, cat. 10634; Vaduz 1992, cat. 62 (not exhibited); Düsseldorf 1998, pp. 431–32, cat. 270; Bregenz 2007, pp. 220–21, cat. 114.

37
***Memoria delle piture* [*sic*] *fatte d' Angelica Kauffman*, December 1781– November 1795, January 1796–November 1798**
Royal Academy of Arts, London, inv. KAU/1

Select bibliography: Manners and Williamson 1924, pp. 139–74; Roworth 1984; Baumgärtel 1998a, p. 21; Knight 1998.

38
***Letter from Angelica Kauffman to the Council of the Royal Academy*, April 1775**
Royal Academy of Arts, London, inv. RAA/SEC/1/7

Select bibliography: Hutchison 1968, pp. 58–9; Hartcup 1954, p. 101; Butlin 1968, p. 31.

39
***Letter from Joseph Bonomi to Benjamin West, with annotations by Benjamin West*, 21 December 1807**
Royal Academy of Arts, London, inv. RAA/SEC/1/28

Select bibliography: Moser 1809, p. 262; Smith 1829, p. 265; Baumgärtel 1998a, p. 38.

ENDNOTES

'She was of her time and the time was made for her' (pages 11–23)
Translated from the German by Fiona Elliott

1 The following draws on Baumgärtel 1990, pp. 103–06; Baumgärtel 1998a, pp. 10–39; and Düsseldorf 2020 (with secondary literature).
2 Rosenblum 1957, p. 288.
3 Christadler 2000, p. 34.
4 Vigée Le Brun 2015, vol. 2, p. 13; for more on the rivalry between Kauffman and Vigée Le Brun, see Baumgärtel 2017, pp. 360–78. A twentieth-century example would be Judy Chicago's *The Dinner Party* (1979) – see Frankfurt 1987, p. 145.
5 Sickler and Reinhart 1810, p. 144.
6 This interpretation of the painting appeared first in Baumgärtel 1987, pp. 279–87; see also Baumgärtel 1990, pp. 191–97; Baumgärtel 1998b, pp. 238–42, cat. 112; Baumgärtel 2020, pp. 52–53, cat. 9; and Rosenthal 2006, pp. 244–48.
7 Rentmeister 1976.
8 Rosenthal 2006, pp. 1–13; for Baumgärtel's discussion of Rosenthal's approach, see Baumgärtel 2001.
9 One of the critics was Peter H. Sturz, letter, 15 September 1768, in Sturz 1779, pp. 7–9; '"Disegno". Theorie und Praxis des Zeichnens', in Baumgärtel 1990, ch. 2, pp. 59–67; most recently, Baumgärtel 2020, p. 17.
10 'Perché il disegno, padre delle tre arti nostri cava di molte cose un guidizio universale, simile a una forma overissima nelle sue missure...', quoted after Panofsky 1960, p. 60, following this approach also in the art theoretical writings of Du Fresnoys (1667) to Reynolds (1783); more precisely in Baumgärtel 1990, ch. 2, pp. 55–67.
11 Kauffman depicts the moment of invention, not the act of drawing.
12 Johann G. Herder to Caroline Herder, Rome, 22 April 1789; see Herder 1988, p. 434.
13 De Rossi 1811, p. 32; see Reynolds's entries in his 'pocket book' for 30 June 1766, 1 and 17 October 1766 in London RA 1986, pp. 339–41.
14 Baumgärtel 1992a; most recently Baumgärtel, in Düsseldorf 2020, pp. 39–43, cats 1 and 2.
15 Herder 1988, p. 401.
16 For more on the 'Settlement on the Marriage' of Kauffman and Zucchi, see Baumgärtel 2008, pp. 36–37.
17 A critical catalogue raisonné is currently in preparation by the author, under the auspices of the Angelika Kauffman Research Project (AKRP), in collaboration with Gabriele Ewenz, Inken M. Holubec and Andrea Parow: www.angelika-kauffmann.de.
18 Note in Kauffman's own hand, Franz-Michael-Felder-Archiv, Bregenz, Sign. AU:56:1.
19 For more on Kauffman's exhibition history, see Baumgärtel at https://www.angelika-kauffmann.de/en/exhibition-catalogues/.
20 Thomas Robinson, 2nd Baron Grantham, to Frederick Robinson, Whitehall, unpublished letter, 30 April 1779, Bedfordshire Archives, inv. L30/14/333/203.
21 See London 1780.
22 Gerard 1893 (1st edn, 1892).
23 *Zucchi Memorie Istoriche*, 1788, vorarlberg museum, Bregenz, inv. A.G. 10; see also Zucchi 1999.
24 De Rossi 1811.
25 Gerard 1893, Preface, p. ix.
26 *The Public Advertiser*, 2 May 1775, p. 2.
27 These were *Ulysses Discovers Achilles Among the Daughters of Lycomedes* (before 1769), *Penelope Taking Down the Bow of Ulysses* (1768), *Vortigern and Rowena* (1770) and *Edgar and Elfrieda* (1769/70; fig. 12). It was Theresa Parker who was interested in acquiring these paintings for Saltram House and came up with a new design to display them on blue damask; see Letter of Theresa Parker to her brother Fitz, 24 August 1775, British Museum, Morley Papers, Add. Mss. 48219
28 First published by Baumgärtel, in Dessau 2018, pp. 250–52, cat. 128.
29 Baumgärtel, in Dessau 2018, pp. 250–55, cats 128, 129.
30 Strong 1978, pp 13, 16–24.
31 The first edition of the *Seven Discourses on Art* was published in 1778; for all fifteen Discourses see Reynolds 1988.
32 *Portrait of the Impromptu VIrtuoso Fortunata Sulgher Fantastici as Muse*, 1792. Oil on canvas, Gallerie degli Uffizi, Galleria Palatina, Florence, inv. 1890, no. 4339; see Baumgärtel 2020, pp. 172–75, cat. 70.
33 *Servius Tullius as a Child, Asleep Beneath the Miraculous Flame* (1785) and *Ulysses Discovers Achilles Among the Daughters of Lycomedes* (1787); see Baumgärtel, in Düsseldorf 2020, pp. 180–85, cats 73 and 74; on Kauffman's works for Catherine the Great, see recently Blakesley 2023, ch. 6.
34 Baumgärtel, in Düsseldorf 1998, pp. 278–86, cats 147–55.
35 Baumgärtel, in Düsseldorf 2020, pp. 110–13, cat. 42.
36 Moulton Mayer 1972, p. 35.
37 See Sterne 2008.
38 Baumgärtel 2016b, pp. 13–62. The author's revision of David Alexander's 'Chronological Checklist of Single Issued English Prints after Angelica Kauffman' (Alexander 1992a) will be published in her forthcoming Kauffman catalogue raisonné.
39 From 1796 onwards Jane Matthews published large-format stipple prints after paintings by Kauffman, including *Death of Alcestis* (1790) after the painting commissioned by Jane's late husband (cat. 34).
40 Many designs for wall paintings, ceilings and fireplace decorations in English residences have erroneously been attributed to Kauffman (see, among others, Manners and Williamson 1924, pp. 129–37). Nevertheless, Kauffman did create two overdoors for Knowsley Hall, Liverpool, the Earl of Derby's seat. For these Robert Adam designed a decorative frame (Sir John Soane's Museum, London, inv. SM Adam vol. 54/7/267); my thanks to Frances Sands for this reference. Kauffman continues to be credited with Adam decorations at, among others, Osterley Park, Hounslow; Harewood House, Yorkshire; and Chandos House, London. However these attributions are very questionable: https://collections.soane.org/drawings?ci_search_type=ARCI&mi_search_ype=adv&sort=7&tn=Drawings&t=SCHEME690. The themes and styles of Antonio Zucchi's designs have a considerable affinity with those of Kauffman, as seen at Kenwood House, Hampstead; Home House, London; Nostell Priory, Yorkshire; Saltram House, Devon; and Headfort House in Co. Meath, Ireland. The author is currently preparing a study of this topic.
41 For more on these 'mechanical paintings', see Birmingham 2009, pp. 72, 220–21, and most recently Fogarty 2013, pp. 116–19, 124.
42 For more on the needlework designs, see Fleischmann-Heck, in Krefeld 2017.
43 Bell 1776–1783; numerous editions followed in due course.
44 Macklin 1800.
45 Goethe 1787/1789; see Baumgärtel, in Dessau 2018, pp. 206–09.
46 Winckelmann 1976, pp. 17–20.
47 See Hogarth 1955.
48 Vasari 1986.
49 Baretti 1781, p. 26.
50 See Baumgärtel 2022.

Angelica Kauffman and the Royal Academy (pages 25–33)

1 Letter from Daniel Crespin to Sir James Grant of Grant, 11 March 1763, partially transcribed in Walch 1977, pp. 101–02.
2 Joshua Reynolds elucidated his concept of the 'Grand Manner' or 'Grand Style' of history painting that the new institution sought to promote in his Discourses presented annually and later biannually at the Royal Academy; see Reynolds 1988.
3 Kauffman was admitted to the academies of Florence and Bologna in 1762 and became a member of the Accademia di San Luca, Rome in 1765 and of the Accademia, Venice in 1782 (see Bettina Baumgärtel, 'Chronology', Angelika Kauffman Research Project: https://www.angelika-kauffmann.de/en/chronology). Italian art academies at this date were, in general, a broader church in terms of membership and expectations of members' involvement than the Académie royale and subsequently the Royal Academy. See also note 13 and Cox 2016.
4 Manners and Williamson 1924, p. 20, citing her letter of 11 July 1766 to her father.
5 Letter from Angelica Kauffman to Johann Joseph Kauffman, 10 October 1766, cited in Manners and Williamson 1924, p. 20, n. 4. Baumgärtel, in Düsseldorf 2020, p. 96, cat. 29 provides an account of their meeting and painting each other's portraits.
6 Letter from Isaac Jamineau, British Consul at Naples, to John Morgan in Philadelphia, 3 November 1767: 'Lord Exeter writes me ... that Angelica was in a prosperous way ... & that she was painting the Queen's picture; which introduced to so many hours of easy & familiar conference with [her] Majesty,

seems to promise the making of this picture', in Marks 1980, p. 24.

7 The animosity between Reynolds and the King and Queen is described by Richard Wendorf in Wendorf 1996, pp. 174–76.

8 An account of the original membership of the Royal Academy, drawn from the directors of the Incorporated Society of Artists and their associates and artists approved by the Royal family, is given in Simon 2018.

9 Kauffman's fellow founder members included four Italians (Francesco Bartolozzi, Giovanni Battista Cipriani, Agostino Carlini and Francesco Zuccarelli), one German (Jeremiah Meyer, joined by another German Johann Zoffany who, along with William Hoare, was nominated a Member by the King in 1769), an American (Benjamin West), a Frenchman (Dominic Serres), another Swiss artist (George Michael Moser) as well as two Irishmen (Nathaniel Hone and George Barret).

10 The 'pleasing guest' comment is from 'An Address from Britannia to the Celebrated Angelica', *The Public Advertiser*, 20 January 1767. The 'English artist' description is from a letter from John Boydell to Sir William Hamilton, 1 January 1793 in the Folger Shakespeare Library, Washington DC, cited in Sillers 2006, p. 296, n. 19.

11 Kauffman features, for example, in an engraving of 1777 depicting *The Nine Living Muses of Great Britain*. This composition was subsequently painted by Richard Samuel as *Portraits in the Characters of the Muses ithe Temple of Apollo* (1778; cat. 19). Although Kauffman seems not to have experienced prejudice relating to her nationality at the Royal Academy, Wendy Wassyng Roworth suggests that attitudes towards other foreign artists within the institution may have contributed to her decision to leave London; see Roworth 2009, p. 155. See also West 1999.

12 Vickery 2020, pp. 4–5. Numerous women, including Moser and Kauffman, exhibited with the Society of Artists but none were among its directors.

13 The French Académie royale admitted six women during the seventeenth century, the first being Catherine Duchemin in 1663, but subsequently passed a series of rules barring, or restricting the numbers of, women members. Reboul was the first woman to be admitted since Rosalba Carriera in 1720; see Williams 2015, pp. 94, 115, 291. There was a longer tradition of women's involvement in both art and literary academies in Italy but this was often in an honorary capacity; see Cox 2016.

14 Williams 2015, p. 94.

15 There never was a written rule officially barring women from Membership of the Royal Academy. The first recorded debate on the matter took place in 1879 when Charles West Cope put forward a motion to make women officially ineligible for membership (RAA/PC/1/16, 11 November 1879, pp. 194–97). This was rejected, the Royal Academicians agreeing that women should remain eligible for election – based on the precedent set by Moser and Kauffman – though not to attend Council or serve as Visitors (teachers) in the Royal Academy Schools.

16 As Kauffman and Moser were unelected founder members, the first woman artist to be elected to the Royal Academy was 78-year-old painter Annie Swynnerton who became an Associate Royal Academician (a now defunct category) in 1922. She was followed in 1936 by Dame Laura Knight, the first woman to be elected a full Royal Academician.

17 Discussions of the representation of Kauffman and Moser in this work include: Baumgärtel, in Düsseldorf 1998, p. 197, cat. 83; Baumgärtel, in Düsseldorf 2020, p. 98, cat. 30; Spies-Gans 2022, pp. 19–21; Rosenthal 2006, pp. 49–52; Rosenthal 1997; and Parker and Pollock 1981, p. 87.

18 Rosenthal 1997, p. 150.

19 Spies-Gans 2022, pp. 19–20.

20 The 'barometer' description is from Hallett 2004, p. 586. It was agreed at an early General Assembly (RAA/GA/1/1, 25 March 1769, p. 16) that 'at the election of Academicians the absent Members shall be permitted to give their suffrages sealed up and inclosed in a letter signed with their own hand and directed to the President'. The first election took place on 27 August 1770, both Kauffman and Moser sending sealed ballots; see RAA/GA/1/, 27 August 1770, p. 38. They both voted in this manner regularly, Kauffman ceasing only once she left London. Her last ballot was sent for the election that took place on 9 April 1781 (RAA/GA/1/1, p. 150).

21 Although both women voted regularly in elections of new Royal Academicians – by sealed letters sent to the President – their participation behind the scenes ended there.

22 Kauffman and Moser's male counterparts were expected to take part in at least some of these duties and, periodically, to attend the General Assembly meetings of all the Royal Academicians. Mary Moser attended General Assemblies on occasion from 1779 (see RAA/GA/1/1, 25 October 1779, p. 133) and more frequently from 1799. There is nothing to suggest that Kauffman ever attended.

23 Baumgärtel, in Düsseldorf 2020, p. 103 points out that Kauffman's friendship with Reynolds was key to her involvement in several potential commissions during the 1770s.

24 Baumgärtel 2020, p. 14.

25 A review from *Lloyd's Evening Post* cited in Brighton 1992, p. 44.

26 They were: *Hector Taking Leave of Andromache* (1768), *Penelope Taking Down the Bow of Ulysses* (1768), *Venus Directing Aeneas and Achates to Carthage* (1768) and *Achilles Discovering Ulysses* (1769).

27 These included Plutarch, Ovid, Tasso, Klopstock, Sterne, Metastasio, Ossian (James Macpherson) and Shakespeare. Baumgärtel discusses Kauffman's 'New Heroines' in Düsseldorf 2020, pp. 135–46. Kauffman's interest in the character of Penelope from Homer's Odyssey is considered in Roworth 2009, p. 37 and Rosenthal 2006, pp. 17–18, 159 and 162.

28 Baumgärtel, in Düsseldorf 2020, p. 78, cat. 19. Kauffman was one of the first artists to exhibit paintings of scenes from English history derived from historical accounts at the Royal Academy from 1770 onwards. In 1769 Samuel Wale showed two scenes from English history ('St. Austin preaching Christianity to King Ethelbert and Queen Bertha' and 'The Queen Dowager of King Edward delivering up the Duke of York to the Archbishop of Canterbury') but these may have been framed prints rather than paintings; see Baudino 2015. Paintings of early English history had been shown at previous London exhibitions but there was greater interest after the foundation of the Royal Academy, and Kauffman's lead was followed by others including William Hamilton and Benjamin West (see Keynes 1999, pp. 296–303.

29 Kauffman also painted after Rapin *Interview of Edgar and Elfrida after Her Marriage to Athelworth*, exhibited in 1770–71 (Saltram House, Devon; National Trust). On prints: Alexander 1992b; in particular, on p. 141, Alexander notes that 'there were more single-issued stipples engraved in England after the work of Angelica Kauffman than any other painter'.

30 Manners and Williamson 1924, p. 38.

31 *The London Chronicle*, 30 April–2 May 1778 reported on her painting of *Calypso Mournful after the Departure of Ulysses*, exhibited at the Royal Academy's Annual Exhibition: 'Miss Kauffman still maintains her character as one of the first history-painters of the age; and so strong is the turn of her genius to that sublime branch of art, that while most of the male pencils in the kingdom are employed in portraits, landscapes &c. she gives us, every succeeding year, fresh proofs of the vigour of her mind by producing something excellent in the historical way' (p. 421).

32 The *London Chronicle*, 29 April–1 May 1777 stated, for instance, that Kauffman 'retains so much of the softness natural to her sex that she always pitches upon such historical subjects as have in them a strong mixture of the tender and pathetic...' (p. 413).

33 Rosenthal 2006, p. 20.

34 Baumgärtel, 'New Heroines', in Düsseldorf 2020, pp. 135–46. Taylor 2021, pp. 115–17 explores the gender dynamics in Kauffman's depictions of Andromache, arguing that despite Kauffman's 'disruption of gender binaries' her portrayals of this character nevertheless tend to emphasise her role as a model of domesticity.

35 Such criticism included frequent discussion of the 'softness' and perceived effeminacy of her male figures. See Baumgärtel, 'Beautiful Young Men as Beau Ideal', in Düsseldorf 2020, pp. 149–57 and Brighton 1992, pp. 82–87. Various rumours circulated relating to Kauffman's private life. Nathaniel Dance, for instance, claimed

that he and Kauffman had been engaged in Rome before she jilted him in the hope of marrying Reynolds, from the account later given by his brother George Dance to the diarist and artist Joseph Farington (see Farington 1978–1998, vol. IX, p 3,192 (entry for 6 January 1808); see also vol. XI, p. 4,038 (entry for 26 November 1811). Manners and Williamson describe Kauffman as an 'accomplished coquette' based on some of these accounts (Manners and Williamson 1924, p. 18).

36 This project was soon halted by the Bishop of London and the Archbishop of Canterbury, who had not been consulted; see Keene, Burns and Saint 2004, pp. 241–2.

37 Letter from Angelica Kauffman RA to the President and Council of the Royal Academy, April 1775 (RAA/SEC/1/7).

38 *Ibid.*

39 See also RAA/PC/1/1, 17 and 18 April 1775, pp. 198–99; Retford 2018; Newman 1986; Butlin 1968; and Butlin 1970.

40 'The Exhibition of Pictures, by Nathaniel Hone, R.A., mostly the Works of his Leisure, and many of them in his own Possession', London, 1775. Hone protested in the accompanying catalogue (London 1775), and in letters to Kauffman published in Smith 1829, that he had 'never introduced … any figure reflecting on Mrs Angelica Kauffman, or any lady whatever' (p. 142). A letter published in the *Public Advertiser* on 15 May 1775 states that Hone's painting was removed from the RA 'on the Complaint of a Female Academician who was supposed (though falsly [*sic*]) to be there represented in an indecent Manner' but most press reports alluded to the slight on Sir Joshua.

41 Eger 2010, p. 3. See also Baumgärtel, in Düsseldorf 1998.

42 Eger 2010, p. 34

43 Murdoch 2001, p. 14.

44 Valentine 2020, p. 18. See also Baumgärtel, in Düsseldorf 2020, pp. 102–9, cats 34–41.

45 Baumgärtel, in Düsseldorf 2020, points out that Disegno was traditionally a male figure and that 'despite being the personification of an abstract concept rather than a real life individual, the drawing female figure – whether intentionally or not – naturally invites associations with women artists and hence with Kauffman herself, who would indeed defy decorum by drawing a male nude, as was argued by the Tate Britain in its 2018 Spotlight Display on Kauffman' (p. 102). See also Spies-Gans 2022, pp. 89–91.

46 Baretti 1781, p. 26.

47 Von Preussen 2018.

48 Cited in Rosenthal 2006, p. 260.

49 Roworth 2009, p. 156 and Roworth 1992, pp. 86–7.

50 *St James's Chronicle*, 9 May 1782. Antonio Zucchi was elected an Associate of the Royal Academy in 1770.

51 The reason cited by De Rossi was Kauffman's father's 'burning desire to see his native land' and to retire to the warmer climate of Italy, stating that this 'demanded her complete separation from a country with which she was connected, and which appreciated and honoured her and to which she confessed attachment and love'; cited in Rosenthal 2006, pp. 259–60. Kauffman exhibited one painting at the Royal Academy in 1782, three in 1786, one in 1788, two in 1791 and one respectively in 1796 and 1797.

1 Staging the Self (pages 37–45)

1 See Bettina Baumgärtel, 'Stagings of the Self', in Düsseldorf, 2020, p. 39.

2 For instance, marking her early decision to pursue a career in art rather than music which she alluded to both at the time and later in life, and also several portraits produced around the time of her move to Italy in 1781.

3 A full account of the portrait, and the circumstances of its production, is given by Baumgärtel, in Düsseldorf 2020, p. 50, cat. 6. Angela Rosenthal also discusses this portrait in terms of Kauffman's 'articulation of a personal mythology about origins – that represents a touchstone for her cultural persona in Italy and in Britain', linking it to literary tropes promoting the moral appeal of 'rural simplicity' and equating purity of mind with 'rural "foreignness"'; see Rosenthal 2006, pp. 257–8 and 261–3.

4 The other – at the Wilson Gallery and Museum, Cheltenham – shows Kauffman as a pilgrim rather than an artist. See Baumgärtel 1987, p. 422, cat. 110; and a more detailed analysis in Baumgärtel 2016a, p. 169.

5 There is no direct evidence for Kauffman's interest in Rubens at this time but she travelled to Flanders in 1781 and other artists of the time were engaging with his work. Reynolds, for example, made numerous pictorial references to Rubens, especially following his visit to Flanders and Holland in 1781, including his portrait of *Mary Darby, Mrs Robinson as Perdita* (1782; Waddesdon Manor, Buckinghamshire). Elisabeth Vigée Le Brun also visited the area in 1781 and painted her *Self Portrait in a Straw Hat* (1782; private collection, copy at the National Gallery, London) the following year.

6 De Rossi 1811; Baumgärtel, in Düsseldorf 2020, p. 50.

7 Baumgärtel, in Düsseldorf 2020, p. 56, cat. 9. In a letter to the director of the Uffizi Gallery, Giuseppe Bencivenni Pelli, Kauffman explained that she had wanted to replace this work since she was living in England; cited in Rosenthal 2006, p. 269.

8 An article in the *Public Advertiser*, 27 January 1776, quotes a letter of 21 November 1775 from Luigi Siries to Angelica Kauffman reporting on the highly enthusiastic reception of Reynolds's self-portrait at the Uffizi. Siries states that this work 'quite eclipsed the portrait of [Anton Raphael] Mengs' among the 'moderns' and also held its own amongst the Old Masters. However, Rosenthal notes that James Northcote, in 1778, reported a somewhat different dynamic stating: '"Mengs" is finished so that you can almost tell the hairs of his beard and Sir Joshua's appears as if it was painted with his fingers'; Rosenthal 2006, pp. 312–3, n. 100.

9 See letter to Pelli, in Rosenthal 2006, p. 269, n. 3, and Baumgärtel, in Düsseldorf 2020, p. 56, cat. 9 regarding the dates of the work and its delivery to the Uffizi.

10 Baumgärtel, in Düsseldorf 2020, p. 56.

11 *Ibid.* The cameo is now in the National Archaeological Museum of Naples. Baumgärtel notes that it depicts the triumph of a goddess, Minerva, over the god Neptune.

12 *Ibid.*

13 The portrait of Michelangelo Buonarroti was given to the Uffizi in 1771 by Lorenzo Strozzi and was thought to be by Michelangelo himself at the time. It is now reattributed to Jacopino del Conte and on display in the Casa Buonarroti, Florence.

2 From Italy to England (pages 47–63)

1 The 'staring in men's faces' quotation is from Rosenthal 1997, p. 147.

2 Baumgärtel, in Düsseldorf 2020, p. 60, cat. 10 gives an account of the portrait and critical response to it, noting that 'Her patron Johann Caspar Füssli the Elder also hailed it as a remarkable achievement for a mere twenty-two-year-old and singled out the great "similarity of character" for special praise.'

3 Desmond Shaw-Taylor, in Nottingham 1987, p. 41, ill. 33; Baumgärtel, in Düsseldorf 2020, pp. 65–7, cat. 13 provides a full discussion of the portrait and Garrick's unusual pose. Rosenthal relates it to portraits by Frans Hals and other precedents; see Rosenthal 2006, pp. 59–69.

4 Lady Wentworth Murray's husband, John Murray, was appointed British Resident at Venice in 1754. He was a noted art collector but also considered to be a dissolute rake. By 1766 he was on his way to a new posting in Constantinople so presumably this was not a concern; see Z. Holmes, 'Murray, John (c. 1714–1775), diplomat', *Oxford Dictionary of National Biography*: https://doi-org.lonlib.idm.oclc.org/10.1093/ref:odnb/71110.

5 The painting itself is untraced but is known from the mezzotint after Kauffman by Thomas Burke published in 1772.

6 Baumgärtel, in Düsseldorf 2020, p. 111, and p. 121, cat. 45; Schmidt-Linsenhoff 1998; and Rosenthal, 2006, ch. 4 'The Inner Orient', pp. 123–53.

7 Kauffman undertook a six-month visit to Ireland in the summer of 1771.

8 Farrington 1978–1998, vol. I, p. 90.

9 Baumgärtel, in Düsseldorf 2020, p. 72, cat. 16.

10 *Ibid.*, p. 76, cat. 19, notes that the story of the heroic Queen Eleanor saving King Edward I was popularised by James Thompson's play of 1739 and that Kauffman may have been inspired by the publication of his complete works in 1762.

11 Baumgärtel, in Düsseldorf 2020, p. 93, cat. 21.

3 Kauffman and the Royal Academy (pages 65–83)

1 Manners and Williamson 1924, p. 20, citing her letter to her father of 11 July 1766.
2 Baumgärtel, in Düsseldorf 1998, pp 188–9, cat. 71; Baumgärtel, in Düsseldorf 2020, p. 96, cat. 29. Reynolds borrowed several motifs from Kauffman's 1766 portrayal of him for his *c.* 1780 self-portrait for the Royal Academy over a decade later, which is exactly the same size as the work she produced. Reynolds also reworked the unusual pose of Kauffman's Garrick portrait for his portrait of *Mrs Abington as Miss Prue* (1771; Yale Center for British Art) while Kauffman seems to refer to Reynolds's portrait of *David Garrick between Tragedy and Comedy* (1761; Waddesdon Manor) in her 1785 self-portrait; see Rosenthal 2006, pp. 69–75, 112 and 274–5.
3 Baumgärtel, in Düsseldorf 2020, p. 96, cat. 21.
4 The painting itself is untraced but is known from the mezzotint by Thomas Burke after Kauffman published in 1772. Baumgärtel, in Düsseldorf 1998, pp. 159–60, cats 51 and 52; Rosenthal 2006, p. 16.
5 Alexander 1992b.
6 Letter from Kauffman to her father, London, 10 February 1767, cited after De Rossi 1811, p. 27; the letter is lost.
7 Letter from Angelica Kauffman to the President and Council of the Royal Academy, April 1775 (RAA/SEC/1/7); see also RAA/PC/1/1, 17 and 18 April 1775, pp. 198–9 and further discussion of this matter in the essay on Angelica Kauffman and the Royal Academy; Baumgärtel, in Düsseldorf 1998, p. 202, cat. 90.
8 Further discussion of this painting, and Kauffman's portrayal feature in the Introduction (pp. 1–31) and ch. 1 (pp. 32–58) of Eger 2010, and also in Rosenthal 2006, pp. 155–9.
9 Baretti 1781, p. 26.
10 Baumgärtel, in Düsseldorf 2020, p. 52, cat. 7. See also Baumgärtel 1990, pp. 197–200. See also Goodden 2005, p. 198 and Rosenthal 2006, pp. 244.
11 Roworth 2011, p. 296.

4 Return to Rome (pages 85–107)

1 Roworth 2009, p. 154.
2 *Ibid.*, p. 156.
3 Baumgärtel, in Düsseldorf 2020, p. 144, cat. 56.
4 *Ibid.*, p. 146, cat. 57.
5 Baumgärtel, in Düseldorf 2020, pp. 128–9, cats 48 and 49.
6 Letter from Joseph Bonomi to Benjamin West translating a description of Angelica Kauffman's funeral (RAA/SEC/1/8, 21 December 1807).
7 Reynolds and other artists of the day also used this costume device. Kauffman depicted Benjamin West in a Van Dyck collar as early as 1763 (see the drawing of West by Kauffman at the National Portrait Gallery, London).
8 Baumgärtel, in Düsseldorf 2020, p. 167, cat. 67, suggests that Kauffman referred to the frescoes at Herculaneum where Thalia's attributes are not only a mask but also the pedum and wreath.
9 *Ibid.*, p. 170, cat. 68.
10 Baumgärtel, in Düsseldorf 2020, ch. 4, pp. 197–208 and 172–5, cat. 70; and Rosenthal 2006, pp. 174–80.
11 Baumgärtel, in Düsseldorf 2020, p. 176, cat. 71.
12 Rosenthal 2006, p. 272.
13 Baumgärtel, in Düsseldorf 2020, pp. 40–41, cats 1 and 2; also Baumgärtel 1990, ch. IV, pp. 131–75; and Baumgärtel 1992a. See also discussion of the painting in Parker and Pollock 1981, pp. 102–03.
14 The Irish painter James Barry cited in Rosenthal 2006, p. 274.

BIBLIOGRAPHY AND SOURCES

RAA/GA: Royal Academy of Arts Archive, General Assembly Minutes
RAA/PC: Royal Academy of Arts Archive, Council Minutes
RAA/SEC: Royal Academy of Arts Archive, Records of the Secretary

Alexander 1992a
David Alexander, 'Chronological Checklist of Single Issued English Prints after Angelica Kauffman', in Brighton 1992, pp. 179–89

Alexander 1992b
David Alexander, 'Kauffman and the Print Market in Eighteenth-century England', in Brighton 1992, pp. 141–78

Ammann 2012
Gert Ammann, '"Ich Maria Angelica Kaufmann von Schwarzenberg im Bregenzerwald Konstanzer Kirchensprengel (aus Zufall in Chur in Graubünden geboren) Witwe des abgelebten Anton Zucchi gottseligen Andenkens [...]": Zur Geschichte der Erwerbungen von Werken der Angelika Kauffmann (Chur 1741-1807 Rom) im Tiroler Landesmuseum Ferdinandeum in Innsbruck. Handschriftliche Dokumente im Vereinsarchiv und in der Bibliothek', in *Wissenschaftliches Jahrbuch der Tiroler Landesmuseum*, vol. 5 (2012), pp. 106–71

Bandettini 1837
Atti della Reale Accademia Lucchese in morte di Teresa Bandettini Landucci fra gli Arcardi Amarilli Etrusca, Accademia lucchese di scienze, lettere ed arti, Lucca, 1837

Baretti 1781
Giuseppe Marco Antonio Baretti, *A Guide Through the Royal Academy, by Joseph Baretti*, London, 1781

Baudino 2015
Isabelle Baudino, 'Works of Historical Fancy? Samuel Wale's Illustrations for Thomas Mortimer's "New History of England"', conference paper, *Fancy-Fantaisie-Capriccio: Diversions and Distractions in the Eighteenth Century*, University of Toulouse, 2015

Baumgärtel 1987
Bettina Baumgärtel, 'Angelika Kauffmann (1741–1807): Bedingungen weiblicher Kreativität in der Malerei des 18. Jahrhunderts', 2 vols, typescript dissertation, Bonn, 1987

Baumgärtel 1989a
Bettina Baumgärtel, 'Freiheit – Gleichheit – Schwesterlichkeit: Der Freundschaftskult der Malerin Angelika Kauffmann', in Frankfurt 1989, pp. 325–39

Baumgärtel 1989b
Bettina Baumgärtel, 'Die Anatomie des Nackenden, Aktzeichnungen von Angelika Kauffmann (1741–1807)', in Unna 1989, pp. 43–44

Baumgärtel 1990
Bettina Baumgärtel, *Angelika Kauffmann (1741–1807): Bedingungen weiblicher Kreativität in der Malerei des 18. Jahrhunderts*, vol. 10 of the *Ergebnisse der Frauenforschung* series, Weinheim/Basel, 1990

Baumgärtel 1992a
Bettina Baumgärtel, *Angelika Kauffmann (1741–1807): Zu Selbstentwürfen von Malerinnen der Aufklärung – Selbstbildnisse im Gewand des Herkules am Scheideweg*, Central Institution for the Promotion of Women's Studies and Women's Research lecture series, vol. 17, Freie Universität, Berlin, 1992

Baumgärtel 1992b
Bettina Baumgärtel, 'Die Attitüde und die Malerei: Paradox der stillen Bewegtheit in Synthese von Erfindung und Nachahmung', *Zeitschrift des Deutschen Vereins für Kunstwissenschaft*, 46 (1992), pp. 21–43

Baumgärtel 1996
Bettina Baumgärtel, 'Angelika Kauffmann, une Européenne à Rome', in Lausanne 1996, pp. 26–34

Baumgärtel 1998a
Bettina Baumgärtel, 'Leben und Werk von Angelika Kauffmann', in Düsseldorf 1998, pp. 16–39

Baumgärtel 1998b
Bettina Baumgärtel, 'Die Malerin und ihre Musen – Allegorien, allegorische Porträts und mythologische Werke', in Düsseldorf 1998, pp. 238–68

Baumgärtel 2001
Bettina Baumgärtel, 'Angelika Kauffmann. Selbsteinschreibungen einer Künstlerin und Fremdeinschreibungen in das Leben und Werk einer Künstlerin', *Symposium Klassizismus und Kosmopolitismus: Kulturaustausch um 1800*, Schweizer Institut für Kunstwissenschaft, Zürich, 6–7 June 2001

Baumgärtel 2004
Bettina Baumgärtel, 'Angelika Kauffmann: Cléopâtre ornant la tombe de Marc Antoine', in Geneva 2004, pp. 239 42

Baumgärtel 2008
Bettina Baumgärtel, 'Künstlerpaare des 18. Jahrhunderts: Angelika Kauffmann & Antonio Zucchi, Adélaïde Labille-Guiard & François-André Vincent, Elisabeth Vigée-Le Brun & Jean-Baptiste-Pierre Le Brun, Maria Cosway & Richard Cosway', in Cologne 2008, pp. 34–47

Baumgärtel 2009
'Angelika Kauffmann und der Freundschaftskult der Künstlerinnen: Bildtypologien der Freundschaft um 1800', in Labouvie 2009, pp. 221–43

Baumgärtel 2011
Bettina Baumgärtel, 'The History of the Gemäldegalerie; and catalogue texts', in Düsseldorf 2011, pp. 82–151

Baumgärtel 2016a
Bettina Baumgärtel, 'Angelika Kauffman – Von Oberschwaben in die Welt', in Bechler and Schiersner 2016, pp. 169–90

Baumgärtel 2016b
Bettina Baumgärtel, 'Angelika an allen Wänden. Die Reproduktionsgraphik nach Angelika Kauffmann', in Stendal 2016, pp. 13–62

Baumgärtel 2016c
Bettina Baumgärtel, 'Die unendliche Reproduzierbarkeit: Das Bildnis J. J. Winckelmanns von Angelika Kauffmann und seine Kopien', in Stendal 2016, pp. 63–84

Baumgärtel 2017
Bettina Baumgärtel, 'Agon der Malerinnen: Angelika Kauffmann und Elisabeth Vigée Le Brun im Wettstreit?', in Lang and Windorf 2017, pp. 360–78

Baumgärtel 2020
Bettina Baumgärtel, 'Die ganze Welt ist verrückt nach Angelika Kauffmann', in Düsseldorf 2020, pp. 10–17

Baumgärtel 2022
Bettina Baumgärtel, 'Rezension zu Johannes Rößler: *Die Kunst zu sehen. Johann Heinrich Meyer und die Bildpraktiken des Klassizismus* (*Ars et Scientia: Schriften zur Kunstwissenschaft*, vol. 22, Berlin/Boston, 2020), *Zeitschrift für Schweizerische Archäologie und Kunstgeschichte* (*ZAK*), 79, 1 (2022), pp. 82–83

Baumgärtel Chronology
Bettina Baumgärtel, 'Chronology', Angelika Kauffman Research Project: https://www.angelika-kauffmann.de/en/chronology

Bechler and Schiersner 2016
Katharina Bechler and Dietmar Schiersner (eds), *Aufklärung in Oberschwaben: Barocke Welt im Umbruch*, Stuttgart, 2016

Bell 1776–83
John Bell, *Bell's Edition: The Poets of Great Britain – Complete from Chauncer to Churchill*, 109 vols, 1st edn, London, 1776–83

Birmingham 2009
Shena Mason (ed.), *Matthew Boulton: Selling What All the World Desires*, exh. cat., Birmingham Museum and Art Gallery, 2009

Blakesley 2023
Rosalind P. Blakesley, *Women Artists in the Reign of Catherine the Great*, London, 2023

Bregenz 1968
Oscar Sandner (ed.), *Angelika Kauffmann und ihre Zeitgenossen*, exh. cat., Vorarlberger Landesmuseum, Bregenz, 1968

Bregenz 2007
Tobias G. Natter (ed.), *Angelika Kauffmann: Ein Weib von ungeheurem Talent*, exh. cat., Vorarlberger Landesmuseum, Bregenz, 2007

Bremen 1993
Bettina Baumgärtel (ed.), *'... ihr werten Frauenzimmer, auf!': Malerinnen der Aufklärung*, exh. cat., exh. in conjunction with the Festival des Historischen Frauen-Kunst- und Kultur-Projekts, Roselius-Haus, Bremen, 1993

Brighton 1992
Wendy Wassyng Roworth (ed.), *Angelica Kauffman: A Continental Artist in Georgian England*, exh. cat., Brighton Museum and Art Gallery, 1992

Brinton 1903
Selwyn Brinton, *Bartolozzi and His Pupils in*

England …, The Laugham Series, London, 1903

Brun 1800
Friederike Brun, *Prosaische Schriften*, vol. 3, *Auszüge aus einem Tagebuch über Rom in den Jahren 1795 and 1796*, Zurich, 1800

Burghley House 1815
A Guide to Burghley House, Northhamptonshire, the seat of the Marquis of Exeter; containing A Catalogue of all the Paintings …, coll. cat., Stamford, 1815

Butlin 1968
Martin Butlin, 'Angelika und The Conjuror', in Bregenz 1968, pp. 29–36

Butlin 1970
Martin Butlin, 'An Eighteenth-century Art Scandal: Nathaniel Hone's *The Conjuror*', *The Connoisseur*, 174 (May 1970), pp. 1–9

Chur 1941
Walter Hugelshofer (ed.), *Angelika Kauffmann*, exh. cat., Kunstmuseum Chur, Chur, 1941

Clark 1981
Anthony M. Clark, 'Roma mi è sempre in pensiero', in *Studies in Roman Eighteenth-Century Painting*, vol. 4, ed. E. P. Bowron, Washington DC, 1981, pp. 125–38

Cologne 2008
Barbara Schaefer *et al.* (eds), *Künstlerpaare Liebe, Kunst und Leidenschaft*, exh. cat., Wallraf-Richartz Museum, Cologne, 2008

Constance 1992
Bettina Baumgärtel (ed.), *'… und hat als Weib unglaubliches Talent (Goethe)': Angelika Kauffmann (1741–1807) und Marie Ellenrieder (1791–1863). Malerei und Graphik*, exh. cat., Rosgartenmuseum, Constance, 1992.

Cox 2016
Virginia Cox, 'Members, Muses, Mascots: Women and Italian Academies', in Everson, Reidy and Sampson 2016, pp. 130–67

Christadler 2000
Maike Christadler, *Kreativität und Geschlecht. Giorgio Vasaris 'Vite' und Sofonisba Anguissolas Selbst-Bilder*, Berlin, 2000

Crivelli 2001
Tatiana Crivelli, 'La "Sorellanza" nella poesia Arcadica Femminile tre sette e ottocento', *Estratto Filologia Critica*, 26 (September–December 2001), pp. 321–49

De Rossi 1811
Giovanni Gherardo de Rossi, *Vita di Angelica Kauffmann, Pittrice* [1811]; reprint, R. W. Lightbown (ed.), London, 1971

Dessau 2018
Bettina Baumgärtel (ed.), *Angelika Kauffmann: Unbekannte Schätze aus Vorarlberger Privatsammlungen*, exh. cat., Kulturstiftung Dessau-Wörlitz, Dessau, 2018

Düsseldorf 1998
Bettina Baumgärtel (ed.), *Angelika Kauffmann 1741–1807: Eine Retrospektive*, exh. cat., Kunstmuseum Düsseldorf, 1998

Düsseldorf 2011
Die Sammlung Museum Kunstpalast, Düsseldorf, Ausgewählte Werke aus den fünf Abteilungen, coll. cat., Museum Kunstpalast, Düsseldorf, 2011

Düsseldorf 2020
Bettina Baumgärtel (ed.), *Verrückt nach Angelika Kauffmann*, exh. cat., Kunstpalast, Düsseldorf and Royal Academy of Arts, London (German and English), 2020

Eastnor Castle 1889
Lady Henry Somerset (ed), *Eastnor Castle*, coll. cat., Eastnor Castle, London, 1889

Edinburgh 1980
Illustrations, coll. cat., National Gallery of Scotland, Edinburgh, 1980

Edinburgh 2001
Scottish Treasures: Masterpieces from the National Gallery of Scotland, exh. cat., National Galleries of Scotland, Edinburgh, 2001

Edinburgh 2008
Stephen Lloyd and Kim Sloan (eds), *The Intimate Portrait: Drawings, Miniatures and Pastels from Ramsay to Lawrence*, exh. cat., National Galleries of Scotland and The British Museum, Edinburgh and London, 2008

Eger 2010
Elizabeth Eger, *Bluestockings: Women of Reason from Enlightenment to Romanticism*, London, 2010

Everson, Reidy and Sampson 2016
Jane E. Everson, Denis Reidy and Lisa Sampson (eds), *The Italian Academies 1525–1700*, London, 2016

Facchin 2010
Laura Facchin, 'Angelica Kauffmann: Tracce per i rapporti tra la pitricce svizzera e l'ambiente fiorentino nella seconda metà del XVIII secolo', in Mollisi 2010, pp. 198–211

Fachini 1824
Ginevra Canonici Fachini, *Prospetto biografico delle donne italiane*, Venice, 1824

Fantastici 1803
Epigrammi alla egregia Signora Angelica Kauffman celebre pittrice, Parma, 1803

Farington 1978–98
Kathryn Cave, Kenneth Garlick and Angus Macintyre (eds), *The Diary of Joseph Farington*, 17 vols, New Haven and London, 1978–98

Findlen, Roworth and Sama 2009
Paula Findlen, Wendy Wassyng Roworth and Catherine M. Sama, *Italy's Eighteenth Century: Gender and Culture in the Age of the Grand Tour*, Stanford, CA, 2009

Florence 1971
Mary Webster, *Firenze e l'Inghilterra: Rapporti Artistici e Culturali dal XVI al XX secolo*, exh. cat., Gallerie degli Uffizi, Florence, 1971

Florence 1979
Marco Chiarini *et al.* (eds), *Gli Uffizi: Catalogo Generale*, coll. cat., Florence, 1979

Florence 2006
Annamaria Giusti *et al.* (eds), *Arte e Manifattura di corte a Firenze dal tramonto dei Medici all'Impero (1732–1815)*, exh. cat., Galleria Palatina, Palazzo Pitti, Florence, 2006

Florence 2010
Riccardo Gennaioli (ed.), *Pregio e bellezza: Cammei e intagli dei Medici*, exh. cat., Museo degli Argenti, Palazzo Pitti, Florence, 2010

Florence Uffizi 2010
Giovanna Giusti Galardi (ed.), *Autoritratte: Artiste di capriccioso e destrissimo ingegno*, exh. cat., Sala delle reali Poste, Gallerie degli Uffizi, Florence, 2010

Fogarty 2013
Barbara Fogarty, 'The Mechanical Paintings of Matthew Boulton and Francis Eginton', in Quickenden, Baggott and Dick 2013, pp. 111–26

Fossataro 2006
Francesca Fossataro, 'Le esportazioni di Carlo Ambrogio Riggi "commesso" di Thomas Jenkins', *Richerche di storia dell'arte*, 90 (2006), pp. 49–52

Frankfurt 1987
Judy Chicago, *The Dinner Party* [1979], exh. cat., Schirn Kunsthalle, Frankfurt am Main, 1987

Frankfurt 1989
Viktoria Schmidt-Linsenhoff (ed.), *Sklavin oder Bürgerin?: Französische Revolution und Neue Weiblichkeit 1760–1830*, exh. cat., Historisches Museum Frankfurt, Frankfurt am Main, 1989

Geneva 2004
Claude Ritschard *et al.* (eds), *Cléopatre dans le miroir de l'art occidental*, exh. cat., Musée d'art et d'histoire, Geneva, 2004

Gerard 1893
Francis A. Gerard, *Angelica Kauffmann: A Biography* [1892], 2nd edn, London, 1893

Giornale Arcadico 1837
Necrology on the poet Teresa Bandettini, died 1837, *Giornale Arcadico*, 69 (1837), pp. 233–53

Goethe 1787/89
Georg Joachim Göschen (ed.), *Goethe's Schriften*, vols 5 and 8, Leipzig, 1787, and Vienna, 1789

Goodden 2009
Angela Goodden, *Miss Angel: The Art and World of Angelica Kauffman*, London, 2009

Gordon 1974
Cathrine M. Gordon, '"More than one Handle": The Development of Sterne Illustration, 1760–1820', *Words: Wai-te-Ata Studies in Literature*, 4 (January 1974), pp. 47–53

Graves 1905
Algernon Graves, *The Royal Academy of Arts: A Complete Dictionary of Contributors and Their Work from its Foundation in 1769 to 1904*, 8 vols, London, 1905

Greer 1980
Germaine Greer, *Das unterdrückte Talent: Die Rolle der Frau in der bildenden Kunst*, Berlin 1980

Hallett 2004
Mark Hallett, 'Reading the Walls: Pictorial Dialogue at the British Royal Academy', *American Society for Eighteenth-century Studies*, 37 (Summer 2004), pp. 581–604

Hartcup 1954
Adeline Hartcup, *Angelica: The Portrait of an Eighteenth-century Artist*, London, 1954

Herder 1988
Johann Gottfried Herder, *Italienische Reise: Briefe und Tagebuchaufzeichnungen 1788–1789*, eds Albert Meier and Heide Hollmer, Munich, 1988

Hogarth 1955
William Hogarth, *Analysis of Beauty: Written with a View of Fixing the Fluctuating Ideas of Taste* [1753], ed. Joseph Burke, Oxford, 1955

Holubec 2008
Inken M. Holubec, '"The whole world is angelikamad [sic]": preparatory layers on canvas used by Angelika Kauffmann', in Townsend *et al.* 2008, pp. 100–09

Hutchison 1968
Sidney C. Hutchison, *The History of the Royal Academy 1768–1986*, London, 1968

Ingamells 1997
John Ingamells, *A Dictionary of British and Irish Travellers in Italy 1701–1800*, Compiled from the Brinsley Ford Archive by J. Ingamells, New Haven and London, 1997

Ittershagen 1999
Ulrike Ittershagen, *Lady Hamiltons Attitüden*, Mainz, 1999

Jones 2018
Saraid Jones, 'Angelica Kauffman at Attingham Park', *The National Trust Historic Houses and Collections Annual 2018*, pp. 32–38

Justi 1898
Carl Justi, *Winckelmann und seine Zeitgenossen*, vol. 3, Leipzig, 1898

Kauffman Memoria
'Memoria delle piture [sic] fatte d'Angelica Kauffman', Venice, December 1781–16 November 1798, from Antonio Zucchi and Angelica Kauffman, MS, Royal Academy Archive, London, inv. no. KAU/1–KAU/4

Keene, Burns and Saint 2004
Derek Keene, Arthur Burns and Andrew Saint (eds), *St Paul's: The Cathedral Church of London, 604–2004*, New Haven and London, 2004

Keener and Lorsch 1988
Frederick M. Keener and Susan E. Lorsch (eds), *Eighteenth-Century Women and The Arts*, New York, 1988

Kenwood 1955
Anne Crookshank (ed), *Exhibition of Paintings by Angelica Kauffmann at the Iveagh Bequest*, exh. cat., Greater London Council, Kenwood House, London, n.d. [1955]

Kenwood 2003
Julius Bryant (ed.), *Kenwood: Paintings in the Iveagh Bequest*, coll. cat., New Haven and London, 2003

Keynes 1999
Simon Keynes, 'The Cult of King Alfred the Great', *Anglo-Saxon England*, 28 (1999), pp. 225–356

Knight 1998
Carlo Knight (ed.), *La 'Memoria delle piture' di Angelica Kauffman*, Accademia Nazionale di San Luca, Rome, 1998

Krefeld 2017
Isa Fleischmann-Heck *et al.* (eds), *Die englische Bildstickerei aus dem späten 18. Jahrhundert: Eine Neuerwerbung für das Deutsche Textilmuseum Krefeld*, exh. cat., Deutsches Textilmuseum Krefeld, 2017

Labouvie 2009
Eva Labouvie (ed.), *Schwestern und Freundinnen: Zur Kulturgeschichte weiblicher Kommunikation*, Cologne, 2009

Lang and Windorf 2017
Astrid Lang and Wiebke Windorf (eds), *Blickränder: Grenzen, Schwellen und ästhetische Randphänomene in den Künsten – Liber Amicorum für Hans Körner*, Berlin, 2017

Lausanne 1996
Jörg Zutter (ed.), *Entre Rome et Paris: Œuvres inédites du XIVe au XIXe siècle*, exh. cat., Musée Cantonal des Beaux-Arts, Lausanne, 1996

London 1775
The Exhibition of Pictures, by Nathaniel Hone, R.A., mostly the Works of his Leisure, and many of them in his own Possession, exh. cat., London, 1775

London 1780
A Catalogue of Mr. Ryland's Exhibition, At Mr. Pollard's Room, in Piccadilly; Consisting of Original Pictures, Historical and Emblematical, Painted by Angelica Kauffman, exh. cat., 'Mr Pollard's Room', London, 1780

London 1996
Ian Jenkins *et al.* (eds), *Vases & Volcanoes: Sir William Hamilton and His Collection*, exh. cat., The British Museum, London, 1996

London 2001a
David H. Solkin (ed.), *Art on the Line: The Royal Academy Exhibitions at Somerset House 1780–1836*, exh. cat., Courtauld Institute of Art, London, 2001

London 2001b
Susan Walker and Peter Higgs (eds), *Cleopatra of Egypt: From History to Myth*, exh. cat., The British Museum, London, 2001

London 2004
John Ingamells (ed.), *National Portrait Gallery: Mid-Georgian Portraits, 1760–1790*, coll. cat., London, 2004

London 2007
Angelica Kauffman in British Collections: An Exhibition to Commemorate the 200th Anniversary of Her Death, text by Angela Rosenthal, Rafael Valls Ltd., London, 2007

London 2008
Elizabeth Eger and Lucy Peltz (eds), *Brilliant Women: 18th-century Bluestockings*, exh. cat., National Portrait Gallery, London, 2008

London Christie 1939
Catalogue of Ancient and Modern Pictures: The Property of the Rt. Hon. The Earl of Rosebery, D.S.O., M.C. ... Messrs. Christie, Manson & Woods, London, sales cat., 5 May 1939

London Phillips 1879
Catalogue of Valuable Property, Removed from Sezincot House, Gloucestershire by Order of the Executors of Sir Charles Rushout, Bart. ..., sales cat., Auction Phillips & Sons, London, 9–12 December 1879

London RA 1770
The Exhibition of the Royal Academy, MDCCLXX: The Second, exh. cat., Royal Academy of Arts, London, 1770

London RA 1772
The Exhibition of the Royal Academy, MDCCLXXII: The Fourth, exh. cat., Royal Academy of Arts, London, 1772

London RA 1776
The Exhibition of the R.A. 1776, exh. cat., vol. 8, Royal Academy of Arts, London, 1776

London RA 1779
The Exhibition of the Royal Academy, MDCCLXXIX: The Eleventh, exh. cat., Royal Academy of Arts, London, 1779

London RA 1791
The Exhibition of the Royal Academy, MDCCXCI: The Twenty-Third, exh. cat., Royal Academy of Arts, London, 1791

London RA 1986
Nicholas Penny (ed.), *Joshua Reynolds*, exh. cat., Royal Academy of Arts, London, 1986

Los Angeles 1976
Ann Sutherland Harris and Linda Nochlin (eds), *Women Artists: 1550–1950*, exh. cat., Los Angeles County Museum of Art *et al.*, New York, 1976

Macklin 1800
Thomas Macklin (ed.), *The Holy Bible: The New Testament. Embellished with Engravings from Pictures and Designs by the Most Eminent English Artists*, 7 vols, London, 1800

Manners and Williamson 1924
Lady Victoria Manners and George Charles Williamson, *Angelica Kauffmann, R.A: Her Life and Her Works*, London, 1924

Mannings 2000
David Mannings, *Sir Joshua Reynolds: A Complete Catalogue of His Paintings*, The subject pictures catalogued by Martin Postle, 2 vols, New Haven and London, 2000

Marks 1980
Arthur S. Marks, 'Angelica Kauffman and Some Americans on the Grand Tour', *The American Art Journal*, 12, no. 2 (Spring 1980), pp. 4–24

Marshall, Russell and Wolfe 2011
David R. Marshall, Susan Russell and Karin Wolfe (eds), *Roma Britannica: Art Patronage and Cultural Exchange in Eighteenth-century Rome*, London, 2011

Milan 2002
Fernando Mazzocca *et al.*, *Il Neoclassicismo in Italia da Tiepolo a Canova*, exh. cat., Palazzo Reale, Milan, 2002

Milan 2015
Fernando Mazzocca (ed.), *Da Tiepolo a Carrà: I grandi temi della via nelle collezioni delle Fondazioni*, exh. cat., Gallerie d'Italia, Milan, 2015

Mollisi 2010
Giorgio Mollisi, 'Svizzeri a Firenze nella storia, nell'arte, nella cultura … ', *Arte & Storia*, 11, no. 48 (October 2010).

Monza 2015
Il fascino e il mito dell'Italia dal Cinquecento al Contemporaneo, exh. cat., Villa Reale di Monza, Milan, 2015

Morrison 1893
Alfred Morrison (ed.), *The Collection of Autograph Letters and Historical Documents, Formed between 1865 and 1882*, vol. 1, London, 1893

Moser 1809
Joseph Moser, 'Memoir of the Late Angelica Kauffman, R. A.', *The European Magazine and London Review*, 55 (April 1809), pp. 251–62

Moulton Mayer 1972
Dorothy Moulton Mayer, *Angelica Kauffmann, R.A. 1741–1807*, Gerrards Cross, 1972

Munich 1978
Barbara Hardtwig, *Bayerische Staatsgemäldesammlungen, Gemäldekatalog: Nach-Barock und Klassizismus*, coll. cat., Munich, 1978

Murdoch 2001
John Murdoch, 'Architecture and Experience: The Visitor and the Spaces of Somerset House', in London 2001, pp. 9–22

New Haven 2011
Martin Postle, *Johan Zoffany RA: Society Observed*, exh. cat., Yale Center for British Art and Royal Academy of Arts, New Haven and London, 2011

Newman 1986
John Newman, 'Reynolds and Hone: *The Conjuror* Unmasked', in London 1986, pp. 344–54

Nottingham 1987
Desmond Shawe-Taylor (ed.), *Genial Company: The Theme of Genius in Eighteenth-century British Portraiture*, exh. cat., Nottingham University Art Gallery and Scottish National Portrait Gallery, Edinburgh, 1987

Nottingham 1991
Ilaria Bignamini and Martin Postle (eds), *The Artist's Model: Its Role in British Art from Lely to Etty*, exh. cat., University Art Gallery, Nottingham and The Iveagh Bequest, Kenwood, London, 1991

Panofsky 1960
Erwin Panofsky, *Idea: Ein Beitrag zur Begriffsgeschichte der älteren Kunsttheorie*, Berlin, 1960, 2nd edn, 1981

Parker and Pollock 1981
Roszika Parker and Griselda Pollock, *Old Mistresses: Women, Art and Ideology*, London and Henley, 1981

Pawłowska 1967
Magdalena Pawlowska, 'A propos de deux portraits féminins d'Angelica Kauffmann', *Bulletin du Musée National de Varsovie*, 8, no. 3 (1967), pp. 72–80

Pawłowska 1969
Magdalena Pawlowska, 'O portretach polskich Angeliki Kauffmann', *Rocznik Muzeum Narodowego w Warszawie*, 2 (1969), pp. 73–144

Pointon 1997
Marcia Pointon, *Strategies for Showing: Women, Possession, and Representation in English Visual Culture, 1665–1800*, Oxford and New York, 1997

Porto 2001
Elisa Soares and José Alberto Seabra Carvalho (eds), *Francisco Vieira, o Portuense, 1765–1805*, exh. cat., Museu Nacional de Soares dos Reis, Porto, n.d. [2001]

Prinz 1971
Wolfram Prinz, *Geschichte der Sammlung mit Regesten zur Tätigkeit der Agenten und Dokumentenanhang*, Die Sammlung der Selbstbildnisse in den Uffizien, ed. Ulrich Middeldorf, vol. 1, Berlin, 1971

Quickenden, Baggott and Dick 2013
Kenneth Quickenden, Sally Baggott and Malcolm Dick (eds), *Matthew Boulton: Enterprising Industrialist of the Enlightenment*, Farnham, 2013

Rentmeister 1976
Cillie Rentmeister, 'Berufsverbot für die Musen', *Ästhetik und Kommunikation*, 25 (1976), pp. 92–112

Retford 2018
Kate Retford, '1775: Nathaniel Hone's *Spartan Boy* "Concealing a Theft"', in Mark Hallett, Sarah Victoria Turner and Jessica Feather (eds), *The Royal Academy of Arts Summer Exhibition: A Chronicle, 1769–2018*, London, 2018: https://chronicle250.com/1775

Reynolds 1988
Joshua Reynolds, *Discourses on Art*, ed. Robert R. Wark, 3rd edn, New Haven and London, 1988

Rice and Eisenberg 1991
Louise Rice and Ruth Eisenberg, 'Angelica Kauffmann's Uffizi Self-Portrait', *Gazette des Beaux-Arts*, 117, no. 133 (1991), pp. 123–6.

Rosenblum 1957
Robert Rosenblum, 'The Origin of Painting: A Problem in the Iconography of Romantic Classicism', *The Art Bulletin*, 39 (December 1957), pp. 279–9

Rosenthal 1996
Angela Rosenthal, *Angelika Kauffmann: Bildnismalerei im 18. Jahrhundert*, Berlin, 1996

Rosenthal 1997
Angela Rosenthal, 'She's Got the Look: Eighteenth-century Female Portrait Painters and the Psychology of a Potentially "Dangerous Employment"', in Woodall 1997, pp. 147–66

Rosenthal 2006
Angela Rosenthal, *Angelica Kauffman: Art and Sensibility*, New Haven and London, 2006

Rosini 1847
Giovanni Rosini, *Storia della Pittura Italiana esposta coi monumenti*, Pisa, 1847

Roworth 1984
Wendy Wassyng Roworth, 'Angelica Kauffman's *Memorandum* of Paintings', *Burlington Magazine*, 126 (1984), pp. 627–30

Roworth 1988
Wendy Wassyng Roworth, 'Biography, Criticism, Art History: Angelica Kauffman in Context', in Keener and Lorsch 1988, pp. 209–23

Roworth 2004
Wendy Wassyng Roworth, 'Documenting Angelica Kauffman's Life and Art', *Eighteenth-Century Studies*, 32 (2004), pp. 478–82

Roworth 2009
Wendy Wassyng Roworth, '"The Residence of the Arts": Angelica Kauffman's Place in Rome', in Findlen, Roworth and Sama 2009, pp. 151–71

Roworth 2011
Wendy Wassyng Roworth, 'Between "Old Tiber" and "Envious Thames": The Angelica Kauffman Connection', in Marshall, Russell and Wolfe 2011, pp. 293–301

Royal Collection 1969
Oliver Millar, *The Later Georgian Pictures in the Collection of Her Majesty The Queen*, coll. cat., The Royal Collection, London, 1969

Saltram 1981
The Saltram Collection: Plymouth, Devon, coll. cat., The National Trust, 1977; Worcester and London, 1981, later edns 1986–94

Schmidt-Linsenhoff 1998
Viktoria Schmidt-Linsenhoff, 'Häuslichkeit und Erotik: Angelika Kauffmanns Haremsphantasien', in Düsseldorf 1998, pp. 60–68

Schulz 1962
Arthur Schulz, *Winckelmann und seine Welt*, Winckelmann-Gesellschaft Stendal, 1961 (Berlin, 1962)

Schwarzenberg 2023
Thomas Hirtenfelder (ed.), *In Szene: Angelika Kauffmann ausstellen*, exh.

cat., Angelika Kauffmann Museum, Schwarzenberg, 2023

Shawe-Taylor 1982
Desmond Shawe-Taylor, 'The Woman's Art Show 1500–1970, Nottingham Castle Museum', review, *Burlington Magazine*, 124, no. 953 (August 1982), pp. 525–6

Sickler and Reinhart 1810
Friedrich Sickler and Christian Reinhart, 'Etwas über Angelika, an ihrem Begräbnistage geschrieben', in *Almanach aus Rom: Für Künstler und Freunde der Bildenden Kunst* [Leipzig, 1810), commentary by Eberhard Paul, vol. 1, Leipzig, 1984, pp. 142–52

Sillars 2006
Stuart Sillars, *Painting Shakespeare 1720–1820*, Cambridge, 2006

Simon 2018
Robin Simon, 'In Search of a Royal Academy', in Simon and Stevens 2018, pp. 2–21

Simon and Stevens 2018
Robin Simon and MaryAnne Stevens (eds), *The Royal Academy: History and Collections*, New Haven and London, 2018

Smith 1829
John Thomas Smith, *Nollekens and his Times: Comprehending Life of That Celebrated Sculptor; and Memoirs of Several Contemporary Artists, From the Time of Roubiliac, Hogarth, and Reynolds, to That of Fuseli, Flaxman, and Blake*, vol. 1, London, 1829

Smith 1878–83
John Chaloner Smith, *British Mezzotint Portraits*, 4 vols, London 1878–83

Spies-Gans 2022
Paris Spies-Gans, *A Revolution on Canvas: The Rise of Women Artists in Britain and France 1760–1830*, New Haven and London, 2022

Stendal 2016
Bettina Baumgärtel (ed.), *Anmut und Aufklärung: Eine Sammlung von Druckgraphik nach Werken von Angelika Kauffmann*, exh. cat., Winckelmann Museum, Stendal, 2016

Sterne 2008
Laurence Sterne, 'A Sentimental Journey Through France and Italy' [1768], in *A Sentimental Journey and Other Writings*, Ian Jack and Tim Parnell (eds), Oxford, 2008, pp. 1–104

Strong 1978
Roy Strong, *And When Did You Last See Your Father? The Victorian Painter and British History*, London, 1978

Sturz 1779
Helferich Peter Sturz, 'Briefe im Jahre 1768 auf einer Reise im Gefolge des Königs von Dänemark geschrieben', in Helferich Peter Sturz, *Schriften*, vol. 1, Leipzig, 1779, pp. 7–9, 32–37

Szymanski 1968
Stanislaus Szymanski, 'Die Polonica der Angelika Kauffmann', in *Jahrbuch des Vorarlberger Landesmuseumsvereins*, 112 (1968), pp. 39–65

Taylor 2021
Jonathan Taylor, '"Employ'd in Works that Womankind Become": Andromache and the Idealisation of Separate Spheres in Eighteenth-century Literature and Art', *Journal for Eighteenth-century Studies*, 44 (March 2021), pp. 101–21

Townsend *et al* 2008
Joyce H. Townsend *et al.* (eds), *Preparation for Painting: The Artist's Choice and Its Consequences*, London, 2008

Treadwell 2009
Penelope Treadwell, *Johan Zoffany: Artist and Adventurer*, London, 2009

Tutsch 1995
Claudia Tutsch, *'Man muß mit ihnen, wie mit seinem Freund, bekannt geworden seyn ...': Zum Bildnis Johann Joachim Winckelmanns von Anton von Maron*, Mainz, 1995

Unna 1989
Horst-Dieter Gölzenleuchter (ed.), *Der weibliche Blick, Künstlerinnen und die Darstellung des nackten Körpers*, exh. cat., Stadtspielwerk Lindenbrauerei, Unna, 1989

Vaduz 1992
Oscar Sandner (ed.), *Hommage an Angelika Kauffmann*, exh. cat., Liechtensteinische Staatliche Kunstsammlung, Vaduz, 1992

Valentine 2020
Helen Valentine, '"The Elements of Art": Four Ceiling Roundels for the Royal Academy of Arts at Somerset House', in Düsseldorf 2020, pp. 18–23

Vasari 1986
Giorgio Vasari, *Le Vite de' più eccellenti architetti, pittori, et scultori italiani, da Cimabue insino a' tempi nostri* [Florence, 1550], eds Luciano Bellosi and Aldo Rossi, Turin, 1986

Vickery 2020
Amanda Vickery, 'Branding Angelica: Reputation Management in Late Eighteenth-century England', *Journal for Eighteenth-century Studies*, 43, no. 1 (March 2020), pp. 3–24

Vigée Le Brun 2015
Louise Elisabeth Vigée Le Brun, *Souvenirs de Madame Louise-Elisabeth Vigée-Lebrun: Texte de l'Edition Originale Illustré de Reproductions de L'Œuvre Réunies par Patrick Weiller*, 3 vols, Paris, 2015

Von Preussen 2018
Brigid von Preussen, '1779: The Muse in the Temple of Apollo', in Hallett, Turner and Feather (eds), *The Royal Academy of Arts Summer Exhibition: A Chronicle, 1769–2018*, London, 2018: https://chronicle250.com/1779

Waagen 1838
Gustav Friedrich Waagen, *Kunstwerke und Künstler in England und Paris*, vol. 2, Berlin, 1838

Walch 1968
Peter Sanborn Walch, 'Angelica Kauffman', typescript dissertation, Princeton University, Princeton, 1968–69

Walch 1977
Peter Sanborn Walch, 'An Early Neoclassical Sketchbook by Angelica Kauffman', *Burlington Magazine*, 119, no. 887 (February 1977), pp. 98–111

Warsaw 1938
Cat. Galerii malarstwa obcego Muzeum Naro, coll. cat., National Museum, Warsaw, 1938

Webster 2011
Mary Webster, *Johan Zoffany*, New Haven and London, 2011

Weinhart 1814
Giovanni Gherardo de Rossi, *Leben der berühmten Mahlerinn Angelika Kauffmann, aus dem Italienischen übersetzt und ergänzt von A. Weinhart*, Bregenz, 1814

Wendorf 1996
Richard Wendorf, *Sir Joshua Reynolds: The Painter in Society*, London, 1996

West 1999
Shearer West, 'Xenophobia and Xenomania: Italians and the English Royal Academy', in *Italian Culture in Northern Europe in the Eighteenth Century*, Cambridge, 1999, pp. 116–39

Williams 2015
Hannah Williams, *Académie Royale: A History in Portraits*, London, 2015

Winckelmann 1976
Johann Joachim Winckelmann, 'Gedanken ueber die Nachahmung der griechischen Werke in der Malerey und Bildhauerkunst [1755], in *Winckelmanns Werke*, ed. Nationale Forschung- und Gedenkstätten der Klassischen Deutschen Literatur in Weimar, Berlin/Weimar, 1976

Woodall 1997
Joanna Woodall (ed.), *Portraiture: Facing the Subject*, Manchester, 1997

Worcester 1882
Worcestershire Exhibition, 1882, Official Catalogue, exh. cat., Worcester, 1882

Zucchi 1999
Giuseppe Carlo Zucchi, *Memorie Istoriche Di Maria Angelica Kauffman Zucchi Riguardanti L'Arte Della Pittura Da Lei Professata Scritte Da G.*[*iuseppe*] *C.*[*arlo*] *Z.*[*ucchi*] [1788], in Helmut Swozilek (ed.), *Schriften des Vorarlberger Landesmuseums* (Series B, vol. 2), Bregenz, 1999, pp. 13–260

Zucchi Indice 1804
Giuseppe Carlo Zucchi, 'Indice Della Seconda Parte Delle Opere di Angelica Kauffmann Zucchi', MS, vorarlberg museum, Bregenz, inv. no. A.G. 12

LENDERS TO THE EXHIBITION

His Majesty The King

The Barrett Swiss Collection in memory of Nona Barrett

BREGENZ
vorarlberg museum

BRIGHTON
Brighton & Hove Museums

The Burghley House Collection

CHUR
Bündner Kunstmuseum

DÜSSELDORF
Kunstpalast

Eastnor Castle Collection

EDINBURGH
National Galleries of Scotland

FLORENCE
Gallerie degli Uffizi

INNSBRUCK
Tiroler Landesmuseum Ferdinandeum, Innsbruck

LONDON
English Heritage, Kenwood
National Portrait Gallery
Royal Academy of Arts
Victoria and Albert Museum

MUNICH
Bayerische Staatsgemäldesammlungen – Neue Pinakothek

NATIONAL TRUST COLLECTIONS
Nostell Priory, The St Oswald Collection
Saltram, The Morley Collection

WARSAW
National Museum in Warsaw

ZÜRICH
Kunsthaus Zürich

and those who wish to remain anonymous

PHOTOGRAPHIC ACKNOWLEDGEMENTS

All works of art are reproduced by kind permission of the owners. Every attempt has been made to trace copyright holders. We apologise for any inadvertent infringement and invite appropriate rights holders to contact us.

Specific acknowledgements are as follows: © The Al Thani Collection, 2019. All rights reserved: cats 28–9 (photo: Prudence Cuming Associates Ltd). Barrett Collection, Dallas: cat. 35. bpk / Bayerische Staatsgemäldesammlungen: cats 2, 36. Bregenz, © vorarlberg museum: figs 2–3; cat. 34 (photo: Markus Tretter). Brighton & Hove Museums: cat. 4. © The Burghley House Collection, Stamford: cats 6, 8, 12–13. Chur, Grisons Museum of Fine Arts: cat. 15. Düsseldorf, AKRP: fig. 6 (photo: Justin Piperger); cat. 11 (photo: Inken M. Holubec). Düsseldorf, Kunstpalast – Horst Kolberg / ARTOTHEK: cat. 32. Eastnor Castle, Herefordshire: cat. 7 (photo: Sam Furlong). Florence, © Gabinetto Fotografico delle Gallerie degli Uffizi: p. 40; cat. 3. © Historic England: cats 9–10, 26. Innsbruck, Tiroler Landesmuseum Ferdinandeum: cat. 1. London, © National Portrait Gallery: cat. 19. London, Omnia Art Ltd: cat. 31. London, © Royal Academy of Arts: fig. 15; cats 24–5 (photo: John Hammond); cat. 17 (photo: Prudence Cuming Associates Limited); cats 37–9; pp. 80–1. Naples, Museo Nazionale di Capodimonte: fig. 7. National Galleries of Scotland: cats 18, 27. © National Trust Images: figs 4, 11; cat. 33 (photo: John Hammond); cat. 16 (photo: Rob Matheson); fig 12. New Haven, Yale Center for British Art: fig. 8. Rome © Accademia Nazionale di San Luca: fig. 13 (photo: Mauro Coen). Royal Collection Trust / © His Majesty King Charles III 2023: fig. 10; cat. 14. Tate: fig. 14. © Victoria and Albert Museum: cats 20–3. Warsaw, © Collection of National Museum in Warsaw: cat. 30 (photo: Piotr Ligier). Washington, National Gallery of Art: fig. 1. Weimar, Stiftung Weimarer Klassik: fig. 9. Zurich, © Kunsthaus Zürich: cat. 5

INDEX

All references are to page numbers; those in **bold** type indicate catalogue plates, and those in *italic* type indicate essay illustrations

BENEFACTORS OF THE ROYAL ACADEMY OF ARTS

THE PRESIDENTS' CIRCLE
The estate of the late Annemarie Aschenagi
Blavatnik Family Foundation
Bloomberg Philanthropies
The Clore Duffield Foundation
Mervyn and Jeanne Davies
The Manny and Brigitta Davidson Charitable Foundation
The Dorfman Foundation
Dunard Fund
Mrs Drue Heinz Hon DBE
Mr Christophe and Mrs Valerié Jungels-Winkler
Mrs Gabrielle Jungels-Winkler
David and Molly Lowell Borthwick
Ronald and Rita McAulay
The McLennan Family
Sir John Madejski OBE DL
The Mead Family Foundation
Mr and Mrs Robert Miller
The Monument Trust
National Lottery Heritage Fund
Julia and Hans Rausing
Sir Simon and Lady Robertson
The Rothschild Foundation
Dame Jillian Sackler DBE
Jake and Hélène Marie Shafran
The Garfield Weston Foundation
The Maurice Wohl Charitable Foundation
The Wolfson Foundation

MAJOR BENEFACTORS
The Band Trust
Matthew Barzun and Brooke Brown Barzun
Aryeh and Elana Bourkoff, LionTree
Sir Francis and the Hon Lady Brooke
The Cadogan Charity
Sir Richard and Lady Carew Pole
Chenevière Travel Award
Adrian Cheng
Jeremy Coller Foundation
John and Gail Coombe
Sir Roger de Grey Memorial Fund
Lady Alison Deighton
Sir Harry Djanogly
The Eranda Rothschild Foundation
The Fidelity UK Foundation
The Foyle Foundation
The Armando Garza-Sada Sr. Endowment for the Arts
Genesis Foundation
J Paul Getty Jr Charitable Trust
Glenbevan Trust
Mrs Grete Goldhill
Horace W Goldsmith Foundation
Mr and Mrs Gounaris-Milner
Peter Greenham Fund
Mr and Mrs Jim Grover
The Alexis and Anne-Marie Habib Foundation
Charles and Kaaren Hale
E Vincent Harris Fund
The Kirby Laing Foundation
Nicolette and Frederick Kwok
Lord Leverhulme's Charitable Trust
Christian Levett and Musée FAMM
The Linbury Trust
Miss Rosemary Lomax-Simpson
Mr William Loschert
Maintenance Fund
Philip and Valerie Marsden
The 29th May 1961 Charitable Trust
The Lord Mayor's Appeal
The Paul Mellon Estate
Milner Educational Trust
Simon Morris and Annalisa Burello
The Batia and Idan Ofer Family Foundation
Christina Ong
Mr and Mrs James Paradise
The estate of the late Miss Constance-Anne Parker
Paulo and Caroline Pereira
J Heritage Peters
P F Charitable Trust
The late Mr John Porter
Ivor Rey Scholarship Fund
Schools Portfolio Fund
The Schroder Foundation
Mr Sean Scully RA
Mr Richard S Sharp
Dasha Shenkman
William and Maureen Shenkman
Oriane Simonet and Nikolaos Andronikos
The estate of the late Mrs Pauline Sitwell
Starr Fund
David and Deborah Stileman
The Swire Charitable Trust
The late Sir Anthony Tennant and Lady Tennant
The Thompson Family Charitable Trust
Patricia Turner Award
Kathryn Uhde
Vandaleur
Sir Siegmund Warburg's Voluntary Settlement
The Welton Foundation
Mr W Galen Weston and the Hon Mrs Hilary Weston

BENEFACTORS
Aldama Foundation
Lord and Lady Aldington
Mrs Allen-Huxley
Joan and Robin Alvarez
The Anson Charitable Trust
Artists' Collecting Society
The Band Trust
Veronica and Lars Bane
Ms Linda Bennett and Mr Philip Harley
Sir Win Bischoff
Charlotte Bonham-Carter Charitable Trust
The William Brake Foundation
The Deborah Loeb Brice Foundation
The Consuelo and Anthony Brooke Charitable Trust
Garvin and Steffanie Brown
Mr and Mrs John Burns
Ilaria Bulgari
Peter and the late Sally Cadbury
Carew Pole Charitable Trust
Dr Edmund Carter
Mr Richard Chang
Sir Trevor and Lady Susan Chinn
CHK Foundation
Mr and Mrs Jonathan Clarke
Mr Andrés Clase
The John S Cohen Foundation
Ms Elizabeth Crain
Crankstart
Mr Michael Cowper
Ina De and James Spicer
The Roger De Haan Charitable Trust
Ron Dennis
The Gilbert and Eileen Edgar Foundation
The John Ellerman Foundation
Mr Richard Elman
Epson
The Lord Faringdon Charitable Trust
Mr and Mrs Stephen Fitzgerald
Mrs Jill Garcia
Mr and Mrs M Gee
The Golden Bottle Trust
Nicholas and Judith Goodison's Charitable Settlement
Antony Gormley and Vicken Parsons
The late Mr Stephen Gosztony
The late Sir Ronald Grierson
Sir Nicholas Grimshaw CBE PPRA
Fiona and Peter Hare
Hauser & Wirth
Mrs Katrin Henkel
Mr and Mrs Julian Heslop
Holbeck Charitable Trust
The Charles Michael Holloway Charitable Trust
Mr and Mrs Jeremy Hosking
Huo Family Foundation (UK)
Harry Hyman and family
The Inchcape Foundation
Japanese Committee of Honour of the Royal Academy of Arts
Chantal Joffe RA
Alistair D K Johnston CMG FCA
Mr Ivan Katzen
Mr Lagrange and Mr Burnough
Sir Christopher Le Brun PPRA and Charlotte Verity
The David Lean Foundation
Mr Nelson Leong
Mr and Mrs Mark Loveday
The Maccabaeans
Dr Lee MacCormick Edwards Charitable Foundation
Mrs McAlpine
HRH Princess Marie-Chantal of Greece
J P Marland Charitable Trust
The Rt Hon the Lord and Lady Marland
The David Ellis Marlow Trust
The late Mr Minoru Mori Hon KBE and Mrs Mori
Sir Michael Moritz
The Murray Family
Lady Alison Myners
Normanby Charitable Trust
Dr and Mrs Orentreich
Mr Charles Outhwaite
PF Charitable Trust
Stanley Picker Charitable Trust
The Pilgrim Trust
Mr and Mrs Maurice Pinto
The Earl and Countess of Plymouth
The Polonsky Foundation
Mrs Tineke Pugh
Red Butterfly Foundation
The estate of the late Mr Ivor Rey
Peter Rippon
Sir Simon and Victoria, Lady Robey OBE
Richard and Ruth Rogers
The Rose Foundation
Sir Paul and Lady Ruddock
The Basil Samuel Charitable Trust
Mrs Coral Samuel CBE
Edwina Sassoon
Guy Senior, in memory of Brian and Mary Senior, Friends of the RA
Louisa Service OBE
David and Sophie Shalit
Archie Sherman Charitable Trust
Mr Brian Smith
Mr Christopher Smith
Sir Paul and Lady Smith
The South Square Trust
Mr and Mrs Roger Staton
Sir Hugh and Lady Stevenson
The Nina and Roger Stewart Charitable Trust
Mr John Studzinski CBE
The late Sir David Tang KBE
Tavolozza Foundation
Tileyard London
Julian Treger
Tresidor Investment Management
Celia Walker Art Foundation
Martin and Anja Weiss
Sian and Matthew Westerman
Chris Wilkinson OBE RA and Diana Edmunds
Mr Peter Williams
Ivor and Caroline Windsor
The Harold Hyam Wingate Foundation
Manuela and Iwan Wirth
The Lennox and Wyfold Foundation
Mr Yuzo Yagi
and those who wish to remain anonymous

MAJOR BENEFACTORS TOWARDS REDEVELOPING THE RA SCHOOLS
The Band Trust
Adrian Cheng
Lady Alison Deighton
Dunard Fund
Mrs Gabrielle Jungels-Winkler
Nicolette and Frederick Kwok
The Mead Family Foundation
Milner Educational Trust
The estate of the late Miss Constance-Anne Parker
Julia and Hans Rausing
Jake and Hélène Marie Shafran
Sir Siegmund Warburg's Voluntary Settlement
The Garfield Weston Foundation
The Wolfson Foundation

MAJOR BENEFACTORS OF THE RA SCHOOLS ENDOWMENT FUND
Chenevière Travel Award
Sir Roger de Grey Memorial Fund
Dunard Fund
The Eranda Rothschild Foundation
Peter Greenham Fund

E Vincent Harris Fund
J Heritage Peters Maintenance Fund
Ronald and Rita McAulay
Ivor Rey Scholarship Fund
Schools Portfolio Fund
The estate of the late Mrs Pauline Sitwell
Starr Fund
Patricia Turner Award
Vandaleur

BENEFACTORS OF THE RA SCHOOLS

Artists' Collecting Society
Charlotte Bonham-Carter Charitable Trust
John S Cohen Foundation
Ron Dennis
Dreamchasing
Dunard Fund
The Gilbert and Eileen Edgar Foundation
Epson
The Eranda Rothschild Foundation
Bianca and Noam Gottesman
Peter Greenham Fund
The Charles Michael Holloway Charitable Trust
Mr Nelson Leong
Leverhulme Trust
Mr and Mrs Mark Loveday
The Maccabaeans
The Machin Foundation
The Normanby Charitable Trust
The Batia and Idan Ofer Family Foundation
Andrés Olow Clase
Christina Ong
Stanley Picker Charitable Trust
Red Butterfly Foundation
The estate of the late Mr Ivor Rey
Peter Rippon
Bianca Roden
The Rose Foundation
Archie Sherman Charitable Trust
The South Square Trust
Sir Paul and Lady Smith
The Stewarts Foundation
David and Deborah Stileman
The Adrian Swire Charitable Trust
The Swire Charitable Trust
Tileyard London
Celia Walker Art Foundation
and those who wish to remain anonymous

BENEFACTORS OF THE RA EXHIBITION PROGRAMME

Blavatnik Family Foundation
Brooke Brown Barzun
Cockayne Grants for the Arts
The David Ellis Marlow Trust
Dunard Fund
Dr Lee MacCormick Edwards Charitable Foundation
Mrs Jennifer Esposito
Wendy Fisher & A4 Arts Foundation
Ford Foundation
The Garcia Family Foundation
Yoav Gottesman
The Huo Family Foundation
The International Music and Art Foundation
Ömer Koç
Simone Krok
The Robert Lehman Foundation
Miss Rosemary Lomax-Simpson
The Magic Trust
Scott and Laura Malkin
Simon Morris and Annalisa Burello
Cate Olson and Nash Robbins
Paul Mellon Foundation
Pro Helvetia
Tavolozza Foundation
The Terra Foundation for American Art
The Thompson Family Charitable Trust
Kathryn Uhde
Peter and Geraldine Williams
and those who wish to remain anonymous

RA BENEFACTORS

The Atlas Fund
CHK Foundation
Joseph Strong Frazer Trust

PATRONS

CHAIR OF RA PATRONS

Mr Matthew Langton

INTERNATIONAL CIRCLE

Mrs Niloufar Bakhtiar-Bakhtiari
Mr Lars Bane
Alexander and Ika Green
Ms Bella Kesoyan
Ms Ida Levine
Mr Nick Loup
Mr Sebastien Mazella di Bosco
Gaukhar Nurgalieva
Mr Thaddaeus Ropac
Antigone Theodorou and Stefan Bollinger
Ms Chizuko Yashiro
Mr and Mrs Basil Zirinis
Ms Mercedes Zobel
and those who wish to remain anonymous

PLATINUM PATRONS

Tim Ashley
Celia and Edward Atkin CBE
Paul Baines
Christopher and Cynthia Bake
Alex Beard and Emma Vernetti
The Deborah Loeb Brice Foundation
Ms Sue Butcher
Kate de Rothschild Agius and Marcus Agius CBE
Mrs Willemien Downes
Hugo Eddis
Charles and Kaaren Hale
Mr Yan Huo
Mrs Elizabeth Lenz
Mr Christian Levett
Mr Nick Loup
Lady Alison Myners
Mr Idan and Mrs Batia Ofer
Mrs Bianca Roden
Jake and Hélène Marie Shafran
Mrs Janet Winslow
and those who wish to remain anonymous

GOLD PATRONS

Mr Stephen Allcock
Joan and Robin Alvarez
Ms Vanessa Aubry
Mrs Georgina Bennett
Sam and Rosie Berwick
Richard Bram and Monika Machon
Molly Lowell Borthwick
Sir Francis Brooke Bt
Mr Thomas E Cantwell
Ms Lisa Carrodus
Margherita Castellani
Varun and Emma Chandra
Ms Natasha Cheung
Alexander Cicetti
The Lady Renwick of Clifton
Maria Cristina Codognato
Vanessa Colomar de Enserro
Christopher and Alex Courage
Dr Juli Crocombe
Mrs Sophie Diedrichs-Cox
Susan Elliott
Swag and Nupur Ganguly
Mrs Carol Gibson Jackson
Dr Chris and Mrs Marjorie Gibson-Smith
Amanda Gowing
Mr Stephen Griggs
Mr Jim Grover
Mr Joshua Harris
Rosalyn and Hugo Henderson
Dame Vivian Hunt
Sir Martin and Lady Jacomb
Mrs Josephine Jenno
Mr Kevin Kane
Sir and Lady Khalili
Ms Maxine Kohn
Sir Sydney Lipworth KC and Lady Lipworth CBE
Miss Rosemary Lomax-Simpson
Ms Olena Lutsenko
Mr Nicholas Maclean
Scott and Laura Malkin
Mr Stephen Marquardt
Louise Nathanson
Simon and Sabi North
Asta Paulauskaite
Maria N Peacock
Paulo and Caroline Pereira
Mr Stuart Piercy
Mrs Ivetta Rabinovich
Ms Melanie Rademacher
Dianne Roberts
Sarah Ryan
Katrina Aleksa Ryemill
Mrs Oliwia Siemienczuk
Mr Richard Simmons CBE
Tim and Lynda Smith
Jane Spack
Mrs Raksha Sriram
Mr Michael Stiff
David and Deborah Stileman
Mr Robert Suss
Nesrin Tisdale
Kathryn Uhde
Miss M L Ulfane
Countess Cornelia Von Rittberg
Mr Waqas Wajahat
Erica Wax
Mr Neil Westreich
Mr Peter Williams
Manuela and Iwan Wirth
David Yates and Yvonne Walcott Yates
Ms Catherine Walsh
Philip and Emeline Winston
Lady Estelle Wolfson of Marylebone
Mr Robert John Yerbury
Mr Riccardo Zacconi
and those who wish to remain anonymous

SILVER PATRONS

Nora Al Angari
Mrs Spindrift Al Swaidi
Ms Katherine Ashton-Young
Mila Askarova
Mrs Leslie Bacon
Mrs Ginny Battcock
Catherine Baxendale
Mr and Mrs Jonathan and Sarah Bayliss
Mrs J K M Bentley, Liveinart
Mr Bollinger
Eleanor E Brass
Viscountess Bridgeman
Mrs Basia Briggs
Mrs Marcia Brocklebank
Mrs Charles Brown
Ms Debra Burt
Mrs Ann Chapman-Daniel
Sir Trevor and Lady Chinn
Ms Evi Chioti
Mr John Clappier
Mrs Jane Clark
Rosalind Clayton
Sir Ronald and Lady Cohen
Andrew M Coppel, CBE and June V Coppel
Cathy Corbett
Edmund Coulthard
Mrs Caroline Cullinan
Monica and Knut Dahl
Mrs Georgina David
Mr Daniel Davies
Mrs Dominic Dowley
Mr and Mrs Jim Downing
Ms Noreen Doyle
Mrs Maurice Dwek
Mrs Marianna E Simpson
Mrs Samira Govers-El Hachioui
Mr and Mrs Jeff Eldredge
Mr David Fawkes
Mrs Stroma Finston
James Freedman
Virginia Gabbertas
Mr Stephen Garrett
Joanna George
Jacqueline and Jonathan Gestetner
Melanie and Piers Gibson
Caroline and Alan Gillespie
Mr Mark Glatman
Peter and Elizabeth Goulds, L.A. Louvre
John Gruzelier, Professor Emeritus
Mrs Margaret Guitar
Ms Han Guo
Ms Kim Habraken
Alex Haidas and Thalia Chryssikou
Mr Christopher Harrison
Sir John and Lady Hegarty
Sir Michael and Lady Heller
Mrs Katrin Henkel
Mrs Pat Heslop
Mr and Mrs Jonathan Hindle
Mrs Susan Hitchin
Anne Holmes-Drewry
Mr Philip Hudson
Mr and Mrs Jon Hunt
S Isern-Feliu
Mrs Caroline Jackson
Sir Martin and Lady Jacomb
Mr Tom Jacomb
Mrs Raymonde Jay
Fiona Johnstone
Mrs Marcelle Joseph
Dr Elisabeth Kehoe
Mrs Kit Kemp MBE
Paul and Susie Kempe
Miss Rebecca Kemsley
Simon and Emma Keswick
Mr Gerald Kidd
Mr and Mrs James Kirkman
Mrs Anna Kirrage
Mrs Latifa Kosta
Mrs Alkistis Koukouliou
Mrs Sybil Kretzmer
Mr Matthew Langton
Ms Isabella Lauder-Frost
Jessica Lavooy
Ms Patricia Lawrie
Mrs Anna Lee
Lady Lever of Manchester
Richard Burger and Rachel Lipson
Mr Jeremy and Dr Julie Llewelyn
Mr and Mrs Robin Lough
Mr George Maher
Olivier and Priscilla Malingue
Mr Richard Mansell-Jones
Philip and Val Marsden
Mrs Janet Martin
Gillian McIntosh
Andrew and Judith McKinna
Itxaso Mediavilla-Murray
Ms Kimiya Minoukadeh
Victoria Miro
Shalini Misra
Simon Morris and Annalisa Burello
Mr Alan Morton
Mr Blair Morton
Mrs Alexandra Nash
Mrs Tessa Nicholson
Ms Minka Nyberg
Emma O'Donoghue
Flavia Ormond
Mrs Harriet O'Rourke
Neil Osborn and Holly Smith
Sir Michael Palin
Mr and Mrs D J Peacock
The Hon Julian Phillimore
Mr Adam and Mrs Michelle Plainer
Mary Pollock
Lady Purves
Mr William Ramsay
Ms Mouna Rebeiz
Peter Rice Esq
Erica Roberts
Miss Elaine Rowley
Sir Paul and Lady Ruddock
Mrs Janice Sacher
Ms Kim Samuel
Mrs Sirkka Sanderson
Mr Paul Sandilands
Mr Adrian Sassoon
Devinyl Schonfeld
Christina, Countess of Shaftesbury
Mr Robert N Shapiro
Mr David Shaw
Ms Elena Shchukina
Dr Shirley Sherwood OBE
Mr Martin Klosterfelde, Skarstedt Gallery
Mrs Jane Smith
Lady Henrietta St George